RIDING
BETWEEN THE
WORLDS

RIDING
BETWEEN THE
WORLDS

EXPANDING OUR POTENTIAL
THROUGH THE WAY OF THE HORSE

LINDA KOHANOV

NEW WORLD LIBRARY
NOVATO, CALIFORNIA

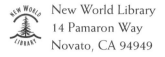 New World Library
14 Pamaron Way
Novato, CA 94949

The material in this book is intended for education. It is not meant to take the place of diagnosis and treatment by a qualified medical practitioner or therapist. No expressed or implied guarantee as to the effects of the use of the recommendations can be given nor liability taken.

Library of Congress Cataloging-in-Publication Data
Kohanov, Linda.
  Riding between the worlds : expanding human consciousness through the way of the horse / by Linda Kohanov.
      p.   cm.
Includes bibliographical references (p. 243).
  ISBN 1-57731-416-6 (pbk. : alk. paper)
1. Horses—Arizona—Tucson—Anecdotes. 2. Kohanov, Linda. 3. Women horse owners—Arizona—Tucson—Anecdotes. 4. Human-animal relationships—Anecdotes. 5. Horses—Psychological aspects. 6. Horses—Philosophy. I. Title.
  SF301.K639 2003
  636.1'001'9—dc21   2003013309

First printing, November 2003
ISBN 1-57731-416-6
Printed in Canada on acid-free, partially recycled paper
Distributed to the trade by Publishers Group West

10   9   8   7   6   5   4   3   2   1

For Spirit,
and all the generous souls who helped him
grow, thrive, and inspire.

CONTENTS

INTRODUCTION

I met Rocky's new owner moments before she rode him in a natural horsemanship clinic. Though I hadn't seen him in almost a year, the little bay Arabian stepped forward and nuzzled my shoulder as Lyndsey and I shook hands. A few moments later, the two entered the round pen and began to demonstrate the various moves they'd learned from their trainer, Jerry Petersen. At one point, Rocky nearly unseated Lyndsey as he turned suddenly and trotted away from the audience. Yet I could see this was only a mild case of stage fright, not the quivering sense of primal fear he once wore like a second skin. Lyndsey was relatively new to the saddle, as was her horse, but their modest performance that day seemed more miraculous to me than any number of famous steeds winning the Triple Crown. Rocky had once been considered psychotic, unsalvageable. The night I met him in the winter of 2000 was supposed to be his last.

Rocky's brush with death is one of those stories that has the power to change lives just by telling it, which I did in my first book, *The Tao of Equus*, and have done many times since in workshops around the country. My encounter with this horse elucidated some profound emotional dynamics that affected not only my equine-facilitated therapy practice at the Epona Center in Tucson, but my relationships with people outside the riding arena. It was Rocky who finally convinced me, once and for all, that the transformative feelings and intuitions I had experienced with my own herd years earlier were not special, not supernatural, and certainly not "just my imagination." Rather, emotion itself was a resonant, multidimensional force that connected all sentient beings. Whether or not humans were ready to acknowledge this consciously, it affected them.

It all started when Becky, a former riding student, asked me to take a look at her mother Nancy's horse as I was about to get into my car one crisp December evening and head off to dinner. The family had recently adopted an abused gelding named Rocky. The sixteen-year-old Arabian was so difficult to catch, halter, and lead that he'd been left on pasture for a decade with little human contact. Nancy, however, felt a strong connection to the horse, whose large soulful eyes held so much promise one minute and so much fear the next. Unfortunately, Rocky's trauma ran deeper than she imagined. During a routine vet exam earlier that day, the horse panicked for no discernable reason. He tried to jump a fence and lacerated his leg in the process. Tranquilizers barely affected him as the vet dodged hooves and teeth to wrap the wound without suffering serious injury himself. All the while, Rocky remained hypervigilant, successfully fighting a drug that would easily have knocked a much larger animal out for an hour.

"The vet thinks we should put Rocky down," Becky told me. "Everyone says he's dangerous. My mom feels terrible, but I don't want her to get hurt."

We walked toward Rocky's stall as a full moon rose above the mountains. Nancy was waiting at the gate. The little horse cowered in the shadows, obviously wary of our presence — and for good reason this time, since we had the final say as to whether he lived or died. I took a deep breath, asked for guidance, and slowly approached him. A number of conflicting images filled my body.

"Has something particularly disturbing happened to you?" I asked Nancy. "Other than what happened with Rocky, are you upset about something in your life?"

"Well...," she said. "I lost my job last week."

"Have you been trying to act happy around Rocky when you're actually feeling sad, angry...trapped?"

"Yeah," she replied tentatively, not quite understanding why I was asking such personal questions about her when Rocky was the one whose life was on the line.

Rocky lowered his head and licked his lips, a sign I had come to read in my own horses as indicating the release of some previously unacknowledged emotion. In this case, Rocky's comfort level seemed directly tied to Nancy's hidden feelings. I walked toward him. He backed away. More images, more sensations seemed to arise from his wounded leg and aching heart. I breathed in sync with his quick, shallow gasps for a moment, then slowly downshifted into a calmer rhythm, radiating a sense of peace and acceptance with my entire body. Rocky began to breathe more deeply in response. I silently conveyed that Nancy was his last chance, that if he couldn't bring himself to trust this woman, his worst fears would indeed come true. I would try to convince her to give him one more month, one more cycle of the moon. The rest was up to him. After a good fifteen minutes of subtle interactions with the horse, he allowed me to briefly touch his shoulder.

"Imagine this," I finally said to Nancy, who now stood quietly, hopefully, about five feet away from Rocky and me. "Imagine that you were raped as a teenager. A few years later, you marry a man who seems very gentle and understanding. Yet once you have that wedding ring on your finger, he thinks you should just get over your conflicting feelings about sex. He suddenly treats you like he owns you. You know he loves you, but he's impatient with you. It doesn't make any sense, but you feel trapped, like you want to run away from this person, who you also realize is your only real hope for connection. Rocky feels like that. He knows you care for him, but just because you officially own him now, just because you pay his feed and board doesn't mean he can automatically let go of all those years of abuse and mistrust. He can't become intimate so easily. Do you know what I mean?"

Nancy stared at me in silence.

"I do," she finally said, shaking her head in disbelief. "Basically, you just told my life's story."

I was shocked. The example I used had popped into my head while breathing in sync with Rocky. I had no idea it related to Nancy's life. I was momentarily speechless, not to mention tired and starving, certainly unprepared for an equine-facilitated psychotherapy session based on a sudden intuition. Nonetheless, I pulled myself together and explained the concept of *emotional incongruity*: the act of hiding one emotion by trying to feel something else.

"You're not doing Rocky any favors by suppressing fear, anger, or sadness," I told her. "Horses have a highly refined ability to sense the feelings of predators and other herd members *at a distance*. Rocky knows what state you're in before you walk through that gate. When you try to muster up a smile and a light tone of voice, while holding back something intensely negative, it makes him feel off balance and unsafe."

In order to survive, I informed her, animals preyed upon in nature have to be sensitive to emotional energy and the intention behind it. Horses, zebras, and deer will often graze unconcerned as a lion who has recently eaten a big meal walks right through their pasture. Yet when an agile carnivore is on the prowl, the herd will scatter long before the cat can get close.

The experience of living with human beings has given domesticated horses even more sophisticated skills. I've seen even the gentlest gelding become noticeably agitated when his handler wears a mask of confidence to hide anxiety. It's as if this person appears out of focus to equine awareness. The body language of someone "putting on a happy face" is incongruent with the rise in blood pressure, muscle tension, and emotional intensity transmitted unconsciously by an individual who's actually afraid, frustrated, or angry. This person may be more of a danger to herself than others, but a skittish horse isn't likely to wait around and find out. Mainstream trainers explain this phenomenon by saying "the horse can smell your fear," but it's subtler and more complicated than that. A secure, well-cared-for animal will often relax the moment his owner simply acknowledges a hidden feeling — *even if it's still there.* Let me say it again: The emotion doesn't have to change in order for the horse to show at least some improvement. The handler just has to make it conscious. When the mask is removed, an animal that was agitated seconds before will sigh, lick his lips, or show some other visible sign of release — exactly what Rocky did when Nancy truthfully answered my questions about her own emotional state.

The observation that horses mirror the "feeling behind the façade" is one of the key principles of equine-facilitated psychotherapy. Most people don't believe it until they see it. Many riders ignore the phenomenon completely because they've been taught to treat horses — and sometimes humans — more like machines than sentient beings. Nancy, of course, was no different until Rocky's life was on the line.

Through my work as a horse trainer and equine-facilitated therapy specialist, I've observed that feelings are contagious. They expand outward like sound traveling through the air and affect others in predictable ways — even across species lines. "We seem to be standing here in silence tonight," I told Nancy, "but we're actually immersed in a sea of vibration. A radio dialed to the right channel could pick up a symphony or a song that would move us both to tears. Well, the equine system is like a huge receiver and amplifier for emotional vibrations. No matter how good you are at hiding things from yourself and others, your nervous system still involuntarily broadcasts what you're really feeling — at a frequency horses are especially good at tuning into."

Musical analogies came naturally to me, but they were more than purely symbolic. As a viola performance major who subsequently made a living as a classical announcer and radio producer for fifteen years, I had numerous opportunities to study the physics of sound and how it travels over the airwaves. I'd also spent most of my life feeling the effects on my body as I rehearsed the same pieces over and over again in ensembles large and small. I was partial to using strings made of catgut, which produced a richer, rounder tone than those of steel. I'd often felt my abdomen and chest cavity resonating with the music, an effect I assumed was related to the fact that my own internal organs mimicked the properties of the strings stretched across my instrument.

Years later, the same principles came into play when I began training horses and noticed that these highly sensitive creatures seemed to send and receive emotion as a gut-level excitation. Over time, I began to resonate with their sensibilities as surely as I had learned to play viola by immersing myself in the music of the masters. If a shock wave of fear swept through the herd, I felt a jolt in my bowels and an electric current shoot up my spine an instant before the first startled colt could throw his head up, turn, and run. As I developed this capacity in the saddle, I could predict a spook before my mare's feet would leave the ground, allowing me to move with a sudden sideways leap as easily as if she and I were a single centaurian entity. This worked both ways, of course. I could always rely on the herd to reflect my incongruities; the sooner I acknowledged and processed my feelings, the sooner we could get down to the business at hand.

Still, when it came to perceiving emotion at a distance, I was like a backwoods fiddler trying to keep up with the world's greatest virtuosos. My horses were light years ahead of me, but I did have an edge with members of my own species. When I first noticed this worked with humans, it was a bit of a nuisance because, like Rocky, I found it uncomfortable to be around incongruent people. I couldn't always tell what the hidden emotion was right away. I learned, however, that when I felt my skin crawl and my solar plexus contract in the presence of someone who looked to be in a good mood, he or she usually had some other, more potent emotion simmering underneath, one that couldn't help but come out sooner or later. If I listened to my gut, I could step out of harm's way much sooner. I began referring to emotional acuity as "the sixth sense," one that civilization relinquished by emphasizing the suppression of feelings, most conveniently as a social control. Creatures with a keen sociosensual awareness cannot easily be lied to or manipulated by outside authority figures; they're only comfortable when authentic feelings and motivations are being acknowledged. The behavior of horses like Rocky illustrates this point dramatically.

In researching these dynamics, I found that emotions are not created exclusively by the mind; they are *not* simply a part of our imagination. Recent work by Candace Pert and other researchers active in the field of psychoneuroimmunology shows that the molecules carrying emotional information (called neuropeptides) are not only generated by the brain, but by sites throughout the body, most dramatically in the heart and the gut. When people have "gut feelings," they're not speaking metaphorically. As animals possessing extremely large and sensitive guts — and hearts for that matter — horses have huge resonant surfaces for receiving and responding to emotional information. Like all mammals, they also have a neocortex, the part of the brain associated with learning and higher thought, though not quite as developed as the human's. Horses, then, are more likely to emphasize emotion over reason. Compared to human beings, these animals are geniuses at sensing the feelings of others, a fact that became clear to me as I moved into equine-facilitated psychotherapy (EFP) and equine experiential learning (EEL), fields employing horses in the work of human development. My herd excelled at helping abuse survivors, addicts, children with attention deficit disorder, and adults with everything from anger management issues and post-traumatic stress disorder to depression. People with less serious career or relationship difficulties developed a greater sense of physical, emotional, and spiritual balance through pleasurable yet challenging EEL activities. Social workers, psychiatrists, and physicians also honed their nonverbal therapeutic skills under the tutelage of my thousand-pound colleagues.

A significant number of our clients, however, were equestrians who had reached an impasse with their mounts. Trainers who encouraged riders to "leave their problems at the gate" simply weren't equipped to deal with the emotional dynamics of these interspecies partnerships. Many so-called "problem horses" were simply mirroring feelings and intentions their owners had no idea they were projecting. Once these people learned how to process emotion as information, rather than suppressing it at all cost, they were able to move forward with a confidence and clarity that enhanced their human relationships as well.

As Nancy and I discussed Rocky's history from this perspective, it became obvious that her attraction to the horse came from what I've come to call *emotional resonance.*

Two beings who've experienced similar difficulties, betrayals, and abuses are like two strings tuned to the same note. Whenever Nancy was in a heightened state of turmoil, I explained, Rocky couldn't help but resonate with her. The intensity would increase if she tried to hide those feelings. In such a state of incongruity, her emotions were fighting her intellect, begging to be expressed. This actually turned up the volume on the sympathetic vibrations exciting Rocky's own unresolved fears and frustrations, causing him to act out these feelings for both of them. I asked her to consider that even though Rocky was afraid of the vet, his reactions were accentuated in the presence of Nancy, who it turned out was not only experiencing feelings related to the loss of her job, but to a series of frustrations with her husband, who was having an affair with another woman in part because of his inability to deal with Nancy's childhood sexual trauma.

"Tell Rocky what you're feeling," I said. "Get it out in the open so he doesn't have to mirror it for you. He won't necessarily understand what you're saying, but by expressing your true feelings, you'll become congruent, and you'll release some of the tension behind those emotions."

For the next ten minutes, Nancy spoke candidly about the violence, shame, and betrayal she experienced. She promised Rocky that she would treat him as she would have wanted to be treated by the men in her life — with respect, patience, and sensitivity to the sometimes unpredictable memories of violent trauma. My eyes began to sting in response to Nancy's story — and to the hope growing stronger in her voice. The moment I let go of my professional distance and allowed the tears to flow down my cheeks, Rocky stepped forward and rested his head in the center of my chest. Just a few minutes earlier I had told Nancy that, unlike human beings, horses don't judge or reject us for what we're feeling; it's the act of trying to suppress our emotions that drives them insane. Rocky took that notion one step further. He showed us that even a horse written off as "loco," a horse considered too crazy to live, could feel safe enough to approach us the moment we let down our guard and began to speak from the heart.

ROCKY ROAD

The month after our first meeting came and went without incident as Rocky accepted the halter and began to follow directions. Nancy made arrangements with me to start him under saddle. My work on *The Tao of Equus*, however, became all-consuming, and I was forced to suspend training sessions until the book was completed. Weaving equestrian, psychological, historical, mythological, and personal insights into a single narrative demanded such concentration that I sometimes got lost driving my car over to visit the herd. In this potent, slightly hypnotic state of creative dissociation, I wasn't present enough to safely teach a simple riding lesson.

In the meantime, another trainer began working at The Ranch on Tucson's east side. I would watch him from a distance as I sat under the big mesquite trees next to my horses, editing the latest chapter of my manuscript and gathering inspiration for another writing marathon. Jerry Petersen specialized in natural horsemanship techniques influenced by clinicians like Pat Parelli, John Lyons, Ray Hunt, and Tom Dorrance. A swaggering man of fifty-plus years with a smooth baritone voice and the wit of a cowboy poet, Jerry also had a certain appreciation for the healing power of horses, having been on the wrong side of the law and his own temper more than once in his younger days. As he absorbed the cooperative, nonviolent training techniques sweeping the West in the 1980s, he found a new sense of balance, not only in the saddle, but in life. He went on to work with thousands of horses at ranches, boarding stables, and in people's backyards, perfecting his own style along the way.

Jerry seemed more comfortable on the back of a horse than walking around on his own two feet. One hot April afternoon, I saw him ride a few surly bucks out of an agitated mare — while talking on a cell phone with a toothpick in his mouth. He never punished the horse for her antics, just encouraged her to keep moving forward until she realized the creature on her back wasn't going anywhere, that it was just plain easier to trot in a circle than flail around in the noonday sun. Nothing a horse could do seemed to threaten or enrage the man — or even raise his blood pressure. For all these reasons, I recommended that Jerry start Rocky.

"This guy has something you can't fake in the riding arena," I told Nancy. "The ability to stay dead calm in a crisis. With a horse like Rocky, that's a definite plus."

Authentic positive feelings like confidence, peacefulness, and joy are just as contagious as anxiety. Yet to horses, no emotion is good or bad. It's just as important for them to recognize when another herd member is afraid or playful, angry or boisterous, depressed or resting peacefully. So-called negative emotions tend to carry a bigger charge because they often must be acted upon quickly to ensure survival. Secure horses, like well-adjusted people, eventually become experts at what empathic counselor Karla McLaren calls "emotional agility," the ability to get the message behind the emotion, adjust behavior, relationship, or environment accordingly, then let go of that feeling and return to homeostasis. Many human beings get caught in the vicious cycle of suppressing and then inappropriately expressing emotion as the pressure reaches critical mass. These people have no business working with a hypervigilant horse like Rocky, no matter how many years they've ridden or how many ribbons they've won. Jerry's ability to stay centered and gather information while others were panicking gave his students — two-legged and four-legged alike — the courage to move into areas that would have traumatized them at the hands of a lesser trainer. They literally borrowed Jerry's focus and confidence until they developed their own.

Even so, I knew that Jerry would avoid engaging Rocky emotionally. The natural horsemanship movement promotes nonviolent training activities that work *with* the equine perspective.

Proponents, however, still see horses primarily as instinctual beings. I had incorporated some of these techniques into my own program and had often recommended that my students attend workshops by Pat Parelli, John Lyons, and Monty Roberts, yet their methods did not explore or acknowledge the depth of feeling, adaptability, or sensory and extrasensory perception I had witnessed in these animals. When *The Tao of Equus* was published later that year, Jerry glanced at Rocky's story and thought the book was way too "far out" to finish reading. The horse's emotional challenges and gifts were so pronounced, however, that the trainer didn't have a choice but to meet his student at this level.

"Rocky would enter states that Vietnam vets describe," Jerry remembers. "Something simple would trigger memories of violent treatment, and he'd just get lost in the terror. Each event took extra time because you had to find what he needed to feel safe. We'd have to break things down into small components and build his confidence around every new thing. But all the time, you had a real powerful sense that there was a part of him that really wanted to do these things. You know, for a lot of horses, being left on pasture with a herd is a better deal than being caught and ridden. But for Rock, that wasn't such a great life either. He was a loner. The other horses would chase him away. He stood there with his head dropped most of the time. He had the appearance of severe depression."

Initially, Jerry asked little of the horse, using "approach and retreat" techniques to gain his confidence. When it came time to ride, he brought in Becky, who had taken lessons with me on her own spirited filly — a wise choice since she was not only an adventurous, agile young woman used to riding inexperienced horses, she had never suffered the abuses her mother endured and wasn't likely to trigger Rocky. The trainer capitalized on the growing connection he and Rocky were developing by remaining on the ground, continually calming the horse with simple leading and longeing exercises as Becky moved closer and closer to mounting position.

"It was a slow process," Jerry said. "Rock couldn't stand to have anyone next to him, so we worked on that for quite a while. Then we worked on putting an arm over his back. He'd bolt sideways a lot in the beginning." Eventually Becky got to the point where she could lean into the horse, then mount bareback for brief periods of time. Despite these giant steps, Jerry still had difficulty getting Rocky past his need for a two-person team confined to the safety of the round pen — until, strangely enough, the trainer himself inadvertently shared his deepest feelings with the horse.

"I'd just discovered that my younger sister was dying," he said. "She was an incredible lady who didn't refer to herself as a cancer victim or a cancer survivor — even though she'd dealt with it for nine years. She called herself the Cancer Dancer. She used to say to me, 'It's an incredible way to live because I don't lose my priorities for long. About the time I get caught in the bullshit, it's time for another bone scan, something that brings me back to what's really important.' Well one night, I got a call about how the cancer had metastasized to the brain. We knew that was it, that she wouldn't survive.

"I went out to The Ranch the next morning, and for some reason there was no one around. I decided I wasn't going to do anything too stressful with Rocky, or any of the other horses for that matter. I just sat in the grass with him on the lead line, thinking about how much I would miss my little sister, who had also been my mentor and in many ways my greatest inspiration. I started to sob, the grief was so intense. Rocky came over and stuck his muzzle right over my heart. I actually felt like he absorbed some of the pain. But it didn't seem to burden him, like he was taking it on. It actually seemed to lighten him."

The following day, Jerry saddled Rocky and rode him through the open desert, alone, for the very first time.

"It was a tremendous turning point for both of us," Jerry said. "My perception was that I was looking to save this troubled horse. But Rocky was able to see out from his own trauma. Rather than me looking to help him, I had this very concrete experience where he was helping me, so it was suddenly more of a horizontal relationship. Something I can't quite define shifted in Rocky as a result. He'd still go into the post-traumatic stress thing sometimes, but never with the same kind of terror. Things moved more smoothly, and he gained so much more confidence through the training after that point. Even folks who weren't that observant about horses started to notice he had changed his herd relationships. He was eating with the other horses. He was defending himself instead of running away. His posture shifted. His coat improved.

"I'd been handling horses for years primarily on a physical level. On an emotional and mental level there was a disconnect. Now I'm beginning to think the physical part is the lesser of the three in importance. You have to stay plugged in to what the horse is doing emotionally and mentally first. Those circuits start working before anything physical happens, but it's a lifetime task to be able to get a working relationship with that feel."

Rocky's ability to support Jerry in the midst of emotions that would have scared most *people* away deepened the trainer's relationship with other horses and inspired him to be more selective in accepting new clients.

"I used to make a living taking anyone who came along, but whenever I tried to teach someone who put purpose ahead of principles, it didn't work anyway. I realized that if someone's primary reason for getting a horse was to serve some kind of ego deal, whether it was getting blue ribbons, passing a test, or showing off for someone else, I didn't want to be a part of it. Love — for the animal, the work, and yourself — has to be the guiding principle, and that demands a continuous awareness and respect for the horse's dignity in whatever task you're dealing with. If you can't accomplish a goal at this particular time without violating that trust, then it's time to stop what you're doing. That's not to say it can't be done, but it does mean you have to change your plans to find the pieces you don't have."

An important part of Rocky's progress involved finding a human partner who could fully appreciate his unusual empathic talents and ongoing difficulties. Jerry was able to provide that missing piece by introducing the horse to Lyndsey, a forty-two-year-old woman with a history of childhood sexual abuse and alcoholism.

At Sierra Tucson a few years earlier, Lyndsey felt a special affinity for these gentle giants when she experienced the power of equine-facilitated psychotherapy, one of the residential treatment center's longstanding and most successful programs. "I signed up to ride every single day I could," she said. "I just couldn't get enough of it. Then I was talking with Jerry, who I'd met through a different program in town, about how I wanted to get involved with horses again somehow, and he said, 'That's what I do for a living.' I thought, well *that's* why we all call him Cowboy Jerry. I just hadn't made the connection."

Though Nancy had subsequently learned to ride Rocky, which seemed to her a miracle in itself, she needed to sell several members of the herd to follow her dream: owning a performance horse capable of competitive trail riding and barrel racing. Still, she wanted to find just the right home for the gelding who had taught her more about the equine heart and mind than she ever imagined possible. When Jerry brought Lyndsey to The Ranch, Nancy knew they had found the right match.

"The minute my eyes met his, there was this instant feeling of love," Lyndsey remembers. "It makes me cry every time I think about how Nancy almost had to put him down. Rocky is the most gentle horse, the most sensitive and forgiving horse. He loves me for who I am. I don't have to put on airs. I don't have to put on makeup. It's given me a whole new perspective on who I am and what I'm worth. And you better believe I would never let anyone hurt him again."

Lyndsey's first ordeal: learning to catch and halter the horse on a two-acre pasture with the rest of Nancy's herd kicking up dust. But she persisted, and before long, Rocky was meeting her at the gate. "I had done some trail riding before," she says. "I thought you just kicked a horse and off he went, pulled on the reins and he stopped. But Rocky demanded I relate to him in a whole new way. Jerry taught me to take it step by step, day by day, to not push it, just let it happen. And it worked! There's still no farrier in this city who can get near Rocky's back feet. Even Jerry can't do that. Rocky loosened up for me though. I can clean his back hooves."

The most startling change, however, took place in Lyndsey. "I've come so much farther in my therapy. I can be more honest and more courageous with people because that's the way I am with Rocky. Being more open with him has been a major factor in my recovery because he sees me exactly for who I am, and there's no judgment.

"My therapist said, 'I can't believe just you owning a horse would make this much difference.' But if you're not an animal person, it's hard to understand, I guess. My brother, who doesn't even own a cat or a dog, was very much against me owning a horse. He finally said to me at Christmas, 'You've grown an awful lot since you got that stupid horse.' I said, 'He's not a stupid horse; he's my Rock Man.' There's a lot of times when I'm on edge, and Rocky is there for me. The principles Jerry taught me to use with my horse, I can also use on myself. I can do a little bit better every day with my own terror, my own lack of trust. That's where Rocky centers me. He doesn't push it with me, and I don't push it with him. He can stand his ground now, and I'm learning to do the same thing."

THE HEART OF THE MATTER

Though I had moved my practice across town several months earlier, I'd heard through the grapevine about the progress the three had made, and I left a message on Jerry's answering service inviting him and Lyndsey to tell their part of the Rocky story for *Riding between the Worlds*. When he called me a week later and asked if we could meet for coffee, I assumed he was simply responding to my request. I was therefore completely taken aback when he sat down, removed his cowboy hat, wiped the sweat from his brow, and apologized.

"The sure bar to knowledge is contempt prior to investigation," he professed in his thick, witty Western drawl. "I was guilty of that with your book. I told people it was full of nonsense before I really looked into it. I wanted you to know that; I wanted to make amends. I'd like you to come to a natural horsemanship demonstration I'm hosting next Saturday. I'll be reading a passage from your book and also showing the progress Rocky has made with his new owner."

"That really means a lot to me, Jerry," I said after a moment of surprised silence. "But when I wrote that book, I didn't expect the majority of people to understand. Half the time I wasn't even sure if I could believe in my own experience. I was often alone with my horses when something like that happened to me, but then Rocky came along, and there were witnesses. Now you're one of them."

The following weekend, Jerry shared his special brand of horse sense with a substantial audience gathered beneath the same mesquite grove where I had sat with my own horses nearly two years earlier, reading my manuscript and watching him train for the very first time. Most of these people had never heard Rocky's story, but those of us who had lived it were there to cheer him on. I waved at Nancy and Becky as Lyndsey proudly rode her Rock Man into the round pen. The little horse shied away from the crowd, more perplexed than genuinely frightened. Jerry's voice, so deep and reassuring, focused horse and rider, and before long the two were trotting around the arena. No bits, tie-downs, or draw reins were used to control this "crazy horse." Lyndsey communicated her wishes from the saddle by virtue of a simple halter and lead rope.

Once again, I felt the tears roll down my cheeks in Rocky's presence, and I thought of one of my favorite quotes, attributed to an "anonymous aboriginal woman" who obviously had much to teach the missionaries and social workers sent to rescue her from life in the Australian outback.

"If you have come to help me, you're wasting your time," she told them. "But if you have come because your liberation is bound with mine, then let us work together."

That, in essence, was what Rocky had been saying all along. Watching him move with Lyndsey under the clear blue sky, I realized that actively trying to fix the world and everyone in it wasn't the surest path to freedom. Quite often it led to hubris, disconnection, and attempts to control those deemed less fortunate "for their own good." True freedom, it seemed to me that luminous October afternoon, arose from the courage to *feel*, the willingness to be vulnerable and the humility to appreciate the wisdom all living beings have to offer. In such an atmosphere of mutual respect, compassion, and sensitivity, no one was likely to be abused or enslaved.

LEARNING TO TRUST

With any phenomenon that stretches the boundaries of consensual reality, people must see it to believe it, and sometimes even that isn't good enough. Logical Western minds demand some theory to explain it, or at the very least, multiple independent observations to corroborate it, and ideally, some procedure for re-creating it at will. Skeptics often require such evidence merely to acknowledge something that has been happening all along, right before their very eyes. These people have to *believe it* to see it. I myself was among them. Whether describing some as-yet-unexplainable aspect of human and equine behavior, summarizing adventurous scientific theories, or researching the archaic myths and long-neglected archetypes that were seeping into my life and work with increasing regularity, the overriding theme of *The Tao of Equus* concerned my personal search for reasons to trust my own experience.

With *Riding between the Worlds*, I'm faced with a new, and in many ways, much more enjoyable task, that of simply reporting what happens when we open our minds and our hearts to the possibility that other creatures have as much to teach us as we have to teach them — not as subjects for behavioral or medical experimentation, but as intelligent, soulful beings in their own right. In this effort, the horse continues to be my guide. The intuitive gifts and sensitivities of this nonpredatory species, combined with its natural penchant for cultivating authentic relationship, make *Equus caballus* especially well suited to acting as a catalyst and a mirror for innovations in human consciousness.

Author, teacher, and medical intuitive Caroline Myss, Ph.D., theorizes that our own species is in the process of moving beyond the limited abilities associated with *Homo sapiens* to a more powerful and refined state of being she calls *Homo noeticus*. In this book I offer evidence to show that horses are also evolving, progressively demonstrating advanced emotional, energetic, and spiritual characteristics as they're given the opportunity to step outside traditional roles as beasts of burden and vehicles for ego gratification.

Not so very long ago, people were ostracized, if not burned at the stake, for relating to animals as sentient beings. The tide is most assuredly turning. I expected more negative response to the unusual theories described in *The Tao of Equus*. Instead I received thousands of letters and emails about the deep, transformative relationships other women and men shared with their horses. They talked about how they felt so alone, unable to discuss the emotions and intuitive insights these animals brought up for fear of being condemned as crazy. With *Riding between the Worlds,* I have the opportunity to share some of these stories, illustrating that personal anecdotes I initially worried were too strange to confess in print are not unique, but rather representative of powerful connections that humans and horses around the world are having with increasing regularity as taboos against treating animals as equals lose influence.

At the same time, I find it necessary to concentrate on horse-human interactions that I've *witnessed* for one simple reason: The most powerful experiences have a significant nonverbal element. Few people can find the words to express their most profound emotions and insights, unless they're interviewed by someone sensitive to these nuances, someone who was actually there to see and feel what happened. I'm *not* reporting these experiences to promote my business in particular. There are many talented equine-facilitated therapy practitioners in this country, and I encourage readers interested in the field to seek out programs established in their own communities. (On my website, www.taoofequus.com, I recommend a number of practitioners whose work I've witnessed, facilitators who guard the horse's perspective and well-being, and keep the client's safety and emotional vulnerability in mind at all times. I also suggest contacting the Equine Facilitated Mental Health Association through NARHA, North American Riding for the Handicapped Association, at (800) 369-RIDE.) While these professionals have many stories to tell, I've found that to capture this work in writing, I have to be present at the session I'm describing. Clients used to suppressing feeling and rejecting their intuition quickly forget important sensations and body language cues. Even experienced equestrians aren't fully conscious of how they respond to nonverbal input from the horses, which is why clinicians promoting a certain method find that some students can perform the exact same moves as the expert and have no impact whatsoever.

In my practice, I encourage students to write their strangest, subtlest, seemingly most irrational impressions down before they leave the barn. I do the same. In this way, we can later reconstruct what took place at a deeper level than reason would otherwise allow. Some of my students and colleagues chose to reveal their names in this book; others used pseudonyms. In two cases, I've combined the stories of several clients with similar issues to further obscure their identities. In this way, I'm able to explore aspects of horse-human interactions rarely shared publicly because they're too personal, too controversial, or too deeply felt to explain.

HIDDEN WISDOM

"Whenever man has left his footprint in the long ascent from barbarism to civilization, we will find the hoofprint of the horse beside it," professed F. Trippet in his book *The First Horsemen*. "Learning to control such a remarkable beast was probably the most exciting development in man's history next to the wheel," asserts *The Encyclopedia of the Horse*. Yet recent developments in the field of equine-facilitated therapy show that the willingness to "get off your high horse," as the old saying goes, allows these animals to perform even more impressive feats of human development, helping overcivilized people reconnect with the wisdom and rhythms of the natural world.

Domesticated horses retain the thought and behavior patterns of their nomadic ancestors. Interacting with these animals on their own terms encourages a fluidity of human thought, emotion, and behavior that sedentary twenty-first-century life makes difficult.

Horses also model the strengths of what are often referred to as "feminine values": cooperation over competition, relationship over territory, responsiveness over strategy, emotion and intuition over logic, process over goal, and the creative approach to life that these qualities engender.

Equine experiential learning, whether practiced formally with a trained facilitator, or informally with one's own horse, first and foremost expands nonverbal awareness. Internet relationships, computer games, cell phones, radios, and flashy multimedia encourage excessive reliance on language and surface appearances. Modern humans are literally mesmerized by words, yet psychologists have determined that less than 10 percent of communication is verbal. Vast nuances of information arise from behavior, emotional import, intent, and more subtle energetic exchanges, qualities so grossly downplayed in postindustrial society that people are losing their ability to function fully and authentically. They tend to judge others, and sometimes themselves, as being good or bad, smart or stupid, trustworthy or suspect based on a few isolated experiences, their often unconscious prejudices, and the opinions of peers. Once this impression is formed, they become increasingly blind to what's happening in the moment. This accounts for a wife with two broken ribs insisting her husband really does love her as she continues to weather his angry outbursts, or a drug addict who ignores evidence of her own sensitivity and intelligence to uphold her parents' mythology that she's the black sheep of the family. When such a person changes for the better, her significant others often find it uncomfortable to alter their static beliefs about her or move beyond the well-worn ways they have related to her for years.

Horses have a gift for "one-trial learning," the ability to process, recall, and elaborate on the lessons gleaned from a single experience. In the wild, they may only have once chance to get it right. Predators, on the other hand, show less facility in this area;

they can make mistakes and live to hunt another day. The equine memory, however, is tempered by an even stronger need to stay alert in the present. If horses are busy planning for the future, reminiscing about the past, or focusing on a single feature of the environment too intensely, a hungry lion moves much closer undetected. This orientation adds immeasurably to the power of equine-facilitated therapy. Unless they've been trained into a state of extreme dissociation or learned helplessness, domesticated horses mirror the truth of what's happening from moment to moment, thus keeping their handlers from becoming mired in projections and illusions. These animals not only reflect incongruities in emotion and intention, they highlight unrecognized strengths and improvements as well. In this way, horses provide a form of biofeedback for practicing self-awareness, emotional agility, and relationship skills that conventional counseling, role-playing exercises, and discussion groups barely access since these techniques are, once again, based primarily in language.

The same principle applies to those aspects of human consciousness often erroneously referred to as "supernatural." Many people who previously sought the advice of professional psychics have developed their own intuitive gifts by working with horses. A number of spiritual counselors have also been humbled. Normally treated as enlightened leaders, they cannot so easily impress a savvy, fully empowered mare or stallion with their reputation and verbal skills. While these animals validate legitimate intuitive strengths, they also reflect areas of imbalance, sometimes with surprising hostility in the presence of people who use meditation practices to suppress unresolved anger — an increasingly common coping strategy psychologist John Welwood has called "spiritual bypassing." Horses simply don't consider empathic, telepathic, and nonlocal forms of consciousness any more remarkable than so-called normal awareness. They model a way of being that moves fluidly through a variety of states most people consider transcendent while remaining grounded and fully present — the ultimate trick, you might say, in bringing nonordinary consciousness into the realm of practical experience.

In this capacity, modern horses demonstrate abilities that have long been alluded to in myth. Throughout the Far East, central Asia, Europe, and the Middle East, traditional cultures depict these animals as mediums between the spirit and material worlds. Certain Celtic tribes, for example, used a white mare as an oracle. Arabic legends also exalt the horse's sixth sense. One story describes a lone rider escaping unexpected attack by acknowledging his steed's nervous whinnies and riding off into the desert hours before his skeptical companions were massacred where they slept. Yet unlike cats, to whom similar extrasensory gifts were attributed, horses were also perceived as carrying riders between the seen and unseen realms, acting as catalysts for creativity, and leading people to myriad forms of lost knowledge. Pegasus spirited the heroes of ancient Greece to the stars of immortality, and the magical waters that inspired poets sprang up where his hoof struck the ground on Helicon, the mountain of the muses. Mohammed received the sacred visions of Islam astride Alborak, the white winged mare who not only took him to heaven but also brought him safely back to earth.

These myths associate equestrian pursuits with images of divine inspiration, but they point to a truth all riders can experience for themselves: Even mortal horses are capable of leading us to hidden realms of emotional, intuitive, and creative vitality. When we respectfully climb on their backs, walk beside them, or sit quietly in their presence, these animals interrupt the hypnotic effects of human conditioning, giving people unusually efficient access to forms of healing, perceiving, and relating they'd previously considered impossible. At the Epona Center, where horses are treated as equals and encouraged to reclaim their full power as sentient beings, clients often feel a surge of emotion the moment they drive onto the property — before they even lay eyes on the herd. "It's like there's a force field surrounding this place," one psychologist told me. "Something shifted in me the moment I walked through the gate."

Defining exactly what shifts in the presence of horses, and why, has been the focus of my research for over a decade. In *Riding between the Worlds*, I delve more deeply into the equine mind and spirit to discover what these amazing creatures have to teach us about the untapped potential of our own species.

CHAPTER ONE

DOES THE HORSE HAVE A BUDDHA NATURE?

S hortly after completing the final draft of my first book, I retreated to the comfort of my herd. Dazed by the barrage of words that had long been circulating through my mind, I was incapable of training or even saddling a horse to ride. Instead, I walked down the line of corrals and flung open the gates. The impulse to run free was overwhelming. Cooped up for too long themselves while I was writing, my horses raced across the property, bucking chaotically through the dust, dodging hitching posts, wheelbarrows, and each other, finally settling around the hay stacked at the edge of a bone-colored wash that hadn't flowed in six weeks. With no fresh grass to nibble, they haphazardly removed the thick blue tarp protecting bales of alfalfa more from sun than from rain. I sat under a gnarled tree and watched them graze Arizona-style, heat waves rising around me even in the shade, blurring the landscape, baking away the chatter in my brain.

A half hour later, when I was as calm inside as I appeared to be outside, my old sage of a mustang Noche turned and stared at me, as if seeing me for the first time. Leaving his celebratory feast, he wandered over and stood next to me, lowering his head, matching his nostrils to the level of my own, transmitting secrets stored in the breath.

Between us, a feeling of ecstasy began to rise. This horse, who had been beaten into submission by his first trainers, had not so long ago found his way back from the dissociative trance that robs trauma victims of their souls. As a part of my equine-facilitated therapy practice, he had gone on to single out, of his own free will, human beings possessing hidden wells of sadness. Time and time again, he would stand beside them, unrestrained, as their hearts melted in his presence, and they finally sobbed out memories they could never speak aloud. Now, this horse, who knew so much about pain, was teaching me something about its opposite.

Though to anyone passing by we appeared to be relaxing in the sketchy shade of a mesquite, Noche and I were ascending. The warmth between us was gathering force, escalating into the rarefied experience of a love I can't adequately describe — a radiant, pulsating combination of gratitude, empowerment, and unconditional regard for all we were and all we had healed in each other over the years. The sensation was feeding back with increasing ferocity. I fought the sudden urge to run away, surprised that something so exquisite could simultaneously seem so threatening. Just when I thought I couldn't bear another minute of it, the feeling began to subside. Noche stayed with me until it dissipated completely. Then he sputtered, shook his head, and walked over to the herd. I started after him, my body contorting in clumsy attempts to regain what I was hoping to escape moments before. "But, but how could you just...leave," I said. "Can't we hang onto that feeling a little longer?"

Noche glanced back, his eyes piercing my heart with an insight that circulated through my bloodstream and flooded my brain with words so clear I could have sworn he spoke them out loud:

"Joy is. Sadness is. You try to lasso one and chase away the other. Yet in finally meeting what you've been craving all along, you're not sure whether to capture it or flee from it, because even great beauty is too wild for you. This is a suffering my kind has never known."

Without the slightest hint of pity or judgment, Noche elucidated the restlessness humans feel. Like every other two-legged creature I knew, I was constantly chasing after so-called positive emotions and running away from the negative. Yet by example, Noche gave me a kinesthetic sense of how to live the Buddhist ideals of nonattachment and nonaversion. He easily saw through the social masks people wear, drawing attention to the truth of what was, while trusting in the wisdom of impermanence. If he felt sadness lurking behind the smiles of my clients, he would step forward and not only dislodge the emotion, but create a safe space where the tears could finally be released. I still don't fully understand how or why he does this, but in his strong, compassionate presence, people are able to mine the depths of despair and come out the other side, finally realizing that, like the thick black clouds of a summer thunderstorm, tempestuous feelings run their course and evaporate, leaving behind a clarity impossible to achieve through suppression.

With a heart open enough to embrace the sorrows of strangers, Noche could also handle a level of ecstasy intimidating to me. As I struggled to contain this overwhelming sense of joy, he flowed into it. As I tried desperately to call it back, he ambled over to the hay pile with the same casual enthusiasm he often exhibited waiting for a carrot after one of our clients made a major breakthrough.

I have seen this horse stand in the rain, the snow, the sun at 110 degrees, with the patience and equanimity he carries in the face of emotions that send most people running for cover. Does Noche have a Buddha nature? Most definitely. But can a horse become a practicing Buddhist? I would have to say no. In Noche's case at least, he doesn't seem to need the practice.

THE COURAGE TO THRIVE

Passing a group of horses huddled together in pasture, I'm often privy to a secret bliss. Sometimes, they're resting peacefully in the shade. Other times, they only seem to be dozing. If I stand with them long enough, I begin to sense waves of feeling moving through the herd, generating a collective subsonic reverie so deep it vibrates through the bones and expands the heart, leaving the ears untouched.

Two years after my mind-expanding encounter with Noche, I have a higher tolerance for the wildness of great beauty, but I'm still haunted by my initial impulse to squelch the joy that rose between us. Since then, I've observed how authentic experiences of love, wonder, and connection can send people into a tailspin just as easily as any negative emotion. Fear — and its accompanying urge to fight, flee, or freeze — has long been known to arise when abuse survivors finally start to feel good. The traumatized nervous system interprets any elevation in arousal, including life-force fluctuations associated with intense well-being, as cause for alarm. Therapeutic techniques involve slowly and carefully separating anxiety from the feeling of being alive. Yet I've also seen successful entrepreneurs, counselors, artists, and educators panic in the face of positive emotions. While this initially seems paradoxical, and even a bit sad, there are numerous reasons for it, some quite logical, others more adventurous. Together they create a picture of the strange position we find ourselves in as our species turns ever so slowly from surviving to thriving.

The U.S. Constitution promises citizens the right to the pursuit of happiness, an ambitious pledge to make, especially in the 1700s. The vast majority of the world's population at that time toiled for the benefit of royalty. Noblemen didn't particularly care if their subjects were happy, or even healthy, for that matter. The ruling class expected people to serve and conform. Religious institutions reinforced this attitude by suppressing all kinds of simple pleasures. Adventurous souls wanting to explore the creative, emotional, sexual, and intuitive dimensions of life were condemned to hell, and sometimes to death. To this day, many people experience repeated surges of fear when they follow their dreams, and feel good as a result of their accomplishments, because the collective memory of humanity reverberates with the dire consequences that so often followed such efforts.

Rigid, narcissistic parents still inflict untold suffering on family members who assert their own needs and desires. Those growing up in abusive environments can feel downright terrified by success. Since the brain creates circuitry patterns in response to experience, physically and sexually abused children develop neural pathways associating stress *and* pleasure with negative, even life-threatening outcomes. Attempts to set boundaries and move toward self-empowerment are met with more violence. These people are wired to expect any rise in self-esteem, personal expression, sexual excitement, love, joy, or connection to end in tragedy or shame. They often pass these debilitating behavioral and emotional patterns onto *their* children, even if, as adults, they manage to break the cycle of overt physical abuse.

The right to seek personal fulfillment, an incredible breakthrough in 1776, remains an unrealized ideal for many people. Over the last two hundred years, men and women of the free world may have grown a bit more comfortable *pursuing* happiness. Most of us, however, aren't sure what to do when we find it, and some are so conditioned to receive punishment for it we barely enjoy it while it lasts. This is perhaps the most frustrating dilemma we face in changing the unconscious patterns handed down by our ancestors.

Serfs, slaves, concubines, soldiers, refugees, and later, factory workers were routinely prevented from experiencing even the most fleeting sense of elation. How could they possibly teach their children to manage the curious power unleashed by emotions like joy, ecstasy, and bliss? The same wisdom eluded their leaders, who were so busy managing and defending territory they had little time to think of anything else. Survival of the fittest was the rule, no matter what socioeconomic class a person belonged to. This mentality affected the so-called objective sciences long after technology offered a sense of physical security unknown to previous generations. In the mid-twentieth century, psychology absorbed the Darwinian tendency to interpret emotion and behavior in terms of survival value. Researchers tried to explain everything from creativity and consciousness to a mother's love and a child's smile as an evolutionary innovation brought about through natural selection.

As society became more industrialized and computerized, so did its metaphors for sentient life. One of our culture's most powerful and damaging myths insists that the universe and everything in it must work according to predictable, mechanical laws. This leads to a marked ineptitude in the more ephemeral realms of feeling, imagination, and intuition. Social institutions deny the wisdom of the body and the senses, deifying the mind in a vacuum, training people to stand in production lines or sit in cubicles at computers, sublimating their physical and emotional needs to the cold, objective logic of consumerism and competition. Many endure the drudgery of meaningless employment, or unemployment, by self-medicating. Recreational drugs, from alcohol to marijuana to television, lull the disillusioned into a comfortable stupor, providing just enough of a high to make a stilted life bearable. Those difficult souls who object through the inconveniences of depression, chronic dissatisfaction, and the proverbial "nervous breakdown" can be fixed with more sophisticated prescriptions and sent back to work. There's no need to pursue happiness with this approach. It comes in bottles marked "Valium," and more recently, "Prozac." With the right dosage, there's no danger of feeling too good. Staying at a nice, complacent, even keel is just what the doctor ordered.

While human beings routinely suppress their emotional and spiritual needs to survive, the ability to thrive demands uncommon courage and awareness, a kind of compassionate, creative intelligence willing to take chances outside conventional thought and behavior. To successfully pursue happiness, one must also work up the nerve to *feel* it, knowing full well that to finally open the heart is to encounter the other outlawed emotions in all their terrible glory. The root of courage, after all, comes from the French word *coeur*, which literally means heart. Most of us have been taught to see this organ as a mechanical pump supporting the fleshy robot that carries a cool, calculating brain around. In this metaphor, strong emotion of any kind is perceived as malfunction. It simply does not compute. At the dawn of the twenty-first century, mainstream culture is no closer to understanding the dynamics of happiness than it was two centuries ago. It has only succeeded in treating people more like well-oiled machines.

Yet it *is* possible to come to terms with a violent past, reclaim the soul, form mutually supportive relationships, and move gracefully through the sorrows and joys of life. If an old mustang like Noche could make this seemingly complex transformation, why not the rest of us? What lost knowledge do horses express through their simple yet profound way of being, and how can we regain a bit of this wisdom for ourselves?

DEEP PEACE

Since Charles Darwin, the behavioral sciences have studied the "classic list" of human emotions: anger, sadness, disgust, fear, surprise, happiness, and contentment. When social psychologist Dacher Keltner established the Berkeley Center for the Development of Peace and Well-Being, he championed research moving beyond what he calls the "self-interested emotions." Based at the University of California at Berkeley, Keltner's brainchild explores "benevolent emotions" like hope, awe, love, compassion, and gratitude. Peace, he says, "is about social harmony *in connection*," and is "based, therefore, on a different set of principles and practices than personal well-being." In this sense, the individual's ability to thrive cannot help but be influenced by his relationships — a colossal conundrum, considering that while modern civilization has successfully curtailed threats from the environment, it hasn't begun to eradicate the pain and suffering that people, and the social institutions they create, inflict on members of their own species. The average human being is much less likely to be chased by wolves, hunted down by lions, and exposed to the elements than he is to be victimized by parents, lovers, bosses, coworkers, and, sometimes, his own children.

Yet, in my work with horses as co-therapists, I've repeatedly witnessed how the suppression of self-interested emotion actually inhibits true connection. Peace, love, and compassion can create social *disharmony* when worn like masks to cover unresolved anger, fear, sadness, and depression. No one has ever illuminated this paradox more clearly for me than my black Arabian mare Tabula Rasa. Her response to a woman with the best human and spiritual intentions illustrated that the art of creating peace and well-being requires much more than most people imagine. And yet the solution, like so many horse-inspired insights, is deceptively simple. It involves recognizing just how interconnected we already are.

The week before an extended equine-facilitated workshop called The Power of Authenticity, one of the participants, "Rhiannon," phoned to inform me she'd shown up early to do some sightseeing.

"Do you mind if I stop by and meet the herd before I head off to California for a few days?" she asked. Her voice felt like cool velvet — the result, I learned, of a morning spent in meditation. In town for forty-eight hours, she'd already visited the local Buddhist center, the vegan restaurant across town, and a number of other alternative attractions most lifelong Tucson residents have yet to explore.

"I'll be teaching until four," I said. "Why don't you come over after that, and I'll show you around."

When I noticed a slim, graceful woman with long, silver hair wandering around the property during my three o'clock riding lesson, I wasn't sure if she was looking for me or someone else. At the large public stable where I based my practice for three years, people I barely knew would come and go at all hours. The stranger standing at the south fence was outside shouting range, yet even from a distance, something about her made the hair on the back of my neck rise. "I hope that's not Rhiannon," I thought.

Sure enough, she opened the gate and walked confidently toward me. "You're Linda, right?" she said.

My gut recoiled in response. "Yes," I mumbled. My throat was constricting, undermining my ability to talk and even breathe. The intervening silence felt unusually tense. I couldn't imagine why my body was reacting so strongly to this gentle and obviously adventurous, intelligent woman.

"Christie's lesson is running a little late today," I finally managed to say as my gray gelding Max began to jig and sidestep — despite his rider's normally successful attempts to keep him calm. "We just need to practice a little cantering. In the meantime, why don't you head over and meet the other horses." I pointed to the corrals housing the rest of my herd and voiced the same recommendation I always make to new clients: "Don't pet them right away. See what happens when you try to connect over the fence without touching them. I'll be with you in a few minutes."

I could barely concentrate on the task at hand. Something about Rhiannon made me feel unbalanced, anxious . . . angry. I silently chided myself for these irrational emotions as Christie and Max galloped circles around me. "What's *wrong* with you?" my inner critic said. "This woman has traveled all the way from Boston to study with you. So what if she shows up a few days early. Can't you give her a few extra minutes of your time? You better pull yourself together and *be nice.*"

As my student led her horse back to his stall, I reluctantly walked toward Rhiannon, agitation increasing with every step despite my conviction to act the perfect host.

"So," I said, trying desperately not to grit my teeth, though I couldn't seem to release the fists hidden in my coat pockets, "which horse are you most attracted to?"

"Well, attraction isn't really the word I'd use," she replied. "I had such a disturbing experience with that black horse over there that I felt too disoriented to look at anyone else."

Rhiannon pointed at Tabula Rasa, the one member of my herd I could count on to welcome newcomers. This confident, gregarious mare had mothered so many people out of their fear of horses that I'd come to rely on her ability to stay calm in the midst of the strongest emotions. When I informed Rhiannon who had singled her out, she looked even more confused.

"Really?" she asked in obvious disbelief. "When I read about Rasa in your book, she sounded like the sweetest, smartest horse in the world."

"What happened?"

"Well, she was standing at the back of her corral under that tree when I walked up. All of a sudden, she ran toward me, teeth bared, flames shooting out of her eyes. If there hadn't been a fence between us, she might actually have attacked me."

To say I was astonished would be an understatement. Rhiannon's description of Rasa reflected how I had felt when this seemingly peaceful woman first greeted me — only, being human, I'd been taught to suppress such flamboyant outbursts and blame myself for the "inappropriate" feelings underneath. While I was certainly glad I hadn't let my emotions run wild, I was comforted by Rasa's reaction. My hands relaxed; my jaw released. The haughty critic in my head could only say, "Hmmmm. . . ."

I invited Rhiannon to sit with me on the straw bales next to Rasa's paddock. Flashes of disappointment and sadness moved across her face as she told me how rejected she felt.

"Rasa doesn't hate you," I assured her, "but she *was* trying to tell you something. She was holding up a mirror for you. Imagine running toward her with the same expression, the same intensity she showed you. What would you be saying?"

Rhiannon took a deep breath and closed her eyes with such a studied sense of calmness I half expected her to adopt the lotus position, but she managed to get into the spirit of the exercise much quicker than I would have thought. Mouth gradually contorting, hands clenching into fists, her gentle demeanor evolved into a picture of absolute rage. "Now let's *finally* have it out!" she shouted with a guttural force that actually made Rasa take a step back.

The Power of Authenticity is an advanced workshop designed to boost creativity, intuition, sensory awareness, and nonverbal communication through reflective activities with horses, while giving participants the experience of building authentic community. People with serious psychological difficulties are not encouraged to attend. Even so, the horses effectively draw out issues of all kinds in even the most conscious, accomplished participants. It took Rasa a matter of minutes to unearth core feelings in Rhiannon that years of meditation and counseling had somehow left unresolved. No way was I going to make her wait until the official start of the workshop to explore the mare's unusual response.

Over the next hour, I learned that Rhiannon had grown up in

a repressive household with parents and siblings who repeatedly complained that she was "too sensitive." Efforts to "toughen her up" seemed to backfire. She remained, in the eyes of her family, too fragile and irrational to ever amount to anything. Several ill-fated romances did little to boost Rhiannon's faith in herself, or other people. Spending time alone, in nature or with her artwork, became her only solace, but the sense of isolation was at times overwhelming. Meditation class, which she originally attended in the hopes of quieting her chaotic emotions, was one of the few places where she could experience some semblance of peace in the presence of other human beings.

After visiting a friend's barn, Rhiannon also developed an interest in horses. She was immediately attracted to their purity of spirit. "You always know exactly where you stand with them," she told me. "Even when Rasa lunged at me, I knew there was no hidden agenda. With most of the people in my life, I never really understand what's going on. When I'm around them for any length of time, something inside me just wants to run screaming in the other direction."

I proceeded to explain the concept of the "feeling bearer," a term my frequent co-facilitator, counselor Kathleen Barry Ingram, had devised to characterize a natural empath who unconsciously acted out or compensated for emotions others refused to own. "You think all these feelings that have been driving you crazy are yours," I emphasized, "but I guarantee you that most of them are not. Your parents, brothers, and husbands had all kinds of fears and frustrations they couldn't face. Just because they put on stoic masks of self-control didn't make it all go away. Those unspoken feelings gathered force and continued to subconsciously affect everyone in your household. *You* routinely released the pressure by crying or raging for no apparent reason. Then, of course, everyone berated you for showing them what they were ashamed to feel." I imagined Rhiannon's family sitting around the dinner table talking quietly about the weather as an arsenal of fireworks bounced off the walls and exploded all around them. "People aren't the separate beings they think they are, but they can bolster this illusion by cutting themselves off from their own hearts. You were never quite able to make that break."

Rhiannon hadn't considered the possibility before. Though she breathed a sigh of relief, another part of her remained skeptical. She had been taught, after all, that feelings were inconvenient, irrational, self-contained sensations that needed to be controlled — and preferably hidden at all cost. The fact that she was incapable of doing this seemed to her a fatal weakness.

"How could I act out emotions that were never, ever discussed in my family?" she asked.

"Please explain to me," I countered, "how Rasa could so effectively mirror the anger and frustration you've been carrying around since childhood seconds after meeting you."

I told Rhiannon that her incongruent presence had affected me as powerfully as it had my mare. I also admitted that I didn't fully understand what was happening until Rasa illustrated, with pure abandon, these feelings emanating from our guest. Before that realization, I thought my agitation arose from some selfish impulse, that I had become so spoiled by success that I didn't want to share a few extra minutes with a woman who'd traveled across the country to attend an Epona workshop. But this assessment was totally off the mark. As my body registered anger, my mind desperately searched for internal reasons to explain it and shame myself for it, when in reality, it was like a blast of irritating smoke coming from someone else's fire.

"It's truly an art form to decipher the intertwining emotional messages circulating through even the most casual relationships," I said. "Some of these feelings are personal, but if we suppress them long enough, they break through our façades of control and well-being, seeping out like stale air escaping a leaky tire and subtly

choking those around us. Because our society hasn't even acknowledged this possibility, it affects us unconsciously. But if we become
aware of the dynamic, we can't so easily be victimized by other
people's feelings — or our own.

"Once Rasa showed me the anger was coming from you, it dissipated in me completely. If it had lessened only slightly, I would
have figured that your hidden anxiety was also triggering some
neglected feeling that I needed to recognize and work on. But I've
at least come far enough in this work to understand that my
intense reaction had nothing to do with 'not liking' you or thinking there was something evil about you, which is the conclusion
untrained empaths often come to when they feel surges of unspoken fear or anger coming from another person."

Rhiannon's eyes widened at this notion. She acknowledged
that the peace she experienced through meditation was, on the
whole, short-lived. Small talk with students right after class sometimes raised her anxiety — more evidence, she decided, that her
continued turmoil reflected a lack of compassion and progress.
She thought she needed to work harder to achieve the bliss she
longed for through Buddhist practice. Yet if some of these errant
emotions weren't hers, maybe she wasn't so maladjusted. Maybe
this curse could be honed into a useful skill.

"It's an interesting theory," she said, "but how do I really know
that Rasa wasn't just telling me to get lost?"

"That's a valid question," I replied. "Let's see how she responds
if you approach her without trying to hide what you've been
taught to reject in yourself. Earlier you gave words to Rasa's
threatening behavior: 'Now let's *finally* have it out.' As you walk
toward her corral again, tell her, out loud, everything that phrase
brings up for you."

Rhiannon hesitated, wary of exposing long forbidden
thoughts and feelings. I obviously didn't have time to establish the
kind of relationship counselors build before encouraging intimate

disclosure. But I did have secret weapon — a sensitive and expressive colleague who Rhiannon knew would never lie to her, categorize her, or, most importantly, betray her trust.

"Rasa's a horse," I emphasized. "She's can't tell anyone what you reveal, and I'm going to stay well out of hearing range. What do you have to lose? Her reaction couldn't possibly be much worse than the first time you approached her, and you still have a fence between the two of you."

From a distance, I watched this woman tentatively put one foot in front of the other as she spoke about things, she later told me, she had never fully admitted to herself, much less another living soul. Had her father beaten her? Did she hate her mother? Was her first husband unfaithful? These were questions I didn't learn the answers to that day, but I could see that a soulful confession was taking place nonetheless.

Rhiannon paused several times along the way, wringing her hands, rubbing her left temple. When her shoulders began to convulse, the tears must have been flowing, though her silver mane strategically obscured any glimpse of her face. The whole time, Rasa repeatedly licked and chewed, yawned and stretched her neck — equine signs of release. As Rhiannon approached the fence, the mare moved gently, almost reverently toward her and stood quietly, witnessing, supporting through presence, if not literal understanding. The woman's voice eventually faded, and the two seemed, for a few moments, suspended in pure being. Rhiannon turned and nodded, inviting me to join them, her moist gray-blue eyes soft yet radiant. All the tension I had felt in my own body seemed a distant, incoherent memory as Rasa let out a colossal sigh. A subtle but palpable feeling surrounded the three of us, like the scent of creosote and cactus flowers hanging heavy in the air after a long-awaited desert shower. I took a deep breath, drawing it into my lungs, my heart, my soul.

"That," I said, when I finally dared to break the silence, "is *peace.*"

RIDING THE PRESENT MOMENT

"Horses are such forgiving creatures," Rhiannon marveled during the opening session of our workshop the following week. She hadn't yet shared the details of her encounter with Rasa, but several of the participants nodded their heads in agreement, having no doubt experienced this equine capacity themselves.

"Why do you think that is?" she asked.

"It's not forgiveness in the human sense," I replied, "because there's no judgment to begin with. It's closer to the original meaning of the word forgiveness: to let go. Only it's not the nature of horses to cling to anything, so there's no need *to let go*. They simply respond authentically to what's happening moment to moment."

"Sounds like a Zen concept to me," said another participant, who was, like Rhiannon, a serious student of martial arts and meditation.

"Well, it's not a *concept* to horses," I replied with a smile, knowing full well where the conversation was headed. "It's a way of life beyond concepts, which I guess is very Zen in itself."

In discussions about horse behavior, Zen terminology often comes up, particularly among people who engage in equestrian activities for personal development. A symbol of freedom in many cultures, the horse models, naturally and effortlessly, many of the qualities promoted by this Asian "way of liberation," as philosopher Alan Watts characterized it. Zen values spontaneous experience as a vehicle for human transformation. Practitioners strive to reconnect with a universal source beyond language, mental constructs, methods, and judgment.

In his classic book *The Way of Zen*, Watts emphasized that this "view of life . . . does not belong to any of the formal categories of modern Western thought. It is not a religion or philosophy; it is not a psychology or a type of science." It is, however, an artful fusion of Chinese Taoism and Indian Buddhism that came into existence when the latter made its way to China around 520 C.E. Originally known as Ch'an, it spread throughout Asia, emerging in Japan in the twelfth century. Zen subsequently infused its adoptive culture with delicate styles of architecture, painting, poetry, and gardening that blurred distinctions between natural and man-made structures, outwardly reflecting the wide-open spaces of naked awareness cultivated through meditation.

In their original forms, Buddhism and Taoism both encourage moving beyond the conditioned persona by emptying the mind of desires, preconceived notions, obsessive preoccupations with the past, and fearful or fanciful projections into the future. Various meditation practices eventually free the individual to respond authentically with the purity and openness of a child tempered by the wisdom and equanimity of a sage. The two traditions, however, diverge on several important points. According to *The Tao of Zen* by Ray Grigg, "Buddhism separates from the world to transcend it; Taoism dissolves back into the world to become one with it." Zen straddles a fine line between the two. "Any discipline in Taoism is used to reenter fully what is already present," notes Grigg. "This is also the case in Zen." Though it fully embraces Buddhism's insights into human suffering, Zen also encompasses Taoism's lightness, playfulness, and appreciative acceptance of earthly experience. Meditation in this tradition releases "the practitioner into the spontaneity and freedom of merely being. The end of all this searching and discipline is a full and balanced life lived gracefully and harmoniously in wonderful simplicity. The sitter returns to the village to become fully engaged in the profoundly ordinary business of day-to-day existence." The rigorous training promoted by some of the other Buddhist sects, however, "does not complete the cycle of leaving, returning, and reaffirming. It spins outward to become removed, unearthly, and austere, reluctantly present in the world as if living were a kind of selfless practice."

If the horse has a Buddha nature, it's definitely of the Zen variety. These animals embody many of the attitudes and skills people develop through this practice, including the ability to engage fully with reality. What seems so difficult for a grasping, hoarding, controlling, competitive human being comes easily to a highly social, intensely aware, nomadic prey animal. Horses are actually hardwired for the state of nonattachment championed by the Buddha. In the wild, they don't defend territory, build nests, live in caves, or store nuts for the winter. They move, unprotected, with the rhythms of nature, cavorting through the snow, kicking up their heels on cool spring mornings, grazing peacefully in fields of flowing grass, despite a keen and constant awareness of predators lurking in the distance. While they react quickly in the face of danger, they also show remarkable resilience in recovering from traumatic events.

Some horses are proud and flamboyant, others more gentle and accommodating, yet they all experience a profound interconnectedness with the herd that doesn't detract from their individuality. They feel what others feel, respond to the information, and then let it go, ready to embrace the next moment with equal attention and enthusiasm. Humans spend so much time and energy judging what should or shouldn't happen, what they *should* or *shouldn't* feel, that they sacrifice their ability to enjoy or adapt to what is happening. While horses certainly have their preferences in life, these animals never lose contact with the fluctuating nature of existence. "Be like a mirror," wrote the Chinese sage Chuang-tzu. "A mirror does not search for or create things, but welcomes and responds to all that comes before it." This in essence describes the eternally reflective mind of the horse.

It's no surprise that people with an affinity for martial arts and meditation find their practices enhanced immeasurably by noncompetitive equestrian activities. In her book *Zen and Horses*, Ingrid Soren describes the insights she gained during her first year of riding. "I felt fully alive," she writes. "Now I could understand Zen Master Dogen's words for real, based on this experience. 'Do not work for freedom, rather allow the practice itself to be liberation.'"

Soren became one with her mount and her surroundings, strengthening "those childlike qualities of absorbed readiness, alertness, and responsiveness" as she found herself too immersed "in the process to have self-centered thoughts that limit the mind." Even though she had studied yoga and other Eastern philosophies for twenty years, she *lived* this knowledge on the back of a horse in ways she never imagined possible, "practicing skill in action," exercising "the art of not trying," learning to "control by going with and understanding" another sentient being. Describing her first gallop as "meditation in action," she came face to face with her logical mind's "limited capacity for problem-solving" and reveled in discovering the "miraculous in the everyday."

"I had to be completely awake," she remembers. "'In the heart of this moment is eternity,' wrote the thirteenth-century monk Meister Eckhart. Horseback riding was verifying this mystic experience for me. Riding seemed to be the ultimate in mindfulness, in absorption, in being present, being there. Those timeless moments experienced in time remain engraved in my memory with an intense clarity, and still inspire awe at both their beauty and their ordinariness. Each one was about being totally present, totally alive. And then it was gone."

Soren makes no apologies for her horse-inspired transformations. "I'm doing this through relationships other than human ones," she states. "And why not? The Buddha says that it is better to travel alone than to travel in the companionship of a fool."

CHAPTER TWO

TORNADO HEAD

Most people aren't fools as much as they are slaves — a bold statement to make in a country founded on the concept of freedom. Yet my equine colleagues have repeatedly made this so clear that I refuse to mince words about it. While overt subjugation has been outlawed, its mental and emotional remnants continue to influence Epona's most accomplished clients. The doctors, artists, social workers, psychiatrists, college professors, and business professionals who attend our advanced human development workshops prove no less immune than people requiring horse-facilitated psychotherapy. Because these insidious patterns have been internalized, and often rewarded in our culture, they're all the more difficult to expel in those who enjoy the trappings of success.

The first hint is a nagging lack of fulfillment, sometimes dealt with through workaholism, alcoholism, chronic spending, sex addiction, or the rampant thirst for advanced degrees and certifications some people pursue to justify their existence. The second, and most telling, symptom is the inner critic. Each person, in effect, carries around a mini tyrant in his head — a debilitating, judgmental voice that stems from a by-product of socialization often called the False Self. Though I obviously didn't invent the term, I use it to character-ize destructive aspects of the ego that limit human potential, causing the average adult to sacrifice her dreams and hide her talents, usually for the sake of acceptance and security. Unless they're intimidated into submission, most horses refuse to cooperate with the False Self, which is how I noticed this phenomenon to begin with. I later real-ized it was the same repressive feature of the civilized persona that people have been challenging for centuries, through art and philos-ophy, through Eastern mindfulness practices and yoga, as well as through more contemplative forms of Christianity and Judaism — all contexts for the revitalization and liberation of that most neg-lected and elusive of attributes: the human soul.

It took a woman with a particularly ornery False Self to bring it to my attention, but I quickly noticed the dynamic affecting all my clients, operating at subtler levels in those who appeared, on the surface, to be living the American dream. "Cynthia" at first seemed a member of the latter category. She called me up after reading *The Tao of Equus* while recovering from a horseback riding injury. Married to an affluent attorney, this genteel, forty-five-year-old Louisiana socialite had purchased an exceptionally well-trained horse named Jasper shortly after her youngest son left for college. The gray thoroughbred gelding, who seemed so secure and accommodating during her test ride, turned out to be, in Cynthia's words, "a real scaredy-cat." Shortly after she finalized the deal, he began challenging her authority on the ground and "spooking at nothing" under saddle. One brisk November morn-ing, he leapt to the side and threw her, breaking her right arm. Much to her family's dismay, Cynthia refused to sell the horse, even though she couldn't bring herself to ride when the cast was removed. Convinced she had developed a mild case of post-traumatic stress disorder, she decided to spend a week at the Epona Center. The woman hoped to work her way onto the back of one of my horses while learning how to train "the spooks and gremlins out of Jasper."

"I feel like something inside me will die if I can't bring myself to ride again," she told me during our first session. "Even I don't understand why this is so important to me. It's the only thing I ever stood up for in my life, but I can't break through the fright no matter how hard I try."

I explained that her own fear, and the unconscious tension it created, could have caused Jasper to shy, giving the impression he was "spooking at nothing." Cynthia insisted she couldn't possibly have been afraid before the accident. "I used to ride bareback a lot as a child," she said in her breathless southern drawl. "I had my own pony, and we won a few shows. But the best times were when my girlfriend and I would race through the woods. We'd slide off laughing sometimes, but we always got right back on. I absolutely love horses, but with three boys, PTA meetings, soccer games, a husband who was trying to make partner, and all those socials at the executive club we belonged to partly to help him make the right connections, I just didn't have the time. I always knew I'd get another horse, though. That's why this thing with Jasper is so demoralizing. I did everything right. I took some dressage lessons to get back in shape. I really researched the market, and I thought I had found the perfect horse. Then what do I do? I fall off and break my arm like some rank amateur in the first month, and I'm too much of a baby to get back on. Do you think you can fix me?"

With her sleek auburn hair and statuesque figure, Cynthia was a potentially powerful-looking woman, yet her demeanor was that of a petite southern belle trying to take over an Amazon's body. Habitually resting most of her weight on her right leg, she held her head slightly to the left in a coquettish manner and gazed, almost shyly, with her eyes cutting to the right. Both shoulders slumped, perhaps to detract from her height. Even so, there was no denying that she towered a good five inches over me. I wondered if her girlish mannerisms, so incongruent and off balance for a woman of her age and size, had somehow contributed to her fall.

I told her we wouldn't be able to "fix" anything until we understood the dynamics involved: "Because fear is especially contagious to a prey animal like the horse, we're going to slow everything down and find out how this emotion affects your body, your breathing, and your ability to think clearly, because all of these things influence your horse's sense of confidence and well-being. Later, we'll take a look at how an insecure horse affects your arousal level, and what you can do to calm things down from the saddle. Let's start with what you feel when you're afraid."

"I feel stupid and worthless," she replied without hesitation.

"That's a judgment your mind makes in response to the fear," I said. "What do you feel *in your body?*" Cynthia had no idea what I was talking about.

I took her through an awareness exercise designed to illustrate how the environment, the body, and the mind exchange information through feeling. The process involved standing in a grounded position known in martial arts as "the horse pose": feet shoulder-width apart, knees slightly bent, arms bent at the elbow and extended outward, like a person loosely holding a pair of invisible reins. Cynthia was surprised to discover how unbalanced and vulnerable she felt in a stance that mimicked the optimum position for riding.

"I'm such a loser," she said. "If I can't even stand here like this without pitching a fit, how will I ever be able to get on a horse?"

I was beginning to notice a pattern. Every time Cynthia got close to feeling anything, she found some way to berate herself and her experience.

"The horse pose is just a tool, not some test you have to pass,"

I emphasized. "Nothing you do or feel or even think can possibly be wrong at this stage. It's all information to help us understand where the fear comes from, what it means, how you're reacting to it, and how it affects the horse you're riding. Based on what is happening, we can then determine what's possible, what *wants* to happen, and from that, the solution will begin to emerge on its own.

"The only thing that gets in our way is fixating on what we think should or shouldn't happen. Telling yourself that you should just be able to get over your fear, or that you shouldn't be disturbed by the horse pose, these ideas don't match up with the undeniable fact that you *can't* 'just get over it,' that you *are* anxious standing in that grounded position. It's especially important to notice when you fall into judgments that disconnect from reality, which is the state of mind you were in when you called yourself a loser just now. Underneath that critical voice are instructive feelings communicating legitimate concerns. Those are what we're ultimately trying to get to by standing in the horse pose."

Cynthia rolled her eyes. "When you talk like that, I feel like I'm standing in a hall of mirrors, looking at my reflection from different angles that go on and on into infinity," she laughed.

"Exactly," I said. "You'll get used to it. There's a purpose — and an end   to it, I promise. But first, you'll learn to engage this reflective, nonjudgmental 'witnessing mind' with yourself and your horse simultaneously."

As Cynthia tried the stance once more, I encouraged her to close her eyes and breathe deeply into her solar plexus. "Don't try to relax," I said. "Don't try to change anything at all. I'm asking you to breathe into the center of your body to draw your consciousness there. We want to know what's happening below your neck right now. What sensation is most prominent?"

"Well, it's still difficult for me to stand like this," she admitted. "It feels unnatural, but that's all I can tell you." Cynthia squinted as her shoulders slumped even more. "I . . . I'm numb below my neck," she said, in contrast to the obvious increase in tension. "Numb and dumb." She giggled nervously, opening her eyes. They were moist with the first hint of tears she was obviously fighting to hold back. "I know you said there's no right or wrong to this, but I'm afraid I'm hopeless because *I can't feel anything.*"

"Numbness, believe it or not, is something," I assured her, ignoring for a moment the fact that she not only interrupted the process by judging herself again, but she was resisting a good cry, which was also something, something big. "When you can't feel anything below the neck, it usually means you've been suppressing so much for so long that you've overloaded your nervous system. There's probably a lot more going on here than the trauma of a single riding accident. Numbness below the neck is a classic symptom of a mind fighting to keep some pretty serious emotions in check. To your horse, you probably feel like a time bomb ticking away. Think about it. The whole lower half of your body, the part your mind is desperately trying to ignore, rests firmly on Jasper's spinal chord whenever you sit in the saddle. Even though you told me over the phone that everything in your life was fine, that you just had some riding-related issues to work through, I have to know now, before we go any further, whether or not you have access to a good counselor when you return home."

"I do," she said quietly, lowering her eyes. "I've been seeing a psychiatrist since I had a bit of a . . . a spell . . . a few years ago. I stop by every once in a while, mainly to get my prescription renewed. I thought Jasper might help me feel good enough to get off all that nonsense. I just had so much stress with three teenage boys. And Jim, well, he was working sixty-hour weeks; he couldn't help much at home. One day I just blew a fuse. It's something we keep *very* quiet outside the family. It may be all the rage to see a shrink in New York City, but people in the South just think you're plumb crazy."

"So there's no history of abuse or anything like that?" I asked.

"Oh no," she replied with a little too much enthusiasm. "I mean we all got the switch when we were bad, but that's the way it was when I was growing up. You caught a whippin' at school if you didn't mind the teacher. My daddy always said that if we got whopped in class, we'd get it twice as bad when we got home, and I have to say it worked. I was a good little girl, much better than my own boys, who never got spanked. I just didn't have the heart for it myself. My kids had an easy row to hoe, and they don't appreciate it one bit."

"Well, even if everybody got whopped back then, it still bred a certain amount of fear and insecurity knowing that the adults in your life might resort to violence at any time, wouldn't you say?" I asked. Cynthia shrugged. "So, let's assume that by finally allowing your body and your emotions to speak, which is what we have to do to get to the essence of fears associated with Jasper, some things might come up that have nothing to do with horseback riding." The cool southern belle standing beside me seemed to wilt ever so slightly. "Even so," I reassured her, "there's a way to keep the flood-gates from bursting open all at once. Do you want to give it a try?"

"Might as well," she sighed, "since I know Jim wants to get his money's worth."

"I think the skills you'll learn will be valuable in and out of the riding arena, but I don't want you to do anything here for your husband's sake, or anyone else's," I stressed. "We need to move at a pace *you* feel comfortable with. Agreed?"

SOLD TO THE HIGHEST BIDDER

Cynthia closed her eyes, this time with greater conviction, breathing much more deeply into her solar plexus. She noticed some pressure in her shoulders.

"Okay," I said. "That's great. That's what we're looking for. But before we go any further I want you to make a deal with your body. I want you to tell it that you'll listen to its concerns, its needs, its memories, from now on, but *only if they're released a little at a time.* Let me say it again because this is important: You'll listen to whatever your body has to say from now on, but only if it releases the information a little at a time."

I encouraged her to repeat this in her own words several times before I continued. "Now, keeping your eyes closed, I want you to breathe into your shoulders. I know this sounds strange, and it is a metaphor. But recognizing that you were able to breathe into the center of your body to draw your consciousness there, do the same thing with the place where you feel the most pressure — again not to relax your shoulders, but to open a dialogue with that part of your body. There's a message in that sensation, maybe more than one reason for the pressure. Breathe into it; expand the feeling; let it get bigger for a moment so it can speak to you. But remember, you don't want to be flooded with information. Clear your mind of any preconceived notions and ask your shoulders to send you *one* image, *one* memory, *one* color, *one* completely irrational phrase. The information may come in a form we can't predict, so be open to possibilities. As soon as you receive even the subtlest wisp of a message, open your eyes."

Cynthia's response was instantaneous. "Wow," she said. "I actually saw something. It was so vivid. I had no idea my body would speak to me like that." She shook her head in disbelief, and then the tears rolled down her cheeks. "I saw my pony, Jellybean, the one I had as a little girl. He stared at me for a moment, so handsome, so happy, so trusting, and then someone put a halter on him and led him away.

"I was afraid this would happen," she added, sniffing and wiping her eyes with the back of her sleeve. "I always did bawl like a baby at the drop of a hat. Here I am a forty-five-year-old mother of three grown boys threatening to cry me a river over something long since dead and buried."

"What happened to Jellybean?" I asked, handing her a tissue and expecting the worst, but the scenario she shared didn't seem so traumatic, at least not at first.

"Oh, you know, I outgrew him, and we sold him to another little girl. I'm sure he went to a good home and all."

"What are you feeling right now?"

"Silly," she said with a self-conscious laugh.

"That's a judgment suppressing the real feeling underneath," I stressed, "and it successfully stopped your crying before you really got started. Where did those tears come from? What did they mean?"

"Sad," she whispered, looking off into the distance, "I guess I'm sad...little bit...still. But I don't want to talk about it anymore right now, okay? Let's do something involving some real, live horses."

We sat down on the straw bales next to an ancient mesquite tree, and I explained how to use the same process in deciding which member of the Epona herd she wanted to work with first: "Just for a change, just for fun, let's ask your body to make the decision. There are seven horses in seven different corrals. Before you walk up to each fence, stand back, in the horse pose, breathe into your belly, and notice what you feel. Don't change anything or judge anything or even try to discover the message right away. The idea is to get a baseline reading using your entire body as a sensing device. Once you've scanned yourself, slowly walk up to the horse, staying outside the fence, and notice if anything shifts. Does your breathing become deeper or shallower in the presence of a particular horse? Do your shoulders feel heavier or lighter? Do you notice a tingling sensation in your gut? Does your heart seem to expand or contract? Do you feel more grounded or light-headed? Do you get any sharp pains or strange images or sudden urges to run away? Whatever comes up, no matter how ridiculous it seems, write it down in your notebook before moving on to the next horse. The subtler and more irrational the information, the more significant it's likely to be. But make sure you write it down or your logical mind will forget most of it simply because it doesn't make sense right away."

For the next half hour I watched Cynthia methodically approach each horse, scanning her body, pausing now and then to write in her journal. When she joined me on the straw bales again, her posture had improved. She seemed content, even pleased — for a moment. Then her shoulders sank as she opened her mouth: "I really don't think I got anything worthwhile."

After a bit of coaxing, Cynthia began to read from her journal, and I realized that her body's awareness system was much more accurate and sophisticated than even I suspected. She had, for instance, felt a "dull ache" in her right knee when she approached Rasa. "It came up suddenly," she said, "and then went away when I moved to the next horse. That's why I wrote it down." When I informed her that the mare had an arthritic condition in her right back stifle, similar to the knee in humans, the woman perked up for an instant before chiding herself once more. "Oh yeah, now I remember; you mentioned Rasa's lameness in your book. Well, that explains it."

"You may have read about it three months ago," I said, "but you didn't know which mare was Rasa; we have several black horses here. Your body gave you a big clairsentient clue. That's pretty amazing, wouldn't you say?"

"Not really," she replied. "I think it was just my imagination trying to impress us both with something I knew subconsciously. I mean, I also read that you had a black stallion named Merlin who was a bit dangerous, and I felt like he was trying to get me to rub his withers today. I knew from the book that he didn't like that sort of thing, so of course I didn't dare reach out. But I was real skittish around that other black fella who was dozing in the shade, even though he certainly didn't look wild and unpredictable."

"*That* was Merlin," I corrected her. "The horse you sensed wanted a good scratch is a sweet, affectionate mare named Comet."

"Lord have mercy, I mistook a stallion for a mare," she said. "How *embarrassing*. I didn't even bother to check the 'equipment.' Am I touched or what?"

"No, actually I'd say you're intuitive and empathic. Your surface mind guessed that Comet was Merlin for some odd reason, but another part of you *knew* which horse to pet and which horse to be wary of, even if he was sleeping peacefully. Do you see, now, how wise your body and your feelings are? Do you also see how you disregard, even sabotage these insights through constant self-criticism?"

Validation of Cynthia's hidden talents didn't quite have the effect I was expecting. A look of abject terror passed over her face, and the tears began to fall. She became, for a few minutes, inconsolable. "Don't do this," she said over and over and over like she was casting a spell that would somehow bring her back from the brink of insanity, which I later realized was exactly what a part of her was trying to do, at least from its own limited perspective. I encouraged her to feel the sense of release that came with a good cry. The suggestion wrenched her free from the clutches of her desperate mantra, and she began to sob in earnest.

"Tell me, what motivated you to come here?" I asked when she began to calm down. Cynthia waded through a list of reasons involving her accident, her horse, her hopes for the future. "Yes, I know all that," I said. "But what made you decide to come to the Epona Center?"

"Your book, obviously," she answered, still blotting her face.

"But what *about* the book motivated you to come all this way?"

"Well, I just cried all the way through it, not always out of sadness, though some of the stories were sad. You touched something in me, I guess."

"Exactly," I said. "Crying isn't always a sign of weakness. Sometimes, tears are power. When I was working on *The Tao of Equus*, I knew that I hadn't quite gotten to the essence of certain stories if I wasn't crying while I was writing. Those tears let me know when I'd hit something deep and authentic. The tears you shed reading it motivated you to get on a plane and come here. *Tears are power!* It's the same in life. Sometimes tears express sadness, frustration, or even anger that needs to be released. But sometimes tears well up when you uncover a part of yourself that was buried under all that's light and logical and socially acceptable. In nature, too much sun is *not* a good thing. The same with our culture's preference for dry reason over feeling. Digging beneath the surface of your persona is like hitting an underground spring in the desert. The water gushes up and creates an oasis for new growth. Could that be part of what you were feeling just now?"

Cynthia's shoulders began to shake and the sobs came once again. She couldn't even nod her head, but I knew the answer was yes.

"I don't let myself cry very often," she said when she was able to speak again. "That sort of thing was discouraged in my family. But I'm even more afraid that if I get started I'll never stop."

"But you *didn't* cry forever," I countered. "No one here shamed you for it. The horses didn't run off, and you didn't go insane." Cynthia smiled.

"To be habitually disconnected from feeling is a dry and desolate state of mind," I emphasized. "It keeps you alienated from the deepest, most precious, most creative aspects of yourself. Knowing this now, do you have the courage to go back into your body and find out why Jellybean came to you so vividly at the beginning of our session today?"

"I already know," she answered softly, pointing at Noche. "When I stood in front of that sad old bay hunched over in the corner, my shoulders began to tingle. Then I saw myself riding

Jellybean. I could actually hear the sound of his breath and feel the wind blowing through my hair. We were both so beautiful and free back then. *Too* beautiful and free."

She reached over, pulled a handful of tissues from the box, and blew her nose. "I wasn't a bad little girl," she continued, "just curious and full of energy. My daddy always complained that I was too big for my britches, and I caught my share of the switch, but he bought me a pony for Christmas one year and that was my salvation. I'd tire myself out with Jellybean, then be a good little girl at home. Then I had the change of life earlier than most girls, and I shot up like a beanpole in the sixth grade — well, not a beanpole *exactly*. One day, Momma pulled me aside and told me I wasn't allowed to gallop through the woods alone anymore because I was 'developing' and the neighborhood boys were looking at me in 'that way.'

"I started riding with this girl down the street named Mandy. She had a horse, and we became good friends, but every once in a while I'd still sneak off on my own. Well, Daddy must have caught wind of it somehow. He up and sold my pony to a little girl in the next county when I was away at church camp that summer. I didn't even get the chance to say goodbye. I was fit to be tied when I got back home and found out what had happened. Daddy said I was too gawky for that pony; he said I looked like a giraffe on a jackrabbit, and he'd gotten a good price for Jellybean. But he wouldn't get me a bigger horse with that money. He told me it was high time I stopped racing around like a heathen and started acting like a lady. He said if I didn't stop my crying, he'd give me something to cry about. I knew he would, too, so I ran to my room and put my pillow over my head and sobbed until the cows came home. But it didn't change a thing.

"Mamma brought me a tray that night, so I didn't have to face him at dinner. I could see she felt bad, but she never spoke out against Daddy, and I suspect she agreed with his decision. I didn't dare bring it up ever again."

"So in some sense your parents sold your soul along with your horse," I said quietly.

Cynthia nodded as her eyes welled up with tears. "I was a proper girl after that. Now that I think back on it, I must have been very depressed, but no one seemed to notice. They liked me better that way."

I wanted to make sure she understood the different meanings behind this painful memory: "So when you said earlier that you were threatening to 'cry me a river over something long since dead and buried,' you were really talking about yourself. You were mourning the loss of your *real* self, your spirit." My sniffling companion reached for another tissue. The box was empty.

"That part of you isn't dead," I assured her, bringing our first session to a close. "I've seen her several times already, and I must say I'm more impressed with her than I am with that coy southern belle who doesn't quite fit into your womanly body." Cynthia blushed, but her shoulders rose ever so slightly.

"Your Authentic Self has been encouraging you all these years to get another horse," I continued. "She's the one who didn't have the heart to spank your children. She refused to sell Jasper. She convinced your husband to send you to Tucson. She's essentially been waving at us all day through some very impressive moments of intuition and clairsentience, through tears, through your conviction to face your fears and ride again. She's the part of you that feels like it will die if you give up riding once and for all. And I think the mask you've been wearing — that false, controlling, critical voice that kicks in every time you *feel* anything — panics big time when you connect with how empathic, intelligent, and powerful you really are. Your False Self has been acting like its very survival is being threatened here. And you know what? Its life *is* in danger."

"Do you think," she asked pensively, "that's what Jesus really meant when he said that you have to die and be born again of the spirit?"

"Well . . . ," I said, momentarily stunned by her insight, "I think that if more churches had interpreted it that way, and supported people in living it that way, the history of the Western world would have looked a whole lot different."

SHINING THROUGH

"Our deepest fear is not that we are inadequate," wrote Marianne Williamson in *Return to Love*. "Our deepest fear is that we are powerful beyond measure. It is our Light, not our darkness, that most frightens us. We ask ourselves, 'Who am I to be brilliant, gorgeous, talented, and fabulous?' Actually, who are you not to be? You are a child of God. Your playing small doesn't serve the world. There's nothing enlightened about shrinking so that other people won't feel insecure around you."

And yet that's exactly what most of us do — not on purpose, and usually not consciously. It's part of the neural circuitry we developed in response to significant life experiences: because somewhere along the line, so many of us were demoralized, ostracized, even profoundly victimized for being "too beautiful and free."

I've worked with at least half a dozen men and women who told me stories similar to Cynthia's. My friend and colleague Melissa Shandley, who works with us at the Epona Center, is one of them. At age seven, she won first place at a state competition on her beloved childhood friend Champ, a handsome dapple gray pony who was considered insolent and even a bit dangerous when she first began riding him. Melissa eventually gained his cooperation not so much through skill as through the deep connection they made. First prize at the Minnesota State Fair, however, brought a sudden end to their relationship. Champ was sold that day, without Melissa's knowledge, to a buyer willing to pay a blue ribbon price. Her first conscious experience with incongruent adult behavior followed in the subterfuge surrounding Champ's departure. "I have a very clear memory of the ranch hands telling me they didn't bring him back from the show," she says. "Then they opened the high wood-paneled stall in the front of the horse van and backed him out. I guess they didn't want to tell me he was sold, but they were trying to send me the message in their cowboy way. Champ was picked up from the Diamond B Ranch shortly after. I can still remember how much I loved him, and it brings tears to my eyes that I didn't get to say goodbye."

No one considered that the little girl's heart might be broken, that there was more to her relationship with Champ than week-end recreation. "There was also an element of shame about winning in my family," she says. "The main message I received at home was to avoid conflict and competition, and success involved conflict. At the very least, I realized that doing well could result in negative consequences. Somebody else noticed Champ because we excelled, and that's why I lost him. Being invisible seemed a much safer place." No surprise that Melissa would grapple with fear of success and emotional connection for decades until she began to process this painful, yet common childhood memory. In the eyes of her parents and riding instructor, Champ was "just a horse," and it was high time for her to deal with life's realities.

Yet this particular reality stems from a survival motif encouraging people to sacrifice soul and sensitivity to live another day, to hide what little they have to avoid confiscation, jealousy, or conflict. While such emergency measures might make sense under certain circumstances, they're passed on to children growing up in peace and prosperity. The pinnacle of this mentality as it relates to human-animal relationships is powerfully depicted in the book and film *The Yearling*. Recognized as a classic coming-of-age story, Marjorie Kinnan Rawling's novel follows a young boy name Jody through his painful passage to manhood. When a rattlesnake bites his father in the swamplands of the Deep South, Jody must kill his first deer and cut out its liver, a folk remedy for snake venom. On the way home, he finds the doe's fawn and begs his father to let him rescue it. Jody's mother, physically and mentally exhausted from a life of poverty, objects. Numb from the devastating loss of several babies, she remains detached from her youngest son's emotional needs. She's more concerned with the stress of having another mouth to feed. Yet Jody's dad, who somehow stayed connected to the wonder and innocence of childhood, grants his son's wish, and for a time, the fawn brightens their world. As Flag matures, however, the deer begins to wreak havoc in the house, knocking over bags of precious grain and breaking the family's modest belongings. Attempts to tie him outside and fence off the garden fail. Shortly after Jody's father becomes bedridden from a tragic accident, the yearling is found devouring the family's modest crop. Jody's parents order him to shoot Flag, who's now seen as a threat to their survival.

After a series of objections, mishaps, and moments of deep personal anguish, Jody pulls the trigger and runs away from home. When he returns, everyone can see that he is no longer a "yearling," but a young man hardened by harsh sacrifices he now knows he will continue to make. Yet he can't forget Flag, or the innocence, vitality, and joy the mischievous young deer reflected in him for a few bittersweet months. Drifting off in his bunk the night he rejoins his family, Jody suddenly calls out for Flag, then cries himself back to sleep.

While *The Yearling* artfully and compassionately portrays the despair of Depression-era rural life, it's usually found in the family section of video stores next to all the Disney movies and fantasy cartoons. Many people grew up with this film, clearly relating to Jody's right of passage as symbolic of the wilder, freer, softer, and more compassionate aspects of themselves they too relinquished on the road to adulthood. Yet in order for civilization to evolve, stories like this must be seen for what they are: poignant illustrations of the hardships that created survivalist patterns in the past, patterns we must all consciously move beyond in order to thrive.

Cynthia's family suffered from a survival mentality that was no longer relevant. Her parents weren't poor. Her father never endured a serious accident or unemployment, yet he often reacted to minor dilemmas as if the world was coming to an end. Cynthia's immigrant great-grandparents were the only family members who had experienced oppression and poverty. Their descendants had all done well in the land of opportunity, but the lack of trust — that "feeling of always waiting for the other shoe to drop," as Cynthia put it — remained pervasive in her family. Selling Jellybean and tightening the reins on their daughter's spirit, her parents injected a cynical, ultimately disempowered mindset that severely limited her search for personal fulfillment, long after she married and left their house.

The way in which this disturbing yet ingenious control system locked onto Cynthia's body, however, turned out to be one of the most fascinating manifestations of the False Self I've ever seen. And the techniques we subsequently developed to loosen its grip enhanced Epona's horse-facilitated therapy practice significantly.

After a two-hour lunch break the first day, Cynthia decided to work with Noche. Her brief encounter with the "sad old bay hunched over in the corner" had inspired the most significant emotional insights of all the horses she'd encountered that morning. I admired her courage and desire to go deeper. Since she was an experienced horsewoman, I handed her a halter and asked her to lead Noche to the hitching post for a little grooming. She entered his corral, creeping, almost wincing, toward him as if she were stepping on glass. The woman felt so sorry for the "poor depressed horse," trying to reassure him with a sweet, indulgent voice reminiscent of baby talk.

She couldn't get near him. The gelding simply moved away at first. Then he snorted and began trotting circles around her, back rounded, neck gracefully curved in that regal posture associated with stallions. Surprised by his vitality, Cynthia was entranced, then visibly frustrated, and finally disheartened as she tried alternately pleading with him and commanding his cooperation, to no avail. The self-deprecating insults began pouring out of her mouth.

"Tell me *who* is speaking right now," I demanded, closing the gate behind me and walking to the center of the corral.

A sheepish yet strangely knowing smile crossed Cynthia's face. "The false character I think," she said.

With that simple realization her shoulders rose significantly. Noche stopped, turned to face us from about twenty feet away and took a step forward. While Cynthia was intrigued by the horse's response, I was even more impressed with how *her* posture had changed so dramatically.

"Just out of curiosity," I said, "stand in the horse pose for a moment."

"I can't believe it," she exclaimed after a brief scan. "I actually feel calmer, more balanced, not nearly as scared as I was before. Maybe there's hope for me after all. Maybe all I needed was a good cry over Jellybean."

"What about your shoulders?" I asked.

"They're *really* tingling," she said, "like a weight's been lifted, like they're coming back to life."

"How do you see Noche now?"

"He had a hard life, but he wasn't defeated by it. When he moves, his spirit shines through."

"Try walking toward Noche, this time letting *your* spirit shine through," I suggested. It was like watching another person take over Cynthia's body. The coquettish southern belle was gone. A tall, confident forty-five-year-old woman strolled across the paddock and reached out to touch Noche's nose. The gelding, who had been standing perfectly still and fully engaged, jerked away on contact. Cynthia's shoulders sank immediately.

"Don't speak yet," I said. "Don't try to change anything. Close your eyes, breathe into your shoulders, expand the feeling, and tell me what happens."

"Oh boy," she said, repeating the phrase several times, her brow contorting in concentration.

I could see the floodgates opening. "Remember," I said, "you don't want to get overloaded here: One thought, one memory, one image, please." I touched her shoulder and brought her back to the present, expecting, by the expression on her face, to hear a horrible tale of rape or some other form of violence. "What did you see?"

"Sweet Jesus," she sighed, suddenly looking more amazed and relieved than frightened. "I have been born, bred, and trained to be a workhorse."

Then she laughed like the entire world suddenly made sense.

BREAKING THE REINS

Cynthia's shoulders were weighed down by excessive responsibility, low self-esteem, and parental pressure to suppress the "unladylike" power her stature implied. Her body, however, communicated the intricacies in much more creative terms. "I saw the darndest thing," she told me. "There was this huge heavy yoke around my neck. It was connected to a cart that was pulling my entire family, not just my husband and kids, but my parents and grandparents, even some of my teachers. My daddy was holding the reins. He had a whip that he'd crack every time I objected to the weight or the path we were taking. And so I just kept plodding along."

We worked for a good thirty minutes with this image to understand its many facets, including how her posture improved whenever she allowed her "spirit to shine through" and how her shoulders collapsed whenever the False Self took hold again.

Finally, we engaged her newfound talent for creative visualization to break the reins and remove the yoke of enslavement. It was a significant turning point for Cynthia, but certainly not an instant cure. Her Authentic Self, as we began to call it, was in a state of arrested development coinciding with the age at which she lost Jellybean. Her sensitive, intuitive spirit still felt just as small and powerless when it faced the tyrant inside as young Cynthia did when she had clumsily challenged her father's authority decades before. What's more, the cruel "wagon master" who'd directed her every move for the last thirty-three years wasn't about to give up without a fight. He repeatedly tried to regain control through verbal intimidation and the imposition of the same submissive postures. On closer observation, this False Self proved to be a kind of split persona that enacted a master-slave archetype. Cynthia was both her own victim and her own perpetrator. Though the nasty creature with the whip resembled her father, the man himself had died twelve years earlier and could no longer wield any direct power over her. He was symbolic of the patriarchal system in general, one that suppressed feeling and intuition, ruling through fear, intimidation, and unquestioning obedience, the quintessential "king" of Cynthia's "house." Trying to beat this vicious complex at its own game proved fruitless. It simply wasn't in Cynthia's best interest to rage, dominate, or trade insults with the tyrant. Any attempt to do so alienated her from her own sensitive nature and her connection to the moment, patterns that automatically heralded the return of the tyrant.

Noche proved invaluable in helping us discover what was helpful simply by standing still when the Authentic Self appeared and running off when her internal dictator took over. All she had to do was calmly notice the False Self, breathe into her shoulders, and imagine removing the yoke or cutting the reins. Sometimes she could hear the old taskmaster screaming bloody murder as she walked confidently toward Noche, but in her mind, the slave driver had become a sad, somewhat comical character throwing tantrums from a horseless cart abandoned by the side of the road.

For quite a while, though, he succeeded in throwing a rope over her neck every time she failed to touch Noche. Cynthia's major blocks to success stemmed from a tendency to take everything personally and an inability to experiment. Four times in a row she reached out to touch Noche's face, and four times in a row he jerked away. It never entered her mind to try a different approach. She automatically assumed there was something wrong with *her*. At that moment, the inner critic would take control, the shoulders would drop, and Noche would step even farther away.

"I just don't think he likes me," she finally said, looking more deflated than ever.

I moved forward, rubbed her forehead and patted her on the nose, saying, "Hi, Cynthia, nice to meet you!"

"Yuk!" she said. Her grimace gave way to a look of recognition. "I get it now." And with that she proceeded to gently touch Noche's neck and eventually rub his withers. Moments later, she put the halter on him and led him out of the corral, moving with a grace and confidence that brought tears to my eyes, the best kind of tears.

Cynthia felt more elated than exhausted as she groomed her new friend, even though, as she put it, she'd "just run a six-hour emotional marathon." As we brought the session to a close, I could see the woman wasn't quite ready to go back to a lonely hotel room. She jumped at the suggestion of taking a chair into Noche's corral and recording the day's events in her journal. As I drove off, she was writing furiously, the old sage mustang standing over her left shoulder as if he approved of every word.

As so often happens, the session didn't end when the human facilitator left. "I sat there for almost two hours," she told me the next morning. "Noche would move away sometimes and come back at other times. I started noticing there was a pattern that followed what was going on inside me. I mean I was just sitting there doing nothing, but he wanted to be near me when I became more...uh...centered, even though that word doesn't come close to describing what I was feeling. And when I got my head to spinning, worrying about what friends at the executive club back home would think, wondering if the whole afternoon was just my imagination, starting to criticize myself again, Noche just didn't care to be near me. After a while, I started to see how long I could hold the first feeling and keep Noche with me without saying a word or lifting a finger. It was like he was exercising something in me, like I was being tuned to...I don't know...sing a new song."

WHIRLWINDS

As the week progressed, Noche mirrored Cynthia's constantly shifting states of mind on the ground and, finally, in the saddle. Together, we learned to differentiate between False Self fears (which usually had little to do with the situation at hand), fears of the body (which contained legitimate safety messages), and fears coming from the horse (which, when recognized early enough, allowed Cynthia to avert a possible spook). We also discovered a great deal about the Authentic Self, a compassionate, inventive, supportive presence that didn't seem to have any fears of its own. Most important, we realized that Cynthia didn't have to battle the False Self at all. She only had to recognize, constantly, that it wasn't *her*, while strengthening the Authentic Self's ability to function independently of her past conditioning.

For over thirty years Cynthia believed that the critical voice inside was her voice, when it was in fact a series of parental and societal dictates designed to keep a young girl in line. The False Self turned out to be nothing more than a collection of habits that had somehow coalesced to form an identity. It had no creativity, no intuition, no ability to experiment, and very little connection to the body and its feelings. With few internal resources to draw upon, this limited persona focused on outside approval, outside appearances, money, security, and social standing. Because it had no imagination, it looked to established methods and protocols for guidance, becoming extremely fearful in novel situations — hence its relentless efforts to keep everything under control and move according to well-worn patterns.

The False Self also had an extremely restricted vocabulary. It tended to speak in "tape loops" as I called them: stern dictates and clichés I later realized so commonly circulated through the minds of every single person I knew (including myself) that the situation became almost comical. In clinics, I began drawing the False Self as a stick figure with a giant whirlwind over its head, symbolizing its cynical, chaotic, yet repetitive declarations. A group of teenage girls from a treatment center I worked with one summer took great delight in officially naming the creature "Tornado Head."

Though some of these messages reflected the concerns of certain age, ethnic, or socioeconomic groups, many of them turned out to be universal. Here's a sampling of the most common False Self themes I've since come across in seminars and private sessions around the country:

"What will the neighbors think?"

"You're not good enough, pretty enough, thin enough, rich enough, educated enough, etc."

"It's just your imagination."

"Who do you think you are?"

"You're a fool, a fake, a loser, an idiot."

"You're just a girl. Women don't do that. Men don't do that."

"Don't cry. Don't be such a baby. You're too sensitive."

"It's just a horse, dog, cat."

"If you can't get it right the first time, you have no business doing it at all."

"Wait until your retirement."

"You can't follow your dreams without this degree or that certification."

"Maybe someday, if you win the lottery. . . ."

Yet I'm sorry to say that winning the lottery would never provide enough security for the False Self to strike out on its own and lead an innovative life. One of the most intriguing and widespread tape loops I've come across in middle-aged women is affectionately referred to as "the bag-lady syndrome" by Epona senior counselor Kathleen Ingram. She first brought it to my attention in December 2000 as a complex that hijacks her mind whenever she makes the most minor changes in work or relationships. I've since heard variations of this dire prediction recited by workshop participants from western Canada to northern Maine: "If you follow that crazy dream, leave that job, or go through with that divorce, you'll die homeless, penniless, and alone, wandering the streets like a bag lady." For one of Epona's apprentices, Fran Nachtigall, a savvy New York businesswoman learning to incorporate horses into her leadership training program, this same phrase is always accompanied by an older version of herself wearing rags and a babushka, pushing a rusty grocery cart through the worst part of town. Imagine my surprise when I glanced at a magazine called *More* while standing in line at the drugstore and saw the following headline: "Bag-Lady Syndrome: Are You Suddenly Afraid of Losing it All?" The December 2002 issue of this *Ladies Home Journal* offshoot featured quotes from a number of successful women admitting to similar fears, including Katie Couric and Oprah Winfrey, who, according to this article by Lynn Schnurnberger, "once kept $50 million in cash as her own 'bag lady fund.' " The most telling moment for me, however, was how close the author's vision of doom was to that of my apprentice. "Last night, I had the 'bag-lady' dream again," Schnurnberger wrote. "I'm wandering around a warehouse district, clutching a paper cup that contains a few coins. Steam is rising out of the sewer grates, and I'm wearing a babushka and a long, soiled skirt."

Even when the False Self manages to come up with some graphic imagery, it still deals in clichés — and grossly overreactive ones at that. Only a neurotic impulse disconnected from reality stashes away $50 million as a buffer. That Winfrey and others like her would fall prey to the bag-lady syndrome seems so ridiculous, however, that it magnifies how the False Self works. For generations in a culture where only well-born men were allowed to own property, pursue higher education, and hold positions that paid enough to support a family, women often found themselves destitute after their husbands died or divorced them, with no prospects for making a decent living themselves. While the situation has changed dramatically in the Western world, painful memories of bag ladies past still echo through the collective feminine psyche, and the terror continues to grip well-educated, highly accomplished women. Men, of course, deal with similar archetypes, and the critical, paranoid voices that go along with them. These repetitive themes become the mental prisons that keep people in survival mode long after an opening for change occurs. Making these patterns conscious is the first step in regaining freedom of thought, will, and action. And yet most adults have grown up so shackled by the False Self's addiction to security and established methods that they haven't developed the skills to live creatively. Every time they try to step into the unknown and follow their hearts, they go blank and lose their bearings. At the same time, the Tornado Head realizes it's losing control and throws a fit that makes thinking clearly outside the box all the more difficult. At this point, most people turn tail and run right back into the cage, which, it turns out, is the most relentless False Self pattern of all, a monstrous force of habit solidified through thousands of years of actual, then self-enforced slavery.

As Alan Watts described it, the alternative involves fostering "a state of wholeness in which the mind functions freely and easily, without the sensation of a second mind or ego standing over it with a club." In effect, the solution comes through cultivating the Authentic Self. Defining this elusive state of being is like trying to measure the limits of the human spirit, but my work with Cynthia and others like her offered some hints that put me hot on its trail. The Authentic Self emerges from the depths like a spring bubbling up through the desert of what the conscious mind can fathom, like a light shining through the body when the yoke of the tyrant falls away. The Authentic Self composes that new song our horses are tirelessly, patiently tuning us to sing. We act in our own best interests when we cut *their* reins and let them guide us now and then, because in the eyes of these reflective, openhearted creatures, we can never be too joyful, too beautiful — or too free.

CHAPTER THREE

FEAR OF FEELING

T he clock flashed 2 A.M. in electric red alert. I was wide-awake, worrying about leading my first workshop in conservative southern racehorse country.

The Savvy Dozen, a Kentucky-based study group devoted to Pat Parelli's Natural Horsemanship techniques, had invited me to the "Bluegrass state" for a seminar exploring the emotional dynamics of horse-human relationships. The setting was perfect: gently rolling hills of endless pasture, dogwood trees beginning to bloom, a herd of Peruvian Paso horses grazing peacefully near a halcyon pond. Kathy and Neal Schroeter, owners of Grizzle Gate Farm, had been consummate hosts, picking me up from the Louisville airport, driving me to media events around town, and putting me up in a spacious second-floor suite overlooking their private equine paradise. We talked for hours about the healing power of horses. A fast-paced emergency room doctor (whose job really *was* a matter of life and death), Neal softened when he discussed how the horses brought out the child in him. Kathy shared some intriguing dreams and intuitions she'd experienced with the herd. The Schroeters and other members of the Savvy Dozen had also established their own volunteer equine therapy organization, Equus Beato (Blessed Horse). They taught Parelli's ground exercises to boys from a nearby detention center and trailered horses to a local nursing home where residents took great delight in grooming or simply touching these regal, gentle animals.

The afternoon before the clinic, I met the Grizzle Gate herd and went over last-minute details. Workshop organizer Beth Roberts was gracious and well prepared. Like the Schroeters, she felt nourished by horses and wanted to explore the connection more deeply.

Why, then, was I so agitated the night before the clinic?

I scanned my body for clues. A charge of nervous excitement radiated through my midsection, but a strange ache in my left shin demanded more attention. It seemed unlikely that I could have injured it walking through a few acres of pasture. I had no memory of tripping or twisting my leg that day, yet the throbbing had steadily increased. I decided to take my own advice and breathe into the sensation, realizing, much to my own surprise, that it carried a message.

"You don't have a leg to stand on," a nasty voice hissed, whereupon my own personal Tornado Head unleashed a seething barrage of insults: "Who do you think you are? You have no business teaching these people anything. They've studied directly with Pat Parelli, for God's sake. Besides, this is the *South*. People here don't want to talk about their feelings, let alone explore them with their horses. That stupid book of yours got you into this mess. All that wild stuff you wrote about couldn't possibly have been real. It was just your imagination, and tomorrow you'll be exposed as a fake. These people are going to tar and feather you and ride you out of town on a rail!"

Once I got over the initial shock, this sinister wraith struck me as incredibly funny. A physical pain signifying that I didn't have a leg to stand on? The Savvy Dozen planning to tar and feather me if I didn't live up to their expectations? The False Self certainly thrived on clichés and exaggeration. It also refused to acknowledge the reality of the situation: that I was invited to Louisville by experienced equestrians with a therapeutic orientation who supported each other in developing emotionally vital relationships with their own horses.

Then another question floated quietly through my mind: What perspective would the Authentic Self have on all this? I brushed my whirlwind-brained critic to the side, and waited for an answer.

"Let's *do* this crazy thing!" exclaimed a confident inner voice riding waves of enthusiasm. "It'll be fascinating to see what works in this part of the country and what doesn't. Gather some information and experiment. Watch how the horses respond tomorrow, identify people's needs and unrecognized strengths — and adapt. That's how new ideas are born."

The ache in my shin disappeared completely, indicating, as I had so often told my clients, that the message had been received and processed to my body's satisfaction. The anxiety in my belly subsided, and I drifted off to sleep, actually looking forward to an early wake-up call.

Contrary to popular belief, fear, frustration, and anger are actually quite reasonable if you know how to work *with* them. When you get the message behind these "negative" feelings, and change something in response, they dissipate on their own. Psychotherapy and sainthood are not prerequisites for emotional mastery. The average person can learn the necessary skills in a weekend, and life itself provides plenty of practice. The problem is that most adults have been suppressing emotion for so long that these simple warnings have fused into monstrous complexes that truly are disturbing when they rear their ugly heads. We've grown up fearing *feeling* itself, and *that* is the root of our discontent.

To put this strange human habit into perspective, imagine the oil light appearing under the speedometer of a teenage girl's first car. Rather than encouraging her to check the manual to see what it means, her parents strongly advise her to ignore it. A week later, she covers this deviant signal with duct tape and continues to drive around, hoping none of her friends will notice. She begins to smell smoke, but she's afraid to check under the hood and too embarrassed to bring the issue up at dinner. When the engine starts to seize, her father tells the confused and frightened young woman that she better get control of that unruly vehicle, or else.

In their purest forms, feelings are no more sinister or irrational than dashboard warning lights, and our attempts to reject them no less ridiculous. In shaming the body's attempts to communicate with the mind, human conditioning makes the situation worse by injecting additional fear, anger, frustration, or embarrassment into the system, creating secondary levels of emotional disturbance. Calming the Tornado Head involves drawing attention back to the core messages underneath the judgments, while developing a more inventive mindset capable of dealing with novel situations.

The night before my Louisville workshop, I really didn't know how my ideas would be received in "conservative racehorse country," and this element of uncertainty agitated the False Self. My conditioned persona had already latched on to the methods I'd learned and developed. It panicked at the thought that some of these techniques might not work in an untried market. Had this fear remained unconscious, it might have caused significant problems the next day. As I'd sometimes witnessed in equine seminars, the clinician would inadvertently shame clients and their horses for "failing to cooperate" with the method. I later realized this was nothing more than the trainer's False Self functioning defensively. Taking the time to decipher the messages behind my anxiety, and engage a more curious, creative spirit, allowed me to use whatever might happen as food for experimentation and innovation. In that single phrase, "Let's *do* this crazy thing," the Authentic Self acknowledged my fears and promised to meet my challenges with a sense of adventure. Both my body and my inner critic felt understood and supported.

The next morning, I taught workshop participants how to use their emotions as information and how to read their horse's misbehavior as communication. We also practiced ways of differentiating between False Self fears and the body's legitimate safety concerns. Based on these simple principles, we created an atmosphere of authenticity and innovation. People began to explore their own frustrations without the threat of social rejection. And whenever they did feel embarrassed, they took comfort in recognizing the critical voice inside as a limiting, artificial sense of self. In this context, the leader wasn't expected to have all the answers. Riders collaborated with their mounts, I collaborated with my students, and the horses showed us all how brilliant they could be when everyone stepped out of the box.

In less than an hour, one amateur equestrian broke through a traumatized gelding's defenses, something that several internationally recognized trainers had already tried to do with increasing yet limited success. Oeste, a striking palomino Peruvian Paso, had been abused by one of his trainers before the Shroeters acquired him. Then, a roughhousing friend of a friend had taken the horse on a horrifying ride without the owners' permission. Oeste thereafter had vacillated between dissociation in the mere presence of humans to abject terror whenever anyone tried to saddle him.

"Pat Parelli helped Neal and Oeste at one clinic because Oeste wouldn't even let you get near his side to mount him," Kathy remembers. "Linda Tellington-Jones also worked with Oeste for four days at Equitana. Finally by the last day, she could sit on him with her sister Robin leading, but the horse was so tense he looked like he was going to explode at any moment. Don West was able to ride him with no trouble, but this experience didn't translate to Oeste feeling safe with anyone else on his back." While each clinician was building on the breakthroughs his or her colleagues had made, Oeste remained wary of anyone who tried to connect with him, including his owners.

Bill Aiton, who traveled up from Nashville to attend the Louisville clinic, noticed the blank look of dissociation in Oeste's eyes right away. "My mother had narcolepsy," he says. "When she got excited or emotional, she would fall into REM sleep. Oeste was just as remote, even though he obviously didn't take it to the same extreme. He was standing in the middle of his stall shut down from everyone. Connection had always been a difficulty for me because I was always wondering what the falling out from the other person was going to be. Here was this animal who was really disconnected, and I wondered what I could do to change the dynamic for both of us."

Bill and his wife, Tricia Dailey, had just bought their first two horses a year earlier. "I didn't have a lot of technique," says the fifty-year-old computer programmer. "I also didn't know what the energy or emotional content of connection would feel like with a horse. But that's what I wanted with my own horses, and I knew Oeste would give me an opportunity to explore that. One of the women at the clinic who actually knew Oeste went into the round pen with him right before me. Even though she was very gentle and loving, he still stayed in that disconnected place. It was like an important part of him, his spirit, wasn't there at all, and it was a sad thing to see."

As Bill entered the round pen, the handsome golden palomino barely acknowledged the man's presence. "I decided to get some movement at least," he remembers. "Kathy and Neal said they couldn't get him to come to them, and this seemed like a really big deal to them. I tried all sorts of ways to draw him to me but it wasn't happening."

Oeste came to life, however, when Bill asked the gelding to move around the circular pen at a trot. The former show horse obviously knew a great deal about ground work, yet no one had been able to "join up" with him, a Monty Roberts term for getting the horse to follow the handler off lead when the animal accepts this person as the "alpha" of their two-member herd. Oeste didn't mind free-longeing from a distance as Bill asked him to change speed and direction through body language. Yet there was something machine-like about Oeste's movements, and he absolutely refused to come near Bill, let alone join up.

On impulse, I suggested something rarely considered among professional trainers because it involved abdicating the human leadership role. "I know this sounds odd," I shouted from the bleachers, "but see if you can get Oeste to longe *you*."

A number of experienced horsemen have since admitted they would have felt foolish trying such a stunt, especially in front of an audience, but the freedom to experiment was palpable in this group. Bill ran playful circles around Oeste. A series of startled expressions crossed the gelding's face: astonishment, confusion, and, finally, something akin to amusement. Wrenched from his dissociative state by the man's unexpected behavior and disarming enthusiasm, Oeste watched Bill's every move with rapt attention. A moment later, the horse took his first step forward. Bill backed up in response, inviting Oeste to move *him* around. The palomino's eyes brightened, and the two began to trade leadership roles so gracefully that at times it was difficult to tell who was choreographing their dance. "At the end, he came up to me and stuck his head under my arm, and we were just buds," Bill remembers. "Everyone had been treating Oeste like this poor sad guy, but he was actually a fun little horse."

"We all saw him in a new light after that," Kathy says. "I think he saw us in a new light too. He gained confidence with horses as well as people. Here's a horse who we couldn't stand next to not too long ago, but we've taken him to the nursing home as part of our therapy program, and he actually lets people in wheelchairs come up to him. One man stepped away from his walker and put his arms around Oeste, and that horse stood perfectly still. He's become our best horse for the nursing home work. There's a patience and a kindness that he shows to the elderly. The other horses are good, but Oeste really shines."

HIDDEN TALENTS

I certainly wouldn't recommend inviting an aggressive stallion to longe the handler. Yet this simple gesture consistently brings disempowered horses back to life, sometimes precipitating their entry into therapeutic work. Many animals with a marked talent for helping humans initially seem sour, moody, or fearful because of an unusually strong ability to detect hidden emotions and think outside the box. These horses are the "high sensitives" of the herd. Standard *de*sensitization techniques can have an unexpected effect, making them withdraw or panic as if they'd been severely abused. As beasts of burden, athletes, and vehicles for ego gratification, they experience unending strife, and quite often end up at the killer's because they can't be "fixed." Human beings face similar dilemmas. Think of an artist entering law school because he was born into a family of attorneys, or a woman with a great political mind whose parents pressure her into skipping college and marrying young. These people are prime candidates for depression and suicide.

In her book *The Highly Sensitive Person*, research psychologist Elaine N. Aron determined that 15 to 20 percent of all mammals, including humans, are "highly sensitive," responding to sights, sounds, and emotions that go unnoticed by others. Using a simple, twenty-three–question test for the trait, Aron surveyed three hundred randomly selected people of all ages, finding an additional 22 percent to be "moderately sensitive." The majority, 42 percent, "said they were not sensitive at all — which suggests why the highly sensitive can feel so completely out of step with a large part of the world."

Often treated as a mild form of pathology in our extroverted culture, high sensitivity can be a blessing or a curse, depending on the context. While HSPs (Highly Sensitive Persons) become easily overwhelmed, emotionally hyperreactive, and often introverted as a result, they also exhibit great creativity, insight, passion, and empathy. These people excel as advisors, artists, philosophers, therapists, parents, and teachers, helping to balance the alpha-style leaders and go-getters of this world. Aron observes that "warrior-kings," as she calls the more proactive members of society, benefit from the counsel of HSPs, who have the foresight and compassion to "look out for the well being of those common folks on whom the society depends," warning "against hasty wars and bad use of the land."

At its best, the HSP perspective fosters a compassionate, innovative approach to life. At its worst, it contends with relentless overstimulation and the persistent feeling of being misunderstood. Many recluses and tortured artists are high sensitives who never learned the emotional management skills essential in coping with their empathic talents — often because they were raised by parents and teachers who found HSPs moody and overreactive for no apparent reason. "Preferring toughness, the culture sees our trait as something difficult to live with, something to be cured," notes Aron. Her book, in fact, was the first to teach HSPs and their loved ones how to deal with dilemmas faced by this minority, challenges that, when overcome, result in benefits for society at large: "(I)f necessity is the mother of invention, HSPs must spend far more time trying to invent solutions to human problems just because they are more sensitive to hunger, cold, insecurity, exhaustion, and illness."

Aron speculates that "since the trait exists in all higher animals, it must have value in many circumstances." Her "hunch is that it survives in a certain percentage of all higher animals because it is useful to have at least a few around who are always watching for subtle signs. Fifteen to 20 percent seems about the right proportion to have always on the alert for danger, new foods, the needs of the young and the sick, and the habits of other animals.

"Of course, it is also good to have quite a few in a group who are not so alert to all the dangers and consequences of every action. They will rush out without a whole lot of thought to explore every new thing or fight for the group or territory. Every society needs both. And maybe there is a need for more of the *less* sensitive because more of them tend to get killed!"

The average horse has a greater awareness of environmental subtleties than the average human. And yet, about 20 percent of the species reacts to this information in more dramatic ways, while upping the ante on what we would consider high sensitivity in people. To ride such a horse into war or competition has never been easy. Some of these animals select themselves out of the process by becoming "difficult" during training. And yet with a trusted handler, these same mounts, like their human counterparts, can become assets to "warrior-kings."

As a boy, Alexander the Great foreshadowed his success by proving to be the only person in his father's army capable of riding the unruly Bucephalus. No one could mount the black stallion, and even the grooms were afraid to lead him. In one of the first historical reports of "horse gentling," the young Macedonian prince took hold of the bridle and turned Bucephalus into the sun so he wouldn't spook at his own shadow. Alexander spoke softly, stroking the horse. Then, at the right moment, the future conqueror leaped onto the stallion's sturdy back and took off at a gallop, reveling in the horse's phenomenal vitality rather than trying to rein it in. The connection between the two deepened over the years. Plutarch wrote that "in Uxia, once, Alexander lost him, and issued an edict that he would kill every man in the country unless he was brought back — as he promptly was."

Bucephalus died at age thirty, a long life for a horse even by today's standards. "During the final battle in India," observed Lawrence Scanlan in *Wild About Horses*, "the horse took spears in his neck and flank but still managed to turn and bring the king to safety before dying. Alexander was overcome with grief, and later named a city after Bucephalus." The legendary king relied on his mount's courage, energy, quick wits, and subtle warnings to help him survive many a battle, suggesting that Bucephalus may have initially seemed so profoundly uncooperative because he was an HSH, a Highly Sensitive Horse, who blossomed under the kindness of a man otherwise known to be ruthless in war.

The Bedouins also took counsel and comfort from their horses, not only in battle but in daily life. Favored mares were actually invited to sleep in the family tent. Some amusing anthropological reports speak of children climbing all over these lounging horses. These Middle Eastern nomadic tribes actually showed a preference for the HSH trait in creating the Arabian, a breed known for its high sensitivity. Animals living in such close quarters with humans, after all, would have to be extra sensitive to the moods and habits of another species. It's no surprise that Arabians have gone on to excel in the counselor and teacher roles twenty-first century horses play in equine-facilitated psychotherapy.

At the same time, equestrians looking for a nice quiet trail horse often accuse the breed of being "too sensitive," if not "downright crazy." Manhandling the Arabian can indeed produce a frantic, misunderstood nightmare. Like Bucephalus, these animals thrive on subtlety, compassion, and respectful communication. Amateur riders with a muted sensitivity quotient do much better with breeds, like the quarter horse, that have a much lower tendency to exhibit HSH characteristics.

CRACKERS

One of the best-known, most talented therapy horses in the Southwest fits the HSH profile, though like so many highly sensitive horses and humans, his behavior was initially interpreted as difficult. He objected to arena work, hated to show, and would consistently spook on the trail. Crackers had the pedigree to perform, which made his unruly behavior all the more confusing. His Arabian father excelled in dressage, as did his brother. His half-Arabian, half-Welsh mother was an accomplished hunter-jumper. For many years, owner Ann Alden, who also bred and raised Crackers, was mystified by the colt's uncooperative attitude. Yet in 1986, she began volunteering at TROT (Therapeutic Riding of Tucson), and her foray into equine-facilitated therapy changed both their lives.

"I was very impressed with what these animals were doing with physical and cognitive disabilities," she says. "Since I had a degree in psychology, I thought there must be a way to combine horses and mental health."

After receiving a master's degree in rehabilitation counseling and gaining certification as a master therapeutic riding instructor from NARHA, Ann accepted an offer to work at Sierra Tucson's fledgling equine-facilitated psychotherapy program in the early 1990s. She brought Crackers with her. The field was still young, and the nationally recognized treatment center was at the forefront of its evolution. Barbara Rector, cofounder of TROT and the Equine Facilitated Mental Health Association (a division of NARHA), started Sierra Tucson's horse therapy program at the request of Reed Smith, executive director of the adolescent unit. She went on to tour the country with her Adventures in Awareness program, teaching others how to employ horses in the work of human development. Shelley Rosenberg, a grand-prix-level dressage rider who later became one of Epona's primary trainers, acted as Sierra Tucson's first barn manager and primary horse handler.

Wyatt Webb later replaced Smith as executive director of the adolescent unit. The former country musician was so impressed with the horses that he went on to create his nationally recognized Equine Experience at the nearby Miraval resort, bringing the power of horse-facilitated therapy to the general public. Discussing many of these early Sierra Tucson experiences in his book *It's Not About the Horse: It's About Overcoming Fear and Self-Doubt*, he cited Crackers as one of the program's stars.

"That horse was ten years old when he finally figured out what he wanted to do when he grew up," Ann laughs. "He really came into his own at Sierra Tucson. We'd almost lost hope that he'd ever find his niche, but he just blossomed in that environment."

Ann insists that she didn't train the Arabian gelding to excel in therapy, she merely created a safe and responsive environment for his own innate abilities to emerge. "After a while, I learned to trust Crackers's intelligence and judgment," she says. "There are people I put on Crackers now who I never would have thought would be safe when I was coming from a conventional training perspective. It's the chemistry between the horse and the client, the spirit, whatever you want to call it. When Crackers picks who he wants to work with, he takes care of them. One of the most important skills the human facilitator develops is the ability to read the horse, to know when he's saying, 'Now that's the person I want to work with.'

"Crackers would do things for people who'd never been near a horse before that he wouldn't do for experienced riders. It's kind of humbling, really. You think you're a horse trainer and then some kid from New York City puts a hard hat on, gets on Crackers, and walks, trots, canters in the round pen without a saddle, without a bridle. Later on, I could teach this person to use his leg to move the horse sideways, so he started to understand the value of channeling his talent and energy to enhance his riding. But the magic that allowed him to ride Crackers so well in the first place came from the connection between the two of them.

"It was amazing to me at first. I almost couldn't believe it was real. I'd try to explain these connections away rationally, but when I saw them happen day after day, I started to realize there was something more to this than just coincidence."

Over time, Ann learned to predict and interpret these "coincidences," acting on them in more sophisticated ways. "I was teaching this woman in her thirties how to groom a horse," she remembers. "Crackers was practically nodding off he was so relaxed. She was standing near his head when I reached down to demonstrate how to clean his right hoof, and I heard her say, 'Ow, he bit me!' I hadn't felt him move. Now if a horse wants to hurt you, there can be serious teeth marks, even blood. I looked up and there was this tiny pinch on her upper arm. I thought about this for a moment and asked her several questions. I asked her to move away from the horse while I went and got her primary therapist.

"I said, 'Excuse me, but does this person have multiple personality disorder?' And the therapist said, 'Yes, how can you tell? It's pretty subtle in this woman.' I explained that I had this hunch that she had just switched personalities, and that Crackers had sensed it."

Ann invited the therapist into the round pen with Crackers and the client. The horse moved around the perimeter off lead. "This woman went through five different alters," Ann reports, referring to the client's ability to shift between different personalities and altered states, "and the horse's behavior changed as she switched from one to another."

This level of sensitivity, however, can be troublesome for counselors with their own unresolved issues. In mirroring hidden emotions and chaotic states of consciousness, therapy horses don't differentiate between clients and facilitators. The "person in charge" has to be just as congruent and alert as the student, preferably more so. Crackers repeatedly comforted and challenged the staff, making it essential for therapists and trainers to be honest about what they were feeling and model quick adjustments to the horse's feedback in front of patients, colleagues, bosses, and subordinates.

"When I was working at Sierra Tucson, Suzellen Holt was the barn manager," Ann says. "One day, she was really busy, rushing through grooming Crackers and talking to me a mile a minute. I needed to tell her something, and she wouldn't even take a breath long enough to let me get a word in. She already had her hard hat on, which has these straps that come down around your ears and clasp below your neck. Crackers reached over, grabbed her ear lobe and shook it gently. She started laughing hysterically and said, 'Okay, Crackers, I get it. I need to stop and listen.' It would be difficult for *me* to reach through those leather straps with my little fingers and grab Suzellen's ear lobe. How did he manage that? You can't train a horse to do these things.

"Another time, one of the psych techs came out to the barn during his break. He was having a hard time in his personal life, and for some reason felt drawn to stand by Crackers. The guy came over after a few minutes and said, 'The most amazing thing just happened to me. That horse offered to take my pain.' I really didn't ask how Crackers conveyed that to him, but the man looked transformed. He had felt this sudden lifting of his emotional pain, and he walked away feeling a whole lot better."

Experiences like these contrasted dramatically with Crackers's marked refusals to work on certain days. "He wouldn't hurt any one, but he wouldn't necessarily cooperate either, and the connection just wasn't there," Ann says. "The emotional experience was very flat for the client. We learned that if he didn't want to work, he'd just stay at the back of his corral and wouldn't engage with anyone. And we learned to honor that. There just was no chemistry, so why bother? After a while, we started noticing this would often happen the day after he had a particularly tense session with someone. Now in a regular riding program, trainers would say the horse has a job to do, and he'd be forced to do it day in and day out, with no exceptions. But the emotional intensity of the therapy work was significant, and we realized that the horses could keep themselves from burning out if we would just listen to them."

WORKING ON HORSE TIME

Burnout is a significant problem for mental health professionals as well, yet few social service agencies contemplate giving employees the same consideration many EFP programs offer their four-legged therapists. Talented counselors are often high sensitives working under administrators with no appreciation for their needs, ample rest being one of them, according to Elaine Aron. The staff is also expected to suppress emotion, something that's doubly taxing for HSPs, who like horses, become agitated in the presence of incongruent feelings. Yet unlike their equine counterparts, therapists are not rewarded for calling attention to the hidden emotions of bosses and coworkers. I've known a number of exceptional addictions counselors who were fired from treatment centers for this reason. Therapists who submit to these standards, however, relinquish a great deal of effectiveness with highly sensitive patients who also react adversely to incongruent emotions. It's a vicious circle, to say the least.

In working with a local adolescent center, I found two of the counselors so stressed and emotionally chaotic that I finally had to discourage them from assisting in or even observing our equine activities. The horses treated these women like patients, yet it was inappropriate for me to interpret this feedback in the group. Their presence created a disruptive undercurrent that I was powerless to address. As the girls learned emotional fitness skills with the horses, these troubled yet highly sensitive teenagers grew more uncomfortable with overworked, underpaid, disgruntled staff, who then felt their authority being undermined.

This experience weighed heavily on my mind as the Epona Center began to expand, and I needed to hire more people. I knew that conventional mental health, business, and farm management paradigms weren't going to work for one simple reason: The horses would forever be mirroring the staff's hidden emotions. How we handled this inconvenience would influence our effectiveness with clients. We began the tenuous process of creating a new model based on "horse values." The experience was alternately traumatic and ecstatic for us all as we stepped outside human conditioning every day. Our Tornado Heads constantly panicked at diving into the unknown, and we had to support each other whenever this happened. Yet it wasn't accurate to tell people to "leave their egos at the door" as we wanted to foster individual empowerment.

Dividing the ego into the False Self and the Authentic Self allowed us to distinguish between internal voices that limited or enhanced each person's unique talents. We had to practice group emotional agility, airing vague intuitions and unpleasant feelings with respect for the information they contained. But when we hit on the right solution, the group would breathe a collective sigh of relief and the discomfort would lift on its own. The most important skill we all developed was the ability to sit with uncomfortable emotions without panicking, the only way to assess the messages behind these troublesome yet ultimately useful sensations.

The intensity of our clinics and private sessions, combined with our organizational challenges, made guarding against burnout a colossal consideration. We were operating as a highly sensitive, interspecies unit, and like all HSPs we needed quiet time to recharge. Overstimulated, chaotic handlers also set off the horses, making a well-rested staff a safety issue. At the very least we had to be congruent. After staying up all night with sick horses a number of times, I had to admit my worry and fatigue in front of clients, which was disconcerting to those who expected counselors to remain neutral and authority figures to appear to have their act together at all times. Yet once these people understood the concept of emotional incongruity, they realized that I was actually more effective as a facilitator, and much less dangerous around the horses, when I briefly conveyed I was tired and overwrought before tackling the task at hand.

As a rule, however, all employees — from the horses to the counselors, the trainers, the barn manager, and the assistants mucking out stalls — were supported in taking time off as needed, sometimes working more than sixty hours during a workshop week, other times fewer than twenty. We set our own schedules, coordinating with the horses' needs. People working at Epona had to be self-motivated, communicative, flexible, inventive, and emotionally courageous. They had to be willing to make mistakes, ask for help, and change their own plans when someone else requested assistance. Those who couldn't uphold these standards weren't shamed or rejected. Some were encouraged to join the volunteer program and absorb the Epona approach through osmosis. Others assisted in roles where they excelled, exploring their personal issues when clients weren't around.

The process sounds remarkably straightforward to me as I summarize it here, but it was actually very messy, like a group of women going through labor simultaneously. Yet as new principles and procedures rose out of the chaos, we became more coordinated, more secure in our ability to adapt — together. I suddenly realized that we were living an idea that first came to me when Rasa joined the herd in 1991. At the time, a strange but compelling phrase would circulate through my mind whenever the mare and I relaxed together:

"The universe is artistic, not opportunistic."

Whether or not this perspective came from the black horse herself, it recommended moving away from a repressive focus on survival to an emotionally and spiritually vital focus on thriving — long before I consciously understood that concept. A decade later,

Epona blossomed because our creative interspecies community operated according to this principle. By fusing our human talents with equine sensitivities, a vague, poetic notion became reality as naturally as winter changes to spring and two streams merge into the same flowing river. The unknown was no longer a cold, heartless void. It was a womb of endless possibility that really wanted to birth our true potential — and didn't expect us to face the night alone. Riding the energy and wisdom of our horses through that dark, formless ambiguity, we learned about the nuances of negative emotions and their place in navigating uncertainty. Because when we couldn't see two feet in front of us, the ability to *feel* was our only saving grace.

CHAPTER FOUR

THE MESSAGES
BEHIND EMOTION

The *fear* of feeling blocks self-knowledge and true connection with others. Yet this particular fear has almost no chance of dissipating until people learn to treat emotion as information. With this in mind, I always present clients with an Emotional Message Chart before we do any significant work. (See Appendix.) Based in part on author and empath Karla McLaren's insights, and on realizations we've gained directly from the horses, this outline summarizes the wisdom behind fear, anger, sadness, grief, vulnerability, frustration, depression, and the suicidal urge. Taking an hour to go over this material saves significant time and confusion when the horses turn on their "X-ray eyes" and participants finally have to acknowledge what they're really feeling.

Most people see fear as a sign of weakness. Yet once they stop fighting it, this troublesome emotion communicates a range of vital insights. At first, the inner critic vetoes the most useful messages. The False Self has a whole list of its own self-absorbed fears usually more about its public image than the situation at hand. Learning which fears to heed and which fears to overcome can be confusing. Yet when handled correctly, this inner warning system functions like radar on a battleship. The naked eye can't see submarines lurking in the depths. The best military minds can't predict their movements. But a mechanism that signals when an enemy sub moves into firing range is quite handy.

In its purest form, fear is the intuitive, focused awareness of a potential threat. When you recognize the danger *and* move to safety, the feeling dissipates on its own. It's so unbelievably simple at this stage. If you get the message, fear disappears. If you don't, according to McLaren, the initial alarm intensifies into worry, anxiety, confusion, panic, terror, dissociation, or over time, a dulling of the senses. Unfortunately most of us are conditioned to judge intuitive and somatic insights as irrational. With little respect for gut feelings, the mind disregards these "premonitions" and keeps moving forward, finally recognizing the danger when it's too late to avoid.

Early in my horse-training career, I had this strange, nagging fear of a seemingly harmless piece of tack: a bit known as the "full cheek snaffle." Actually, it wasn't just any full cheek snaffle; I had used this style before. It was the one a physician across town had recently bought for his new horse.

While attending a medical conference in California, "Greg" had visited a breeding farm owned by some colleagues. There he met a magnificent paint gelding named Thunder and immediately imagined the two of them riding off into the sunset. It seemed the perfect way to relieve stress and enjoy the trails near his rural desert home, so he paid cash for the horse and arranged to have him trailered to Tucson. Thunder, however, refused to cooperate with Greg's vision. After the disgruntled doctor got thrown a few times, he came across my brochure at a local feed store and gave me a call.

During our initial consultation, I could see that Thunder's tendency to buck wasn't related to aggression or abuse; he was simply a young, energetic horse with an inexperienced rider. Greg, who seemed both sensitive and athletic, needed to develop some basic equestrian skills while Thunder was schooled a few days a week by someone who could teach them both how to *bend* rather than *lean* into turns. Greg's lack of confidence in the saddle was exacerbating the problem. Whenever horse and rider leaned into a curve, Thunder would buck slightly to regain his balance, which confused Greg, who held his breath, tensed his legs, and began to fold over into a fetal position — a classic fear response. Thunder would then move faster to escape whatever seemed to be scaring Greg. This was not the relaxing style of trail riding the doctor had in mind; he wanted to get *away* from the hospital, after all. Still, I didn't think it would take more than a month or two of training to help stabilize their relationship.

I never felt nervous in Thunder's presence. He was respectful, intelligent, and pleasant to ride. Yet for some odd reason, I cringed every time I had to tack him up, most notably when I reached for his bridle. On the advice of a friend, Greg had bought Thunder a typical full cheek snaffle, which has two prongs resting outside the animal's mouth on both sides. This feature holds the bit in place, keeping it from sliding across the horse's tongue when you pull on one rein or another.

I couldn't for the life of me figure out why this mundane contraption made me so nervous. At the time, I failed to notice that there was a minor difference between Greg's Western head stall and the English bridles I'd used with full cheek snaffles in the past. The latter had little loops that secured the prongs to leather straps running along the horse's face. On Thunder's standard Western head stall, the prongs free floated unattached to the rest of the bridle. Some vague, subconscious awareness knew this miniscule variation spelled trouble, especially for a woman. My gut was trying desperately to warn me, but my mind could make no sense of it.

And so my False Self proceeded to shame me for this weakness at every opportunity. "Here you are, a trainer supposedly special-izing in problem horses," it chided, "and you're afraid of a stupid bit. What an idiot! You'll never succeed in this business." This sort of self-imposed humiliation, of course, did nothing to address the original fear. Neither did the positive affirmations I used to boost my self-esteem back to a functional level. No matter how many inroads I made with Greg and his horse, my radar still flashed red alert.

One day, after a particularly satisfying ride, I found out exactly why I was afraid of the full cheek snaffle. Both Greg and my hus-band, Steve, walked up in time to see me trot and canter a much more agile, confident horse in Thunder. I was proud of how I had transcended my fears and conquered my inner critic. Greg com-plimented me on the gelding's progress as I dismounted. Thunder stood quietly beside me for quite some time as we all talked. Then he casually leaned into me, probably to shoo a fly from his face. In a split second, Thunder somehow hooked the left prong of his full cheek snaffle under my bra, and lifted me off the ground. I was flailing around five feet in the air, my chest hopelessly attached to the horse's face as he raised his neck higher and higher, stepping backward faster and faster, not quite sure what to do with the fran-tic human riding his head.

Thankfully, the average bra isn't designed to support a full-grown woman dangling from a moving horse. It finally ripped in two, and I slumped to the ground. Standing up in a daze, I actu-ally pulled this tattered undergarment through a significant hole in my T-shirt with my two male companions looking on in startled fascination.

Steve turned to Greg and said the first thing that came to mind: "That horse of yours, he must be a breast man." The three of us exploded into laughter.

We were still giggling during Greg's riding lesson the follow-ing week. The galloping gynecologist said it was the funniest thing he'd ever seen. And I learned that my body's natural warning system deserved respect.

DANCING WITH FEAR AND CONFUSION

No matter how well I describe fear's benefits, most clients need their own "broken bra" experience to drive the point home. Joe Esparza and his wife, Ris Higgins, who run Leadership Outfitters in Montana, made several trips to the Epona Center to master the techniques they've since incorporated into a progressive leadership retreat for executives and entrepreneurs. After checking into a classy Tucson hotel during one visit, Joe felt a vague paranoia when he entered his first-floor room.

"It didn't make any sense," he remembers. "I suddenly had this urge to go back to the front desk and get a room on the second floor. But we were tired, and I didn't want to cause any trouble."

Joe and Ris were robbed that night as they slept. The gutsy intruder entered through a sliding glass door that opened to the courtyard. Had Joe followed his intuition and moved to a higher floor, he probably never would have learned why he didn't feel safe in that pool-side room, but his wallet, computer, and rental car would have been there the next morning, saving him hours of calls to insurance and credit card companies.

In responding to fear's most subtle cues, the mind has to release its compulsion to know *exactly* what the problem is before taking the action — or inaction — the body recommends. Yet once this trust begins to form, the benefits are obvious. One calm spring day, after moving my stallion Merlin across the property for a breeding session, I was overcome by a sense of impending disaster as I led him back to his corral. Scanning the path ahead, I saw nothing out of the ordinary, and the horse himself appeared unusually calm. Still, the tension in my solar plexus increased — until I turned around and headed back toward the breeding pen. My gut told me to leave the stallion there overnight. When I haltered him the next day, the feeling was gone, even though a much feistier Merlin tried to nip me in the cool morning air. I walked him back to his stall without incident, never learning what horrible fate might have awaited us if I had ignored my fear the afternoon before.

I've since realized that it's easiest to sense these red alerts when working alone. Groups tend to obscure our purest internal messages because other people's emotions and actions are contagious, making it harder to identify what our own bodies are trying to tell us. Luckily, our subconscious minds have devised a variety of failsafes or "intensifications" of the original feeling. When we recognize *worry, anxiety,* and *confusion* as fear's attempts to turn up the volume, we're given a second or even third warning before wandering into peril. If we ignore these alarms and proceed through naïveté or willfulness, the feeling escalates into *panic, terror,* or *dissociation* as the danger becomes inescapable. In other words, we enter flight-or-fight mode. In a last-ditch effort to save us, the self-preservation instinct hijacks the neocortex, and we lose conscious control over our actions. In a colossal paradox, logic must collaborate with feeling in its earliest, subtlest stages for higher thought to prevail in the long run.

Sometimes fear creates a cringing tension in the solar plexus for a different reason: To *keep* us from dissociating. This usually happens when we're engaged in a physical activity, such as riding a horse, where full-bodied awareness in the moment helps to prevent accidents. If, by breathing into the constricted area, the feeling suddenly dissipates without pointing to any specific danger, the fear was merely cautioning us: "Stop talking, daydreaming, intellectualizing, and *stay in your body!*"

The False Self finds fear especially troublesome since the emotion often recommends an unexpected change in plan. The conditioned persona wants things to unfold according to established schedules and methods. With little imagination and no ability to respond authentically in the moment, the Tornado Head is more afraid of altering course and sailing into the unknown than it is of going down with the ship. This tendency is exacerbated by the inner critic's obsession with public image. It really can't bear to look foolish, no matter what the stakes. Rather than fumble through uncertainty, making mistakes along the way, it would much rather play the Titanic's dignified, well-heeled captain.

And yet, even the False Self's fears carry important messages. They tell us that we need to strengthen our ability to experiment, to dream, to adapt — to finally work up the nerve to play the fool, and find genius in disguise. In equine experiential learning, the round pen is a means toward this end: an open space for collaborating with a species that doesn't play by the persona's rules. The horse becomes both a mirror and a companion on the journey toward self-realization. A much more inventive, empowered spirit emerges as we not only gain confidence in taking chances, we recognize fear as a friend. It alerts us to possible blocks and dangers along the way, teaching us to adjust fluidly to what *is*, allowing us to dance with the constantly shifting currents of a life lived artfully, consciously — and, ultimately, joyfully. When fear is no longer seen as the enemy, it can't possibly intimidate or betray us; it can only save the day.

I've had enough experience with this profoundly misunderstood emotion to consider it a trusted ally, especially when I'm leading seminars with horses I don't know. During a women's empowerment workshop in Platteville, Colorado, I had the opportunity to work with an unusually wide range of horses. The workshop was sponsored by psychotherapist Jill Eldredge, who had been developing her own equine-facilitated practice for five years, and horse trainer and breeder Jean Brandenberg, who lived within walking distance of Jill. The two combined several members of their respective herds for this event. Jill's contingent included a couple of quarter horses, a paint, an Arabian mare, and a dark bay thoroughbred gelding. Yet they all looked like ponies compared to Jean's two-thousand-pound Belgian draft horses.

While her older mares lived up to the breed's gentle reputation, they were on the verge of giving birth that weekend and couldn't participate. Instead, Jean led her two-year-old stud colt and her three-year-old gelding over to the workshop site at Jill's ranch and turned them loose in the arena. These brothers proceeded to play like foals, running, bucking, and twisting in midair, a sight all the more impressive because they were twice as large as any other horse on the property. Now, at a workshop for advanced riders, these gravity-defying draft horses would have created some intriguing yet manageable challenges. But this seminar was designed to accommodate women with no background in the equestrian arts. My stomach took a flying leap into my throat watching Jean's Belgians rear up thirty feet in the air, taunting each other with flailing hooves as big as my head.

When I shared my concerns with Jean, she insisted the brothers were well trained in natural horsemanship techniques. She proceeded to direct the three-year-old through a surprising array of movements, which he performed with uncommon grace for an animal his size. The two-year-old wasn't quite as skilled, but he proved to be a willing and respectful partner. As a guest clinician, I didn't have time to develop a relationship with these horses myself, and I was skeptical of their ability to support people experiencing fear or performance anxiety during the workshop. The brothers drew so much confidence from Jean's quiet, loving, yet firmly assertive presence. She seemed key to their participation. I noted my body's response as we discussed a variety of options, from allowing people to simply observe the Belgians, to including these horses in the full range of activities. My gut relaxed completely when we concluded that they could engage in round pen work with the more experienced equestrians. They could also be groomed by beginners, but only if Jean acted as horse handler.

The morning of the workshop, the Belgian brothers were on their best behavior. I couldn't tell if they felt more secure in their new environment or if they had simply played themselves into a state of exhaustion. The women seemed delighted with them, and when it came time to choose partners for the grooming exercise, several amateurs were drawn to these gentle giants. Yet as we were heading toward the hitching posts, Jean's husband called. One of the pregnant mares was distressed. Jean jumped into her truck and headed down the road, promising to call us when she knew if the horse was in labor.

Jill and I proceeded with the grooming, confident the Belgians were docile enough that day for an amateur to groom them under our direction. These horses were already bringing up constructive insights in some of the participants, and we didn't see any reason to interrupt the process. As we were handing out halters and grooming kits, however, I lost my concentration. I had facilitated this exercise hundreds of times in all kinds of locations, but I couldn't seem to make the final decision as to who should groom what horse at which post with what handler.

My face burned with embarrassment. After several attempts at organizing the activity, I finally blurted out the obvious: "I'm confused."

The women stared at me with wrinkled brows as I continued to fumble around, searching for the answer: "I'm confused because . . . I'm *confused!* And confusion is . . . an intensification . . . of *fear.*"

Since we'd already gone over the Emotional Message Chart that morning, several of the participants nodded thoughtfully.

"I'm little nervous myself," Jill admitted, looking as perplexed as I felt. I wondered if we were both sensing the hidden fears of someone in the group. I began to scan the clients and the horses, suddenly realizing that my confusion increased every time I directed my attention toward the Belgians.

"I get it now," I finally said, pointing to the two handsome draft horses staring longingly over the fence. "Yesterday when I met those guys, they weren't nearly so calm and collected; they were leaping around the arena like torpedoes. They may be bigger than all the other horses here, but they're still adolescents, and one of them is essentially a stallion. In a new environment, with people they don't know, they could be unpredictable."

I explained that younger horses doing emotional work with humans need a trusted handler to lend them confidence. Though I was sure some of the women would be disappointed, I realized my body had interrupted my ability to think straight for a reason, reminding me that it wasn't safe for beginners to lead or groom the Belgians without Jean present.

Much to my amazement, the entire group breathed a collective sigh of relief. Several participants said they too had felt a vague insecurity — which lifted completely when I spoke my concerns out loud. My organizational abilities returned full force as I renegotiated the grooming assignments, leaving our two largest herd members out, for the moment. Jean returned later that day, and the Belgians proved to be a spirited, yet thankfully safe, addition to the rest of the workshop.

And everyone present got an impromptu lesson on the benefits of confusion — which seems, at first, a sign of ineptitude. Yet when treated as information rather than weakness, this mental glitch indicates that some crucial factor is being ignored, and the plan needs to change accordingly.

ANGER'S GIFT

Like fear, rage can override reason. The shame that ultimately follows such an outburst seems to confirm the need to keep this primal feeling under wraps, but continued suppression is not the answer. Rage is an intensification of anger, a protective agent that has been so grossly misunderstood we've almost lost our ability to make sense of it. When this habitually maligned emotion shows up, it means that someone has invaded your physical or psychological space, perhaps unconsciously, perhaps with the intention to control or take advantage of you. Either way, the surge of energy that accompanies anger helps you stand your ground when someone tries to violate your boundaries. Catching the message early is what keeps this instinctual power from turning violent. Still, it takes courage and awareness to use anger judiciously. You must be willing to tell someone to back off the second they step over the line — because the sooner you face this minor discomfort, the less force you will ultimately have to use.

Horses are great for teaching this neglected art. Their size motivates the handler, simply out of safety, to command respect. Once a disempowered client learns to hold her own with an energetic, emotionally perceptive thousand-pound being, her ability to set boundaries with her own species comes much more easily. In the process, she discovers that anger is the alarm that goes off when someone tries to push her around.

Most Americans are good at protecting their "stuff." Yet they may be under the impression that to get more stuff — land, money, promotions — they're obliged to let certain people manipulate them. As nonterritorial beings, horses illustrate that healthy boundaries have nothing to do with material ownership. To gain their cooperation, you must protect your personal space without violating theirs.

Finding this balance is primarily a nonverbal skill. Some of the women I encounter believe that "it's mean to set boundaries." They quietly ask or tearfully plead for respect, but their body language says, "Walk all over me." In the round pen, they try to seduce, bribe, or even guilt-trip the horse into cooperating, but their empty words have the opposite effect. The refusal to engage the slightest hint of power creates a vacuum that unconsciously sucks others into their space. These women don't understand the

difference between establishing boundaries and aggressively stepping on someone else's toes. They "don't want to hurt anyone." Yet
every time they fail to stand up to a person with unreasonable
demands, their bodies still feel the violation, no matter how diligently their minds ignore the truth. Over time, this unrequited
anger gathers force, expressing itself inappropriately — like when
a child spills a glass of milk at dinner, inadvertently triggering his
mother's repressed rage. This loss of control adds to the parent's,
and ultimately the child's, belief that "anger is bad," when it's really
the *misdirection* of this emotion that causes so much trouble. The
turning point comes when a woman realizes that to avoid hurting
others later, she must use her power *now*.

The unconscious diversion of anger onto an innocent by-
stander is a relic of the dominance-submission paradigm. This
archaic mentality doesn't recognize the concept of personal boundaries, so it virtually outlaws anger. Slaves with a strong sense of self,
after all, don't act like slaves. To force them to give up their lands,
relinquish their culture, squelch their dreams, and work without just
compensation is a gross boundary violation solidified through
relentless demoralization. The descendants of serfs and pre-union
factory workers carry the rage of generations, with no models for
sensing or setting boundaries in the present. Climbing the social
ladder by accumulating wealth or advanced degrees becomes the
most obvious way to escape the underling's fate. Kings who wield
the power of life and death over their subjects have evolved into
managers who take advantage of employees, tenured professors
who put Ph.D. candidates through hell, doctors who shame and
intimidate their interns, and parents who treat their children like
possessions. Those subdued by this demented version of authority
take comfort in the promise that someday, if they play by the rules,
they'll have their own flunkies to torture.

And so the cycle continues. People groomed for this lifestyle never learn to stand up for themselves thoughtfully and

appropriately. They become victims or bullies, usually a combination of both. Even those who consciously try to break the pattern lack the skills to pull it off. After submitting to a boss who repeatedly asks too much, a middle manager may resist the urge to deflect that anger onto his employees, and feel tremendous guilt when he eventually loses control with a loved one. To prevent this from happening again, conscientious cowards engage in drugs, sex addictions, and other self-destructive behavior to diffuse a rage turned inward. Yet anger in its purest form is nothing less than a call for self-respect and integrity — and the courage to reinforce them both.

NO MORE MISTER NICE GUY

In some families, deflected anger expresses itself through racial bigotry and hate. Other times, it twists into what I call the "nicest guy in the world" syndrome. I most often encounter this personality type in my work with battered wives. Some of these women have trouble leaving abusive marriages because their husbands appear to be such warm, generous souls — to outsiders. Image is everything to these men. They patiently endure all kinds of difficulties at the office, and they literally can't say no to a friend in need. Over time, of course, these men feel used. Anger rises justifiably in response, warning them to change their compulsively benevolent behavior. Yet in doing so, they risk losing the public approval their egos crave. So they find ways to diffuse this rage privately, at home, with devastating consequences for immediate family members.

The nice guy phenomenon also wreaks havoc in marriages with no sign of physical abuse. "Marian" came to Epona after learning that her husband "Bob" was having an affair. The two had recently celebrated their twenty-first wedding anniversary, and their only son had just announced his engagement to a college girlfriend. The juxtaposition of happiness and hopefulness for her child, mixed with the sadness and betrayal she felt in her own marriage made it difficult for Marian to function at work. Even with antidepressants and regular visits to a psychiatrist, she seriously considered resigning from her job as a school counselor. She just didn't seem to care about her students anymore and felt she was doing them a disservice. A friend who had attended one of my women's empowerment workshops practically dragged Marian out to Epona, hoping the horses would help her reclaim her life.

"I have no energy," Marian told me, "no real interest in anything at all. I must really be desperate to think that a bunch of horses can pull me out of this rut. But at this point, I'm willing to try anything."

Over the next three weeks, the herd uncovered some dynamics she was unable to access through talk therapy with her psychiatrist and discussions with the marriage counselor she and her husband saw biweekly. Her obsession with words and concepts was a large part of the problem. With a master's degree in child psychology, Marian said all the right things, practically analyzing herself into a stupor at times. Exceptionally bright and witty, even in her depressed state, she had no doubt used her conversational skills to form a vast network of friends. These people came forward to support her during this difficult time, calling her, taking her out to lunch, begging her to go shopping, yet increasingly finding that Marian would rather stay home. This dramatic behavior change frightened her family. The couple had previously enjoyed an active social life. After Marian discovered that Bob was sleeping with a colleague, she became increasingly despondent and reclusive. Six months later, everyone was worried, including her repentant husband.

Getting Marian out of her head and into the moment was a significant challenge, even in the round pen. She would intellectualize everything, to the point of asking all sorts of questions about equine behavior while completely ignoring the fact that a real, live horse was slowly herding her around the arena. In a similar way, she mulled over complex theories for why her husband was "seduced by that other woman" while finding excuses to keep from relating directly. Though she felt wounded by the affair, she insisted he was "a good man, the best really." Bob was an outgoing, congenial accountant and philanthropist who served as deacon of their church. He was "deeply concerned" for his wife's well-being, and "sincerely sorry" for his "indiscretion," as he put it. Though he at first believed equine-facilitated therapy was "a load of manure," he agreed to attend a couple of sessions at the end of the month because "the horses really did seem to be raising Marian's spirits."

After some profound work together, the two realized their marriage not only suffered from Bob's reputation as the nicest guy in the world, but from Marian's unconscious agreement to uphold this illusion. Bob was the first person friends would call when their cars stalled and they needed a ride. Since he had worked as a mechanic before completing his college degree, he'd sometimes spend the weekend fixing these broken-down vehicles at cost. The Elks' club and the church relied on him to lead important, time-consuming committees. Bob and Marian gave a significant portion of their income to charity and were forever attending fundraisers and politically advantageous social events. That is, until Marian's depression.

Through his open, welcoming demeanor and relentless good deeds, Bob was used to charming the most reserved strangers, but the horses saw right through him. Several refused to come up to the fence, and one pinned her ears back, raising her leg to kick when he tried to seduce her with sweet talk. The man was convinced these animals were "stupid and dangerous," until he noticed how congenial they were with his wife, who'd already done some extensive work with the herd. He also saw, unequivocally, how these same horses relaxed and approached him when he finally admitted that he "might be a little aggravated." At first, Bob was confused and embarrassed, afraid of facing the pent-up emotions inside. But once he and Marian understood anger as a protective emotion that intensifies into *rage, sarcasm, boredom, apathy,* and finally, *depression,* they began to see their marital difficulties from a new perspective.

Bob felt used and drained, though he'd never consciously acknowledged it. While his mind focused on the rewards of public admiration and prestige, his body seethed with anger at having his boundaries so flippantly violated that he couldn't help but take it out on the one person he trusted most. Bob never hit Marian, nor did he embarrass her in public. Yet at home, his constant, mean-spirited jokes about her weight, his criticism of her housekeeping abilities and mothering style, and his occasional fits of rage (ending in an overturned chair or a broken dish) took their toll.

"Bob was pretty stressed sometimes, taking on a lot at work and church," Marian said. "I know he didn't mean to hurt me. I tried to go to the gym after school and keep up the house better to take the pressure off us both, but sometimes I was too tired, especially when our son was still living at home. After a while I just didn't feel as sexy as I used to."

Both spouses disconnected from their feelings by focusing on other people's needs. Saying yes to too many favors, Bob diffused his anger through sarcasm, and through the rage attacks that always took place when his son was away from home. Marian saw these private emotional outbursts as a kind of intimacy, a part of her husband he didn't show anyone else. Even though Bob's mis-placed anger hurt her deeply, she endured his emotional abuse without objection, preferring to make excuses for him. Rather than supporting him in saying no to the people who were sucking him dry, she propped him up to go back out into the world for another round of good deeds.

Marian's bottled-up anger intensified into an apathy that initially — and understandably — manifested as sexual disinterest in response to her husband's persistent jokes and insults. This culminated in a full-blown depression when Bob finally stepped over the ultimate line in their marriage. Yet as the couple began to see negative emotions as allies in their search for a more soulful connection, the marriage transformed into a more satisfying partnership.

FOLLOWING THE ENERGY

Depressed people feel self-conscious, dimwitted, and embarrassed by their predicament. Yet according to Karla McLaren, this debilitating state is nothing to be ashamed of. In her audiobook *Becoming an Empath*, she characterizes depression as "the stop sign of the soul." This "ingenious stagnation," as she calls it, takes over when people refuse, over an extended period, to acknowledge anger, fear, sadness, or grief. Marian's episode resulted from ignoring all four of these important signals. Attempts to lift her mood through medication resulted in a temporary surge of well-being that leveled out and then began to plummet, requiring a higher dose just to keep her functioning. For this reason, I suspected that Marian's depression would persist until she deciphered the messages behind her long-suppressed emotions — and began to follow their advice.

While some depressions *do* result from chemical imbalance (and respond well to antidepressants as a result) many cases stem from a deep-seated, intuitive objection to major life choices. After repeated warnings, the psyche finally hinders the False Self's compulsive reenactment of destructive patterns by draining all energy from the mind and the body. According to McLaren, people who can't engage this protective mechanism blindly stumble into situations endangering their health, their sanity, and their purpose in life: "In a world where we're taught to ignore our emotions, dreams,

and true passions, where we enter blindly into the wrong relationships and the wrong jobs, depression is our emergency break."

One of the most efficient ways out of this emotional quagmire
is to ask two questions: "What currently drains my energy?" and
"What new direction gives me energy?" For most people, the difficulty lies in accepting the answer. Sometimes, this energy trail
leads a lawyer to pursue photography, a seemingly irrational or, at
the very least, irresponsible impulse for a man born into a family
of attorneys. Sometimes, it demands that a battered woman leave
her husband, even though everyone else thinks he's the nicest guy
in the world. In my case, a bout of depression in the early 1990s
mysteriously pushed me away from a successful, rather glamorous
career as a music critic toward the initially vague notion of working with horses to help people. At first, it seemed ridiculous to
switch from radio and print journalism to the equestrian arts. I
resisted for months. Some wise, persistent force finally squelched
my skepticism by shutting off all power to the safe, ego-satisfying
activities with which I identified myself. It got to the point where
I had to down an entire pot of coffee to write a single music
review, and even then, my mind was sluggish and full of fog. Yet
whenever I managed to drag myself out to the barn, I seemed to
have endless enthusiasm for cleaning stalls, grooming horses, and
riding in the desert heat. So many creative ideas and insights
would flood my brain when I was relaxing with the herd that I
kept a notebook in the tack room. The research I did during the
seven years leading up to writing *The Tao of Equus* spanned subjects
that seemed to have no practical purpose at the time. Yet all I had
to do was follow the burning need to know, and I was blessed with
endless energy and concentration.

If depression's message were so easy to accept, the psyche
wouldn't have to resort to such tactics — and that's the genius
behind the stagnation: After months of lying listlessly in a dark-
ened room, the attorney finally steps out to shoot some pictures.

His wife and parents are thrilled to see him take an interest in something, anything. "What the hell," they say. "Let's buy him a new camera!"

Depression is the Authentic Self's last-ditch effort to assert itself in a climate that fosters a rigid, socially sanctioned persona. If thwarted, the psyche moves into far more dangerous territory. According to McLaren, intensified depression leads to the *suicidal urge*. Some internal force finally lays down the law and sentences a relentlessly controlling False Self to death. Unfortunately, far too many people who've reached this stage mistakenly attempt, or succeed, in killing the body as well.

In certain cases, the suicidal urge results from chemical imbalance or chronic pain, requiring medical, psychological, *and* spiritual support to keep such a person from trying to end his suffering in a moment of profound fatigue. More often, however, this extreme impulse absolutely does not want to end physical existence. McLaren insists it "emerges when our lives are already endangering our souls. . . . What needs to die is our attachment to falseness, lovelessness, lies, and spiritual emptiness." Here, the dark night of the soul "exists in direct proportion to the dawn that awaits us."

Research on the relationship between chronic stress and serious diseases like cancer suggests that if a person does not get the support she needs to alter her lifestyle, she may face a slow, agonizing death over time, even if she resists the notion of actually killing herself. The inability, or outright refusal, to respond when every fiber of one's being is calling out for change is arguably a passive form of suicide.

When interpreted correctly, however, this desperate bid for authenticity rallies some impressive untapped resources. The questions McLaren advises us to ask the suicidal urge are dramatic for this reason: "What must end now?" and "What must be killed?"

"If you ask these questions prayerfully and ceremonially," she says, "your suicidal urge will tell you that this draining behavior, this soul-killing relationship, this painful addiction, this weakness and self pity, this pathetic story about why you can't do your art [shows that] you've forgotten who you are, but *I remember.* If you let it speak, your suicidal urge will stand up for your lost dreams, and it will help you clear away everything that threatens to kill them. It will remind you of your forgotten goals."

NO TURNING BACK

As he begins to express his artistic yearnings, the depressed attorney will no doubt face a series of "Change back!" reactions from friends and relatives. This term, which I first encountered in *The Dance of Anger* by Harriet Lerner, Ph.D., describes the attempts people make to keep a maverick family member from altering old, painful patterns. Parents, spouses, and colleagues don't *consciously* try to hold this person back; they want him to get better after all. It's more of a knee-jerk reaction to sensing that they'll be forced to change some outmoded behaviors and perceptions in relation to his innovations. The attorney's conviction to finally follow his heart seriously challenges his lifestyle. Though his wife wants him to be happy, her False Self will most assuredly want him to "change back" to the compliant, dependable bread winner she married ten years earlier. She may seem supportive one day and negative the next because of this inner conflict.

For Marian to move out of her depression — and stay married in the process — both husband and wife had to undergo a complete overhaul of their habitual responses to other people. Bob had to start saying no more often. Marian had to stand up to him when he released his anger at home. And together, the two had to face the disappointment friends, colleagues, and church officials initially expressed as Bob learned to *feel* just how many good deeds he could handle in a given week, using the slightest rise in anger to gauge where to draw the line. In this effort, the couple not only benefited from visits to a marriage counselor, they mastered the non-verbal dynamics of boundaries and assertiveness with the horses. Bob realized that these powerful creatures were actually more cooperative when he relinquished his seductive, good-guy persona and related to them in an honest, straightforward manner. He also noticed how the anger simply disappeared when he used its volatile energy to hold his ground. These equine-inspired insights gave Bob the courage to deal with the numerous "change back reactions" he encountered in renegotiating his role at work and church. The couple's efforts to support each other during this difficult time were exemplary. Yet Marian's grief, not her anger, proved the final hurdle in mending their relationship.

During a pivotal session with the Epona herd, Bob was grooming Noche in preparation for some round pen work. As he so often does with strangers, the formerly abused gelding pulled away as the man reached up to brush his forehead. When I explained Noche's background, Bob backed off completely for a minute. Then, speaking to the horse in a calming tone that wasn't the least bit condescending, he began to stroke the horse's neck. Marian sat under a nearby mesquite, watching her husband intently as he gained Noche's confidence with uncommon grace and sensitivity. Finally, the horse leaned into Bob and let him touch his face.

Marian suddenly burst into tears.

"What now!" Bob exclaimed with an agitation that surprised Marian and me both. "What more do I have to *do* to *make this right?*"

The woman stood up, walked over, and rested her hand on her husband's shoulder.

"I just saw a side of you that I thought I'd lost," she said quietly, "a kind, healing man who really *does* know how to help people. I can't explain it really, but I saw it come out when you were comforting Noche."

Marian's face glowed, her still-streaming tears reflecting the intensity of the desert sun.

"I miss you," she continued, still trying to hold back the sobs, "and I forgive you, I really do. But I'm like Noche. I was hurt. I was betrayed, and I can't automatically act like everything's all right, even though we're living a better life now. Noche has people who love him. He knows he's in a better place, but sometimes he still needs gentleness and understanding to help him trust again."

Bob looked away from Marian. "I just feel so ashamed when you cry," he mumbled, kicking at a stone next to the grooming box. "I'm the cause of your pain, and sometimes I wonder if you'll ever get over it. I really don't know what more I can do. I barely know how to make love to you after...you know...after what happened."

"You can treat me like you treated him," she said, pointing to the wise old grandfather of the herd. "You weren't the one who abused him. You weren't ashamed when he pulled away from you. You didn't take it personally, but you were there for him in this sensitive, strong, and gentle way, simply because that's what he needed. Can you help me trust again that way? Can you hold me while I cry the tears I need to cry? Can you let *me* tell you when it's okay to touch my face?"

"I can...at least...do that," Bob replied, his own eyes misting. A single tear rolled down his cheek as he took his wife's hand.

HEALING WATERS

Some people are more afraid of sadness than anger. They act like they'll dry up and blow away if they release all the tears they've been saving up for years, and they can't bear to see anyone else cry. I have to assure such clients that I've never, ever seen anyone die of sadness. A person might become depressed and suicidal from suppressing it, but the original feeling is both healing and life-affirming.

According to Karla McLaren, this misunderstood emotion "restores flow" to the system "when loss is imminent and *in our best interest.*" More specifically, it "brings the healing waters of tears and physical release to us," and "removes log jams in our psyches" so we can live authentically again. Sadness is often a part of grief or depression, but in its purest form, it's a healing agent that motivates us to let go of what no longer serves us so we can embrace the next stage of growth and creativity. McLaren emphasizes that we must ask two questions of this emotion: "What must be released?" and "What must be rejuvenated?" If we can't release our attachment to old patterns and destructive relationships, we can't be rejuvenated, and the sadness persists. The concept is as basic as remembering to wash rancid wine out of a glass before pouring in the new.

Until he understood the message behind sadness, Bob felt helpless and quite often shamed by his wife's tears. Aware of his discomfort, Marian had been crying for months in secret, caught in that too-common limbo between release and rejuvenation. Yet hiding her feelings to make Bob more comfortable was precisely what got them both into such trouble in the first place. The two subsequently realized that underneath Bob's anger was a deep well of sadness he'd suppressed his whole life, feelings he was taught to squelch by mentally reciting that ubiquitous False Self edict: "Real men don't cry." Marian recognized that sharing sadness would require a much more profound level of trust than Bob's private expressions of anger ever did. Yet to work with these emotions more efficiently in the future, the couple also needed to grasp the difference between sadness and grief.

With sadness, people decide when and how to release what no longer works. With grief, the loss or death has already occurred. Grief is so painful because anything that takes form — a relationship, a method, a lifestyle, a business, a human body — solidifies and then struggles to endure beyond its capacity for change.

When it finally breaks apart, or fails to function, grief arises in direct proportion to how attached we had become to it. Sometimes, of course, a loved one dies before his or her time. Either way, the only question to ask of this emotion is "What must be mourned?" And the tears that come in waves over months, or even years, help us let go of what seemed so suddenly and rudely snatched away from us.

Marian's sadness pertained to old relationship patterns she had to *willingly* move beyond in order to create a more satisfying and meaningful marriage. Her grief arose from the shattered image of Bob's fidelity, something she ultimately had no control over. Once Bob understood Marian's sadness and grief as life-*renewing* processes, rather than repeated guilt-trips for having an affair, he was able to hold her through the tears without taking them personally. He also realized that some of the anger he had expressed to Marian over the years was more accurately a resistance to the rising currents of sadness that had plagued him since childhood. Once he learned that this heart-wrenching emotion had a purpose, he was able to comfort *himself* with the same compassion and grace he showed Noche, and Marian was more than happy to support him, privately and intimately, in exploring this long-neglected feeling.

MIXED EMOTIONS

Now, here's the tricky part when it comes to working with emotions: Some are "look-alikes." Anger and frustration look, or more accurately feel, alike, but the messages behind them are different. The same goes for fear and vulnerability. Yet just as two words with different meanings can sound alike, the mind is perfectly capable of interpreting these nuances once it becomes fluent in the language of feeling.

Vulnerability often comes up in equine-facilitated activities, and it took me a while to decipher its meaning. The key lies in separating it from the body's natural warning system. After working with hundreds of clients, I started to notice a particular kind of fear overtaking those who were suddenly confronted with feelings, insights, and even gifts they'd hidden for years. When the horses mirrored authentic emotions, some participants felt raw and exposed, "like an egg, cracked out of its shell and left quivering on the sidewalk," as one woman put it. This psychological vulnerability had nothing to do with physical danger or memories of previous traumas. Even so, these people initially wanted to run as far away as possible from this new information, or fight it tooth and nail.

Vulnerability marks the point where an old coping strategy, behavior pattern, or perception is being challenged — or a previously repressed part of the self is being revealed. This threatens the persona, which has no power to act in innovative ways. The False Self can literally feel like its life is threatened in moments like these — and indeed the way of life in which the False Self thrives may be altered significantly by acknowledging the truth, precipitating drastic changes in one's job and relationships. The persona might even go into its own flight-or-fight mode if the person hasn't developed a sufficiently confident and adaptable Authentic Self. Panic results when the conditioned mind tries to "run away" from the insight. Rage arises when the False Self tries to fight or violently suppress the insight. To keep someone from escalating out of control when vulnerability takes hold, it helps to ask the following questions: "What belief, behavior, or perception is being challenged?" and "What or who can help you integrate this new information?"

The messages behind vulnerability and frustration are related, yet the latter feels more like anger than fear. Sooner or later, everyone who works with horses experiences this rapidly increasing sense of irritation, usually when the animal refuses to cooperate with a favorite training trick or coping strategy. Frustration means that you're employing a technique in work or life, or an influence in relationship with another being, that simply isn't effective. Rather than look for alternatives or ask for help, you're trying to force a breakthrough using familiar methods that, while they may have worked in the past, currently produce little or no result. If you keep pushing, frustration explodes into a rage that often reverts to severe, hurtful dominance tactics. If you decide to give up and go home instead, frustration intensifies into a feeling of utter powerlessness. Either way, you failed to ask the right questions: "Where is the block?" "What can I do differently?" "Who can I ask for ideas or assistance?"

To make things a bit more complicated, anger itself sometimes has a secondary message. Over the years, I've noticed that highly sensitive people, like horses, feel agitated in the presence of someone who's incongruent. They usually interpret this sensation as anger, when in fact it's an alarm signaling that they're interacting with a person who is not what he appears to be — who may, in fact, be wearing a mask of happiness, friendliness, courage, or control, when he's actually feeling aggressive, sad, or fearful.

If you're an empath or high sensitive, the most efficient way to read anger is to first sense if someone has stepped over a boundary. If not, the person may simply be incongruent. By asking yet another question — "What is the emotion behind the mask, and is it directed toward me?" — you can determine whether the person is hiding something in order to take advantage of you, or if he's simply sad, angry, or fearful for personal reasons. In the latter case, the anger, which is really agitation, often subsides when you notice the incongruity and realize the person may act unpredictably because of his conflicted emotional state.

Which brings me to the "Ph.D. level" of emotional intelligence: managing empathic insights. At this point, you recognize that what *you're* feeling may not be what you're feeling, but what someone else is feeling. The contagious nature of emotion is, of course, a controversial notion completely ignored by most people and vehemently challenged by skeptics who see it as some kind of psychic mumbo jumbo. Yet after repeatedly witnessing how horses mirror the emotions of others, I'm convinced the so-called sixth sense is real. Searching for scientific corroboration of what I sometimes call "shared emotion" has become a hobby of mine, and I'm pleased to report that the evidence is rising.

Back when I wrote *The Tao of Equus*, I could only find one term for the phenomenon outside mystical and New Age circles: anthropologist E. Richard Sorensen's concept of "sociosensual awareness." In many ways, I still prefer this term because of the lilting, almost musical way it rolls off the tongue. Sociosensual awareness also has a decidedly positive connotation compared to "affect contagion." I sometimes use this expression when describing how people feel victimized by others' emotions. Affect contagion also carries more weight with skeptics because of its medical connotation. I came across this phrase in *Healing the Soul in the Age of the Brain* by psychiatrist Elio Frattaroli. His definition recognized that the hidden emotions of one person could affect another. While he framed this as something akin to a communicable disease, he recognized that it couldn't be explained away as transference or countertransference. He subsequently learned to use affect contagion in his practice — in one case to accurately sense a client's unspoken suicidal mood when conventional psychological tests, and the opinions of respected colleagues, insisted the man had no self-destructive intent.

The most intriguing description of shared emotion I've encountered comes from Lyn Buchanan, a retired U.S. Army officer trained in remote viewing, the psychic ability to perceive the details of a particular place, as well as other people's thoughts and experiences, at a distance. His book *The Seventh Sense* describes how the military has been methodically cultivating this ability in intelligence personnel for the past thirty years, using it as a data-collection tool during the Iran hostage crisis, the Chernobyl disaster, and the Gulf War. Buchanan, who began teaching these techniques to civilians after the Army declassified a good portion of its research, refers to this sixth sense as "ambience." It essentially involves the ability to gauge the unspoken emotional tone of a person, place, or situation.

"Your psychic sense is not the sixth sense," he insists. "It is the seventh. People [who] attend the CRV [Controlled Remote Viewing] training hope to develop their psychic sense. But perhaps the most surprising and life-changing side effect of taking a CRV course is that it develops not one but two brand-new senses.... Science says that something has been proven when it can be shown to have predictable, dependable repeatability. The sense of ambience is predictable, dependable, and repeatable. But, since there is no body part associated with it, it is ignored as a human sense by the scientific world. It is also ignored in education, child development, and personal training. It is therefore drastically underdeveloped in most people."

While CRV courses hone all the senses in preparation for expanded awareness, ambience is the one Buchanan focuses on the most before taking people to the next level. The results are similar to what Epona clients report after engaging, through equine experiential learning, what I'd been calling shared emotion, sociosensual awareness, or affect contagion. "[These people] now realize they had been walking around mostly asleep for years, and now they are finally awake," he writes. "They begin to see the world in such completeness and beauty that they pick up the paintbrush or pen and begin creating works of art. They go at their jobs with a new and more complete understanding and begin to excel easily, where before, they got along, at best."

I believe, like Buchanan, that "the sense of ambience is not psychic, but as people learn it, they develop a keen ability to perceive things to which other people are virtually blind. People who develop this sense often report that friends and acquaintances have started asking them, 'What are you? Psychic or something?'"

After working with both trained and natural psychics in the military, for the police, and now for the private sector, Buchanan has "become convinced that probably more than 90 percent of everything that passes for psychic is nothing more than the person's innate ability to read the ambience of the person in front of them. . . ."

In reading his description of this natural, yet long-neglected ability, I was amazed and gratified to find that Buchanan and I had observed similar principles at work. The first and most obvious insight concerns the human reliance on language as a block to sensing emotional nuance. "English is very sparse in ambience words," he notes. "Because ambience awareness is not a major part of our language, it is not a major part of our thought process."

The second principle suggests that it's easier for people to sense dramatic differences, rather than subtleties, in the emotional tone of a situation. Buchanan cites an old and somewhat disturbing science experiment: "If you place a frog into hot water, it will immediately jump out. But if you place that same frog in cold water, then slowly heat the water to boiling, the frog will sit there and be boiled alive. . . . Humans, like frogs, are much more sensitive to change than they are to constant conditions. Therefore, if you leave a room that is safe and enter another room that is also safe, you don't notice the ambience in the second room, as you are accustomed to it. But if you leave a safe room and enter a dangerous place, you will notice the sudden change in ambience immediately. We are naturally sensitive to sudden, large changes in ambience, but rarely ever to small ones."

People who tap this underdeveloped sense through the equine-facilitated work go through a period of agony and ecstasy similar to what CRV students experience: "Since I have started training people to become more sensitive to the world around them," Buchanan reveals, "I have seen their creativity and happiness soar, their marriages and parental relationships improve, as do their work situations, life paths, and spiritual closeness with God.... But you can't become more sensitive to the world without also becoming more sensitive to the sorrows within it. While that may not be pleasant, it is nonetheless an unavoidable side effect, so let this be fair warning."

For this reason, learning to sit with uncomfortable emotions — without panicking — is an essential skill in managing the gift of sociosensual awareness. Clients integrating this ability need to take brief "time-outs" to discover what they're feeling before engaging with family members, friends, and especially large groups. The trick is to step into a quiet office or bathroom before walking into, say, a business meeting. In this private space, the person does a body scan to get a baseline reading before facing the collage of emotions he's sure to experience in the conference room. This way, he's more apt to pinpoint emotions hidden behind the masks of professionalism people wear, in part to hide their true motives in competitive situations. The body scan also gives the newly initiated empath an emotional baseline for telling the difference between his emotions and those of others. The pressure of disturbing emotions lessens noticeably when you recognize they're not yours.

Most people are unconsciously empathic to a certain extent. They just don't know how to use the information to their benefit. A woman in a good mood might meet a few colleagues for dinner. As the meal progresses, she feels increasingly agitated, though the conversation remains light and superficial. Not realizing the man sitting next to her is facing a nasty divorce, she nonetheless gets hit with the affect contagion of his rage and mistrust. As her body registers anger, the woman's mind desperately searches for reasons to explain it internally. By the time she drives home, she's convinced the fight she had with her own husband two days earlier must not have been resolved after all, and she's ready to start it up again when the poor man meets her at the door.

Unrecognized empathic talents explain why codependent people go out of their way to calm and support others. They just can't get comfortable when someone else in the household feels sad, angry, frustrated, or depressed. This same concept, in fact, explains why horses so willingly cooperate with their human caretakers. As sociosensual beings in the extreme, these animals only feel good when their riders feel good.

Sometimes a new client asks me how she can reward her mount for doing well. In addition to some standard equestrian protocols, I encourage her to send him a feeling of pure pleasure every time he makes the slightest effort to understand what she wants. Training becomes much more enjoyable for both parties, because in order to transmit a congruent feeling to her horse, she must literally feel that pleasure herself.

Occasionally a new rider balks at the assertiveness necessary to motivate her horse, insisting, in her inexperience, that training is a form of cruelty.

"Let me put it this way," I always say. "If your husband really wants to see a movie you don't much care for, you might go with him because you know it will make him happy — and you both have fun at dinner afterward, partly because he's in such a great mood. If the horse appreciates your company, he'll be willing to do all kinds of things he wouldn't do on his own, simply because he gets an emotional charge from the sheer elation you experience riding him."

Good feelings, after all, are contagious, too, and *that* is the empath's reward.

CHAPTER FIVE

THE MUSIC
OF CONNECTION

A fter enduring her mother's death and a traumatic event in her eldest son's life, "Dinah Jeffries" resolved to be joyful in 2002. She had been helping Kathy Schroeter develop a Louisville-based horse therapy program, and riding Apache, a particularly affable member of the Grizzle Gate herd. Yet when it was her turn to enter the round pen at my Kentucky clinic, she took a much more assertive horse with her.

"Apache had stolen my heart," she says, "but I knew I had to work with Mariposa, the alpha mare of that herd, who doesn't tolerate fools. I was drawn to her because she's what every centered woman hopes to be, undaunted and confident."

Still, Dinah had no idea how to interact with this strong feminine figure. She was fragile and visibly ashamed of her vulnerability. I asked her to define more clearly why she'd picked an aloof mare she described as "all business."

"It was all I could do to stop from shouting out, 'Because I'm really a masochist and can hardly wait for all of you to share in my humiliation,'" she remembers. "But I just stood there stupefied. And then came the profound answer, 'Uh . . . I don't know; I just knew I had to.'"

Considering Dinah's New Year's resolution, I suggested she experiment with ways of simply having fun with the horse. Yet she remained physically and psychologically immobilized, unable to draw on the basic ground training techniques she had learned, much less create a more personal approach. Her fellow workshop participants tried to support her by clapping in rhythm, singing a cheerful invitation to dance with the horse. When this left Dinah unmoved, they shouted some increasingly whimsical ideas from the bleachers: "Go for it," they encouraged. "Get Mariposa moving. Pick up the whip. Run around with her. Try some cartwheels. Make some funny faces. Let yourself go!"

"I was paralyzed," she says. "After several attempts at flapping my arms around like a wounded crane, my time in the round pen was becoming painful to experience, let alone witness. Had everyone else seen my inability to feel or know joy?"

Dinah had fallen into freeze mode, a less widely understood aspect of the flight-or-fight response common among victims of rape, childhood abuse, and life-threatening accidents. I could see that to get to the joy she so deeply wanted to embrace, Dinah would have to break through some feelings that frightened her, yet we were both treading on thin ice. While this particular workshop, The Art of Freedom, explored the emotional dimension of the horse-human connection, it wasn't designed to delve into personal trauma. I had no idea what tragedies Dinah might be harboring, but I didn't feel it would be constructive to explore them in front of the group, especially since I'd be flying back to Tucson the next day and wouldn't be able to support her or even recommend a trusted counselor in her area. Yet I also couldn't leave Dinah in this heightened state or she would feel betrayed by the round pen experience itself.

Equestrian clinicians regularly deal with people suffering from post-traumatic stress disorder for several reasons: Amateurs intimidated by their mounts often refuse to seek help until they have a serious accident. Lifelong riders encountering their first "highly sensitive" horses sometimes inadvertently create unpredictable mounts with conventional techniques and get hurt in the process. Add to this the fact that abuse survivors are often profoundly attracted to frightened, misunderstood animals, and you begin to understand why clinicians who pledge to "do no harm" need to master some basic emotional fitness and trauma resolution skills.

The problem is exacerbated by some talented trainers who don't feel comfortable with their own species. These innovators may have incredible show records, but as teachers of human beings, they can be insensitive, overly demanding, and even competitive with the very people who come to them for help. I can't count the number of amateur equestrians who've contacted me after leaving such seminars feeling hopeless and humiliated.

The holistic horse world proves no more enlightened in this respect. Clinicians espousing the benefits of organic food, herbal supplements, homeopathic remedies, natural hoof care, massage, acupuncture, energy work, and telepathic animal communication are just as likely as conventional trainers to ignore or vilify emotion. In trying to find a more balanced approach to emotion, Karla McLaren observed that many leaders in the holistic field at large see feelings other than peace and joy "as signs of imbalance, of incoherent thinking patterns, of insufficient detachment, and of poor or improper spiritual development." These people are endlessly devising therapies and metaphysical practices to get rid of negative emotions. Yet too often no one takes the time to get the message behind the feeling, and so it persists or returns. This requires endless cycles of treatment, transcendence, or release, invariably followed by the habitual resuppression of emotion, which then leads to uncomfortable blocks, again needing treatment, transcendence, or release.

The sacred triangle of mind, body, spirit conveniently leaves out emotion, and in this respect, "alternative" techniques retain one of the most troublesome features of mainstream science and religion.

McLaren, an empath with a history of childhood sexual abuse, came face to face with the ramifications of this tendency as she struggled to handle her own sensitivities. "I have searched diligently, but I have not discovered a Western view of emotions that explains each one of them in enlightened or useful ways," she emphasized in her groundbreaking book *Emotional Genius*. "My search also led me into spirituality, metaphysics, and energetic healing. In those systems, I found some useful ideas and tools to help me manage my empathic skills — but no functional understanding of emotions. Much of our modern metaphysical curriculum is infected (in my opinion) with an unbalanced, ascendant belief system that doesn't make room for the necessary passages of human life. In many spiritualist or metaphysical belief systems, the body and its ills, the world and its upheavals, the mind and its opinions, and the emotions and their pointed needs are all seen as stumbling blocks that must be overcome, or interruptions that must be transcended."

In his book *Toward a Psychology of Awakening*, psychotherapist John Welwood calls this *spiritual bypassing*. "While still struggling to find themselves, many people are introduced to spiritual teachings and practices that urge them to give themselves up," he writes. "As a result, they wind up using spiritual practice to create a new 'spiritual' identity, which is actually an old dysfunctional identity — based on avoidance of unresolved psychological issues — repackaged in a new guise. In this way, involvement in spiritual teachings and practices can become a way to rationalize and reinforce old defenses. For example, those who need to see themselves as special will often emphasize the specialness of their spiritual insight and practice, or their special relationship to their teacher, to shore up a sense of self-importance. Many of the 'perils of the path' — such as spiritual materialism (using spiritual ideas for personal gain), narcissism, inflation (delusions of grandiosity), or group-think (uncritical acceptance of group ideology) — result from trying to use spirituality to shore up developmental deficiencies."

One of the most telling symptoms of spiritual bypassing involves finding "ways to transcend your personal feelings altogether. This is a major pitfall of the spiritual path, especially for modern Westerners. The attempt to avoid facing the unresolved issues of the conditioned personality only keeps us caught in their grip."

Yet this is precisely the behavior that many religious leaders and holistic healers promote, as McLaren found during her search for a more soulful way to approach her feelings. In order to "be more spiritual," she "strained to be emotionless and nonjudgmental," to "have only joy in my heart." But this proved to be a dead end: "I saw quite clearly that happiness and joy could become very dangerous if they were trumpeted as the emotions of choice — as the only emotions any of us should ever feel. I can't count the number of people I've seen whose lives imploded after they disallowed the protection of anger, the intuition of fear, the rejuvenation of sadness, and the ingenuity of depression in order to feel only joy. In short, I've found throughout my life that what we were taught about emotions is not only wrong — it's often dangerously wrong."

In taking some of her cues from dreams and intuitions, some from years of experience working with fellow abuse survivors, and significant inspiration from the remarkably fluid ways that animals respond to emotion and trauma, McLaren became the first researcher to systematically categorize the wisdom behind fear, anger, sadness, grief, depression, and the suicidal urge. Her work was essential to my understanding of how horses operate as master empaths, and how they help humans reclaim these natural abilities.

"Emotions exist to help the body protect and heal itself at all times — before, during, and especially after trauma," she writes. "They also serve as a vital connecting link between the body, the spirit, and the mind. Emotions are fluid, ever-changing, and extremely versatile energies. Emotions *move* — and they carry massive amounts of energy with them. They're completely truthful (if sometimes painfully so) and completely healing, as long as we approach them correctly, use them honorably, and treat them with utter respect."

Those same statements could be applied to the horse itself, an emotional genius who lives by this code, and in the process, teaches human handlers how to ride the power of authentic feeling.

SYMPHONIES OF EMPATHY

The art of emotional agility must be practiced before it becomes second nature in a crisis. Yet those who've spent their entire lives trying to put on a happy face, while holding all those other "nasty, unenlightened" feelings at bay, find the prospect as daunting as starting the violin at age forty. I often use this analogy with students learning to process their long-neglected emotions. At first, these people feel stiff and uncoordinated. At times, they may even squeal like screeching cats. Yet no one masters an instrument without enduring a host of ugly honks and choking wheezes — and no beginner is shamed for missing notes. It would have been so much simpler, of course, if we'd all taken lessons as children. But that's the price we pay for living in a culture where logic rules with an iron fist, and the "Three R's" are the only courses to survive educational budget cuts. In fact, when clients and colleagues ask me why I seem to have no fear of feeling, I attribute it to the fact that my public school system fostered an award-wining music program.

I don't have a formal degree in psychology, though I've done extensive independent research to enhance the Epona program and write about the results. All my higher education — and much of my time from ages eight to thirty — was devoted to music. When I really thought about it, this explained my seemingly natural gifts for sensing, supporting, and most significantly, *flowing* with the feelings of others in therapeutic situations.

At its best, music is a language of pure emotion that moves body, mind, and spirit simultaneously. At the time I was learning the linear skills of reading and writing, I was practicing the nonverbal art of symphonic resonation, merging my growing expressive abilities with those of up to eighty other people in full orchestra. While popular songs tend to focus on one or two emotions, great classical works cover a surprising array of feeling. My fellow musicians and I would move through passion, joy, tragedy, rapture, jubilation, despair, exuberance, hopelessness, transcendence, power, gentleness, peace, pathos, ambiguity, and triumphant resolution. If we made somebody in the audience cry, that was a *good* thing. People didn't pay us to play happy tunes all evening. They wanted the full panorama, and if we did our job well, they left feeling elated and alive.

We rarely discussed these nuances; we all knew we were trying to capture the indescribable. The notes on paper triggered something we could draw out and show others through the sound, as if each instrument was a portal to the individual soul, that harmonized with some nameless force coordinating all our efforts into a symphony of shared experience much greater than the sum of its parts. These moments on stage and in rehearsal were worth the woodshedding in lonely practice rooms and the conflicts in the hallways, those desperate attempts to jockey for position and prestige. What would it take, I wondered, to let go of our egos and live what the music taught us?

To me, partnering with a horse felt like music in motion. The raw energy of a thousand-pound being took shape in concert with the rider's sensitivity, courage, focus, and skill. And yet one important member of this duo lacked an ego in the classic sense, changing the rules of improvisation significantly. Whatever the horse reflected to the handler was devoid of ambition and ulterior motive. In this sense, riding became an adventure in self-discovery more honest than many purely human works of art, which can lapse into emotional indulgence, the flipside of suppression. Horses, so sensitive to minute changes in emotional nuance, taught me to ride the fine line between these opposites. Over the years, I also learned that these animals could sense the difference between spiritual bypassing and *truly* enlightened responses. Horses modeled an *embodied spirituality*, one that was both fully present in this world and deeply connected to the soul's divine origins.

Yet to share this equine-inspired wisdom with others, I had to point to nonverbal realities with words and procedures, much like a music professor systematically teaches the theory of scales, chords, counterpoint, and orchestration to students who will someday create their own symphonies. In this effort, I combined aspects of Karla McLaren's work with Peter Levine's research on trauma resolution, Elaine Aron's insights into highly sensitive people, and my colleague Kathleen Ingram's holistic counseling perspectives, among other influences.

I also struggled to articulate the dynamics of shared emotion my horses were demonstrating daily. Over time, I realized that terms I'd been collecting to describe this phenomenon could be used to characterize its nuances. For instance, when a workshop participant becomes infected by the emotions of a fellow group member, I use the term *affect contagion* to emphasize that the sadness or anger the first person feels really belongs to someone else. *Clairsentience*, a heightened form of affect contagion, involves feeling someone else's bodily sensations, usually pain, in your own body. *Empathy* also involves feeling what others feel, only more consciously. With affect contagion, you're *inadvertently* infused with someone else's unconscious or incongruent emotions. I now use empathy to specify the act of *willingly participating* in another person's emotions.

Ambience more specifically relates to the feeling of a place. An emotionally potent event creates lingering impressions. In the most extreme example, the ambience of a house where a murder took place feels noticeably different than the ambience of one where a joyful celebration was held. Horses are extremely sensitive to ambience, which is one explanation for why they spook at "nothing." The other major reason stems from affect contagion — emotions coming from other horses or from distressed, incongruent handlers and riders.

With *emotional resonance*, two people who've experienced similar betrayals or abuses trigger each other, causing one to overreact to and reinforce the other's fear, anger, sadness, or grief. Horses with a history of trauma easily draw out the unresolved emotions and repressed memories of human abuse survivors — which is why such animals make great therapy partners in an EFP setting *and* wreak havoc in barns where students are encouraged to "leave their problems at the gate." For riding instructors, the most troublesome aspect of emotional resonance stems from its tendency to draw traumatized horses and traumatized people together. A frightened, flighty, dissociative incest survivor should never attempt to rehabilitate a frightened, flighty, dissociative horse, yet such a person will invariably feel "at home" with this animal. She'll insist on buying him over the calm, quiet teacher horse she really needs. In her audiobook *Advanced Energy Anatomy*, Caroline Myss calls this "The Law of Magnetic Attraction," using the term to explain why two previously unacquainted alcoholics, or two rape victims who've never met, will "accidentally" sit next to each other during her workshops, and as the weekend progresses, find out just how much they have in common.

While this phenomenon sometimes results in like-minded people or horses reinforcing old trauma patterns in each other, emotional resonance can serve an important role in healing. Alcoholics Anonymous, Incest Survivors Anonymous, Alanon, and other such programs employ sponsors who've suffered the same abuses or addictions as newcomers. These wounded healers, who now function more effectively, can still tune into the frequency of the original trauma and vibrate sympathetically with those who need their help. Through emotional resonance, sponsees feel the same sense of being "at home" with their sponsors that an abuse survivor feels with her abused horse. Yet as an emotionally healthy sponsor vibrates sympathetically with his sponsees, he can actually raise their vibration, so to speak, giving them, in his presence, the experience of the more balanced "chord of well-being" they'll someday be able to hold on their own. (More about the power of resonance in chapter 8.)

Another benefit of emotional resonance pertains almost exclusively to human-equine relationships. For years, I puzzled over how readily my horse Noche would move toward someone on the verge of a good cry — when he normally couldn't stand associating with strangers. He actually seemed to incite, or "loosen," these tears, allowing the client to hug him and sob into his neck. This same person, trying to brush him or put a fly mask on him, might not be able to approach him the next day. Over time, I got the distinct impression that Noche was, in part, riding *their* tears for his own purposes. He wasn't the least bit traumatized by these emotional outbursts; they actually had a healing effect on him. Was he, I wondered, releasing his own unresolved sadness through emotional resonance?

Horses, contrary to popular belief, can cry, albeit one or two tears at a time. I've seen it happen a dozen times in situations where the animals had good reason. Yet they can't engage in that cathartic sobbing humans use to discharge strong emotion. As

Karla McLaren suggests, tears are the "healing waters" that remove "log jams in our psyches." If so, animals who haven't evolved to cry effectively might seek out opportunities for emotional resonance.

Oeste, the Schroeters' Peruvian Paso, seemed to be doing just that with a woman at the Kentucky clinic. When Regan Leo went to halter the palomino and lead him to the round pen, she found herself fighting the urge to cry. "I began to sob uncontrollably," she remembers, "and I didn't know why. I was afraid that I would upset Oeste."

As the three of us walked toward the ring, I discussed my little theory, explaining that she might actually be doing Oeste a favor by letting those tears flow. This gave her the courage to dive into her inexplicable grief. In the process, she discovered just how much she had in common with the horse.

"Oeste had been a showpiece for his previous owners because of his incredible beauty on the outside," she says. "Time was never given to find out who he really was, to get to know him for the incredible being he is. I realized then that I had been a showpiece, for my ex-husband." And Regan cried for the misunderstood, unappreciated beauty in them both.

This wave of emotion, potent as it was, didn't last long; neither did it have a debilitating effect. "I'm not what I consider an experienced horsewoman," Regan emphasizes. "I love horses, but I hadn't had any Pat Parelli training like most of the others in the workshop. Oddly enough, after all that intense emotion, I learned a few new Parelli games very quickly that day. Whatever movement or task I asked Oeste to do, he responded, as if he and I were one. There was a light beaming inside me that felt as bright as a Hollywood spotlight. I had always felt a strong connection to Oeste helping my friend Kathy Schroeter at her farm. The last day of the workshop, I learned that Oeste was not only a soulmate, I was the instrument through which he could cry the tears he could not cry. The experience changed my life."

ONE URGE TO RESIST

Shared emotion carries at least one destructive by-product: the compulsion to aggressively "fix" friends, loved ones, horses, and group situations. This urge arises mostly because people don't realize they're empathic or understand how to process emotion effectively. A person in emotional pain essentially infects others with his unpleasant feelings. When this dynamic remains unconscious (as it most often does in a culture that sees emotions as irrational, self-contained, and shameful) those around him will rally to help, or more accurately, *make* him "get over it" as soon as possible, mostly so that *they* can feel better. Powerful positive emotions, believe it or not, produce a similar panic in stoic people who value good sense and proper deportment. To catch someone else's joy is to feel out of control, and they'll fight it, even to the point of *creating* depression in exuberant family members through sarcasm, apathy, soul-deadening criticism, and, in some cases, domestic violence.

There's simply no getting around it: To give a loved one time to decipher the meaning behind a troubling emotion, you have to be willing to endure the discomfort with him. You have to resist the urge to distract him, medicate him, shame him, punish him, or give him a cookie if he promises to be a good boy and stop crying. And you can only fathom taking this route when you trust the wisdom of authentic feeling. Rather than correcting the situation for him, or abandoning him to his anguish, you *can* have a profound effect by offering what horses like Rasa, Noche, and Rocky do naturally. They move in closer and stand next to the person in turmoil. They participate empathically, remaining fully present with what *is* happening, creating a psychological container of support. Kathleen Ingram calls this "holding the sacred space of possibility." It's a fully engaged form of patience: open, nonjudgmental, respectful of a person's inner wisdom. It allows him to more easily connect with the genius inside, what I like to call the Authentic Self, what other writers and psychotherapists prefer to call the True Self, or in Carl Jung's case, the "Self" (as opposed to the small-minded "self" or persona). This creative presence is fully capable of deciphering the meaning behind what the conditioned personality sees as misbehavior. To the Authentic Self, everything is information: the body, with its aches and pains, irrational feelings, and sudden intuitions; the False Self, with its storehouse of methods, socially conditioned responses, relentless dictates, and critical tape loops; the shadow personality, which defiantly acts out what the False Self has rejected, usually at the most embarrassing, inopportune moments.

I've sometimes heard God referred to as "the One who sees everything and still smiles." He, or She, apparently made the Authentic Self in this image. When the True Self, the soul — whatever you want to call it — emerges from its inner prison, it carries with it the courage to fully participate in the ten thousand joys and the ten thousand sorrows of life, flowing through pathos and ecstasy like Itzhak Perlman reveling in a tempestuous performance of the Sibelius Violin Concerto. As it gains power, the Authentic Self collaborates with life, improvising an original composition of such poignancy that it inspires awe in those who hear it — and fear in those who cling to the cage. At the same time, the fully empowered, fully embodied spirit senses, more profoundly than ever, the needless suffering of others. And while it wouldn't presume to fix them for their own good, it knows that it will never rest until others free themselves from the bonds of internal slavery. At this point, every authentic creative act becomes a beacon, a soul song capable of calling others to live the truth of who they really are.

In this effort, as I've so often found, the horse is more than willing to travel the nether regions between freedom and captivity with us, offering to carry the lost child of divine origins back to the world that once rejected it. Decked out in full riding regalia, this majestic beast of burden was the ultimate symbol of conquest, of man's power over nature, over other men, and over his own "base" instincts and emotions. But when a weary warrior finally steps out of the saddle, removes his armor, and asks his mount to accompany him beyond the boundaries of civilized protocols, the horse becomes the champion of his Authentic Self.

TRUE COMMUNITY

The False Self and the Authentic Self certainly weren't new ideas when I incorporated them into my work. References to these two conflicting aspects of the human psyche can be found in religious and psychological texts the world over. But as I watched the horses respond to people in different yet strangely consistent ways, depending on which "self" was active, I amassed a great deal of practical knowledge about the phenomenon. The truth of the matter is, people have been waxing philosophical about freedom and enlightenment for centuries without significantly changing their behavior, least of all in groups. When human beings get together, they almost can't help reinforcing the same patterns of social conditioning their ancestors rebelled against or tried to emigrate away from — only to inadvertently re-create them again in whatever new world, new religion, or new political movement originally promised change.

Horses, however, have an uncanny ability to see through the False Self's trickiest maneuvers. Given half a chance, these animals quite naturally draw out and reinforce the Authentic Self. Of course, they act like any other slave when dominated into submission. But unlike human serfs, horses are remarkably resilient when they sense an opening. It's like they've been waiting, for thousands of years, to catch us off guard so that they can help us remember who *we* really are — in part, I suppose, so they can finally be appreciated for who *they* really are.

Just as I diligently searched the literature for evidence of shared emotion, I became for a time obsessed with accounts of the False Self–Authentic Self dilemma. I was thrilled to find numerous writers throughout history documenting the same dynamics I had first observed with the help of my horses, sometimes using the exact same vocabulary. Among the most powerful yet accessible of these books are Alice Miller's *The Drama of the Gifted Child* and John Welwood's *Toward a Psychology of Awakening*. In *When the Heart Waits*, Sue Monk Kidd eloquently sums up this seemingly universal experience of awakening:

"Is it possible, I asked myself, that I'm being summoned from some deep and holy place within? Am I being asked to enter a passage in the Spiritual life — the journey from false self to true self? Am I being asked to dismantle old masks and patterns and unfold a deeper, more authentic self — the one God created me to be? Am I being compelled to disturb my inner universe in question of the undiscovered being who clamors from within?"

As Epona's interspecies staff answered those questions with a resounding *Yes!*, we became more adept at helping other people recognize and strengthen the Authentic Self. We were repeatedly awestruck at how talented this aspect of the psyche could be in negotiating relationships and life challenges. Over time, eight skills proved universally relevant in building partnerships and communities capable of *supporting* authenticity. In the process, we moved from instinctively engaging these abilities to consciously promoting their development.

I eventually formalized the list and began handing it out at seminars. Though the need for these skills arose at different times and in different combinations during the experiential work, opportunities to strengthen them all invariably arose during a typical weekend workshop. Still, it was helpful to explain them in a certain order since the latter four principles were easiest to engage when the first five were already in place:

EIGHT ESSENTIAL SKILLS FOR AUTHENTIC COMMUNITY BUILDING

1. Using emotion as information.
2. Sitting in uncomfortable emotions without panicking.
3. Sensing and flowing with the emotions of others, again without panicking.
4. Reading "misbehavior" as a form of communication.
5. Understanding the dynamics of shared emotion: distinguishing between instructive personal feelings, conditioned (False Self) emotional patterns, affect contagion, empathy, ambience, and emotional resonance.
6. Resisting the temptation to aggressively "fix" people, horses, uncomfortable situations, etc.
7. Creating a psychological container of support, what Kathleen Ingram calls "holding the sacred space of possibility." This fully engaged form of patience is crucial to tapping innovative solutions that arise from the eighth ability:
8. Activating the Authentic Self.

PREPARING THE WAY

In equine-facilitated human development programs around the country, participants sometimes find the horses *too* efficient in unearthing intense emotions. After a powerful session, some of these people are turned loose with the recommendation that they see a counselor or come back in a week for another EFP session. In the meantime, they're left reeling from a Pandora's box of long-suppressed material — without the personal skills to process these explosive feelings. Adequately preparing clients for what may happen goes a long way in averting the possibly overwhelming effects of diving into experiential work.

Just as in psychology, with its divergent approaches of cognitive therapy, shock treatment, antidepressants, Freudian analysis, somatic psychotherapy, and other methods, a number of well-defined styles have emerged in programs employing horses as agents for transformation. Terms reflect differences in emphasis and approach, with Equine Assisted Psychotherapy (EAP), Equine-Facilitated Psychotherapy (EFP), Equine Experiential Learning (EEL), Equine-Facilitated Mental Health, Equine Assisted Growth and Learning among the more common monikers. Yet as these activities have gained more respect and acceptance, some disturbing trends have also appeared. I can't count the number of times I've heard therapists with little or no horse experience report that they attended a three-day EAP workshop that "qualified" them to do "this amazing work." The fact that some counselors come home with a "Level I certification" does not mean they can create a safe container for catharsis when they step out of the office and into the round pen. It takes practice to simultaneously help both species modulate their arousal in tense situations, while reading the complex nuances of equine behavior communicating both the client's and the horse's constantly shifting mental and emotional states. These people didn't become psychotherapists in a weekend, and they shouldn't expect to delve into the highly specialized field of equine-facilitated therapy without additional research and supervision.

Most EAP or EFP training programs require mental health practitioners to join forces with "equine specialists": trainers or riders with significant horse sense. While this is a good way to get started, it can also create a false sense of security. Conventional training techniques do *not* necessarily apply to therapeutic activities — at least not without some modification. Even advanced dressage instructors need more than a three-day seminar to assimilate this new way of interacting, and their own fears and prejudices invariably come up along the way. Sometimes a client's feelings trigger the horse handler's suppressed emotions. In such cases, an inadequately prepared "equine specialist" may be of no use whatsoever to the counselor for the rest of the session. Since horses also mirror the therapist's incongruities, the opposite has actually been known to happen, leaving the trainer to stabilize a frantic or dissociative counselor. For this reason, Epona's apprenticeship program spends the entire first entire week evaluating and supporting future practitioners in exploring their own issues. Therapists and horse professionals are supervised in facilitating each other — with a herd already experienced in this work acting as the ultimate teachers.

While many EFP innovators have developed highly effective practices through their own talent and independent study, the question of certification has been coming up with increasing regularity, as it always does when a new field takes off. One organization has stepped forward: EAGALA (Equine Assisted Growth and Learning Association). Their Level III certification demands at least 300 hours of documented sessions and attendance at increasingly advanced seminars, among other requirements. I don't agree with certain aspects of EAGALA's approach, yet Level III does exhibit the integrity, educational goals, experience, and research and publication requirements that produce credible professionals in this field. The problem is that many people call themselves certified EAP practitioners after attending a single Level I workshop. Some social service agencies actually see this as a legitimate qualification, when in fact it's nothing more than a three-day introduction to the field that *anyone* can attend. Ethically speaking, Level I should be referred to as a "prerequisite" for certification. EAGALA's Level II is more accurately a work-study vehicle similar in commitment and time requirements to Epona's yearlong apprenticeship (though the philosophies of these two training programs are as different as behaviorism and archetypal psychotherapy). Teams pairing counselors and equine specialists lead sessions at Level II, but they're still in a crucial development stage benefiting from supervision and support.

Aside from EAGALA's efforts, the EFMHA division of NARHA is the only other North American organization with the resources and expertise to oversee the field. In the early 1990s, NARHA developed a multileveled certification process for therapeutic riding instructors who work with physical and cognitive disabilities. Even so, the organization has been moving much more cautiously toward certifying people in Equine-Facilitated Mental Health. At the publication of this book, EFMHA was still researching standards and practices with special attention to the safe, humane treatment of therapy horses — something the EAGALA program has already been criticized for not attending to more closely. EFMHA board members emphasize that these animals must be treated as sentient beings with their own needs and unique perspectives. Figuring out how to ensure that therapists respect the horse's rights — or even determining what those stated rights should be — is no small task. After several years of deliberation and experimentation, EFMHA plans to launch its own certification for mental health professionals in 2004.

Trainer and clinician Chris Irwin, author of *Horses Don't Lie*, recently discussed his concerns in a website essay titled "E.A.P.–ed Off!" which he will reportedly include in a new edition of his book. Initially a supporter of equine assisted psychotherapy, he has since observed that "the majority of the practices seem to be based in setting both the horse and the human up for failure. For example: A very common game is to hand a client (who has no experience with horses) a halter and lead rope and say to them 'catch that horse' and perhaps even 'then lead it over the bridge.' The person has no clue how to approach the loose horse, let alone halter and lead the horse correctly, and getting the horse to walk over the bridge is almost comical. It becomes clear that the goal is to see how the client responds to stress, performance anxiety, and, most often, failure."

Irwin shows some insight in assuming that "the horse is essentially used as a catalyst to provoke human emotions so that the therapist can make the metaphorical leap from relations with horses to relations with people." Yet the facilitators he encountered somehow missed the point that these animals can detect hidden emotions *at a distance* — that they relax, lick, and chew when people simply become congruent. Counselors who don't understand this crucial factor tend to rush clients into direct experiences, or "games," that really can be traumatic for both species. Don't get me wrong. These same activities can be enjoyable and empowering for everyone. Yet just as a mundane kitchen knife can kill, and a whip can either torture a horse or gracefully communicate changes in speed and direction, proper sensitivity and timing are crucial in facilitating even the most rudimentary EAP games.

The problem, at its most basic level, seems to arise from some programs' stated philosophy of "using the horse as a tool," which attracts some counselors with little regard for the animal's emotional well-being. "How do the horses feel about being subjected to people who are confusing, invasive, contradictory, and often frustrating?" Irwin asks, and rightly so. "Throughout this process, the horse has had, in the truest sense of the word, people who are ignorant of its needs basically using it as a tool for their benefit. All too often I see horses who are clearly demonstrating that they are not happy with our games. Leave it to humans to design a feel-good experience for people with horses but completely forget about the needs of the horse."

Of course, this same statement could be made about mainstream equestrian activities that force horses into all kinds of compromising positions to stroke the human ego. This attitude, however, is doubly destructive in a therapeutic context. To treat a horse as a tool is to model the same attitude perpetrators of emotional and sexual abuse adopt with other people: considering a sentient being as some *thing* to be used for one's own enjoyment or fulfillment, to be put away and ignored when no longer amusing. For this reason, programs sensitive to the needs of both horse and human generally offer some introductory material on "equine culture." They also employ reflective activities that initially take place over the fence, allowing facilitators to evaluate the emotional responses people have in the presence of individual horses, and vice versa, before clients are allowed to lead and groom the animals.

Over the years, I've learned that even seminars designed for experienced equestrians benefit from the same preparation before riders enter the arena, regardless of how well they know their horses. Taking a mere eight hours to explore the dynamics of shared emotion is a drop in the ocean compared to decades of suppressing feeling and functioning in a dominance-submission paradigm. Still, people chomping at the bit to saddle up aren't so thrilled with the idea — until the group encounters a person, like Dinah Jeffries, who responds traumatically to a seemingly benign activity like playing with a horse in a round pen. In fact, the full importance of what Dinah ultimately accomplished at the Kentucky clinic only makes sense when you understand how workshop participants are primed for such moments through the emotional fitness and community-building skills introduced the first day.

THE SAINT IN THE CENTER

After discussing the Emotional Message Chart and leading the group through some awareness exercises, I encourage participants to gather information about the herd using their bodies, their feelings, and their intuition. This can be intimidating, especially when I ask them not to touch the animals, a simple request that brings up both challenges and unrecognized strengths. Some participants are initially mystified or even aggravated by the fact that I don't want them to pet the horses. As we discuss their concerns, many realize their desire to touch is actually a covert form of control, a way of holding someone at arm's length while feigning intimacy. These people are subsequently surprised at how insecure they feel approaching a thousand-pound creature with their hands behind their backs or at their sides — even when that horse is standing on the other side of the fence.

For other clients, the temporary moratorium on petting opens up a whole new world. Some experience a rush of information through the gut and the heart. Smells ignored moments earlier take over. A subtle toss of the horse's head suddenly seems rich with meaning. And the mind begins to think in images rather than words. By the time participants circle up to discuss these insights, however, their inner critics are running amok. For this reason, I always send them out to scan the horses with notebooks in hand. "Write down everything you feel or think, no matter how ridiculous," I stress. "The subtler and more irrational the information seems, the more significant it's likely to be — and the more likely you are to forget it as you walk back over to the group, just as you often forget important details of your dreams by the time you pour your first cup of coffee."

Our culture's attention to feeling and imagery is so underdeveloped that most people at first catch only brief, disjointed glimpses of what the body can sense and communicate. These subconscious observations become even harder to access as they're sifted through the persona's limited beliefs and dictates, leaving somatic and intuitive insights little outlet for expression except in dreams. When the mind *consciously* converses with the body, some people feel like they're "dreaming while awake," as one man put it. The sensation can be disorienting, even frightening. The facilitator's ability to create an atmosphere of openness and loving support is crucial even at this early stage.

To outsiders, the "no touch" exercise looks like a group of people milling around some horse corrals taking notes on a whole lot of nothing. Yet this deceptively simple activity not only enhances sensory awareness, it allows people to glimpse the power of ambience, emotional resonance, and other nonverbal insights.

It builds trust between the mind and the body, and between the participants themselves.

As they compare notes, people realize they're not alone in dealing with critical internal voices that try to block all kinds of useful information. In other words, they begin to see how the False Self works before that concept is officially introduced. Ideally, the facilitator also models how the Authentic Self processes "irrational" or "embarrassing" feelings and ideas. While the False Self lapses into ruthless, habituated judgments about what should or shouldn't happen, suppressing or fighting anything that doesn't fit into its limited worldview, the Authentic Self engages a compassionate discernment of what *is* — before determining *what's possible*, or *what wants to happen*.

I formally introduce the False Self–Authentic Self metaphor in preparation for the next activity: *reflective* round pen work. Here the round pen isn't used as a training venue, but as an open space for connection and cocreation. In contrast to *active* round pen work, where the student attempts to longe, ride, or dance with a horse, reflective round pen interactions allow people to explore the shifting currents of feeling and intuition that arise *in relationship* to a four-legged emotional genius. At first, these subtle sensory insights are easily obscured by conventional equestrian agendas. For this reason, it's helpful to exercise feeling and intuition without the added pressure of trying to make the animal perform a particular move. Later on, we can apply these same abilities to active round pen exercises where the student draws on somatic input to fulfill a specific horse-training goal.

The concept sounds reasonable enough. Yet as I learned early on, the parameters essential to reflective work — open space, cocreation with a non-human being, and lack of a specific agenda — initially throw False Self into a panic, almost without exception. For purely practical reasons, I have to assure students that while the conditioned personality freaks out at the thought of entering the round pen without a predetermined task to perform, each person nonetheless possesses another, more innovative source of wisdom. Toward this end, I find it helpful to hand out a simple stick-figure drawing illustrating the idea of leaving the False Self outside the gate:

I soon realized, however, that the Tornado Head, the horse, the rider, and the instructor at the center symbolized different facets of each person's psyche. The horse not only represents the flesh-and-blood animal we propose to interact with creatively but our own body's instincts, intuition, and emotions, which most of us were taught to rein in and control like an unruly three-year-old stud. The rider personifies the mind, which holds the intellect, will, focus, and ambition to motivate the "horse" to accomplish certain tasks as needed. And the riding instructor symbolizes the Authentic Self, a being capable of interpreting the meaning behind the horse's body language and apparent misbehavior while coaching the mind in how to respectfully collaborate with, rather than dominate, the incredibly sensitive creature it rides.

The gargantuan size of the False Self in the figure depicts its almost-overwhelming presence in our lives, the arrows beside it signifying that it draws its energy, knowledge, and motivation from external sources: outside approval, security, wealth, social standing, methods, peer pressure, and validation through degrees, certifications, and other forms of praise authority figures bestow on us for jumping through the right hoops. The whirlwind over its head, of course, represents clichéd thought loops spinning in fearful frenzy as the False Self towers over us with an intimidating display of its dubious power.

The riding instructor, on the other hand, is both fully grounded in this world and connected to a higher source, yet its relatively small stature acknowledges that in most people, the Authentic Self is less developed. In some students, particularly those from abusive backgrounds, it may be so small that it barely has a voice at all. Yet through the initial act of creating a sturdy boundary between the conditioned persona and the true self, the latter finally has the space to grow, an arena in which to practice its own way of relating to the body, the emotions, and the mind. The False Self may still scream bloody murder over the fence, but it can't get inside and force the newly individuated soul into submission. Through this process, inner wisdom begins to shine out. The rider takes the reins and saddle off her mount, experimenting with her own version of natural horsemanship under the tutelage of a compassionate, imaginative inner teacher.

If I were to depict the evolution of this process, I'd draw increasingly larger, brighter representations of the riding instructor to contrast with a smaller, fainter Tornado Head. The False Self eventually defers to the Authentic Self, occasionally shouting helpful suggestions over the fence based on the methods it learned and the degrees it earned. The disappearance of the False Self, or more accurately the soulful integration of its useful yet limited knowledge, precludes the use of the round pen all together, and the Authentic Self quite naturally grows beyond this useful yet artificial boundary, accompanying horse and rider on a journey through unmapped territory. Eventually, the three would become one — a fully integrated, wholly indescribable being of unlimited scope and potential. Though I've never met anyone who reached this point, it would, I suppose, mark that state of grace known as "enlightenment."

JUST YOUR IMAGINATION

In the meantime, there are all sorts of fascinating things to learn in the round pen with a horse milling around at liberty. I mean this both literally *and* symbolically, of course, but for the moment we'll concentrate on actual human-equine interactions. Through reflective work, participants practice authentic community-building skills as they sit outside the arena, holding the sacred space of possibility for each individual who enters, sensing empathically what happens inside, supporting the Authentic Self as it makes its first shaky attempts to assert itself, resisting the False Self's urge to fix certain things for people and judge everything else into submission. The entire group benefits from each person's experience. Students not only gain confidence in deciphering the wisdom behind previously troublesome feelings, they begin to differentiate between *intuition, projection,* and *transference.*

The False Self treats all three of these concepts as suspect, particularly intuition, which it either casually sloughs off as "just your imagination," or more dramatically rejects as evidence of "insanity" or "the devil's work," depending on whether you were indoctrinated into the cult of reason or a fundamentalist church. Yet intuition is none of these things. It's simply a catchall term for our ability to gain accurate information through nonrational means.

At a workshop in Tucson, Monique Brignoni, an intelligent, experienced, quite reasonable equestrian from Switzerland, was embarrassed by the bizarre, nonsensical images she received interacting with various members of the Epona herd. After a bit of coaxing, she finally shared one of these garbled insights with the group, assuming that it was her own subconscious trying to send symbolic messages about her "obviously chaotic" psyche.

"It was so ridiculous," she said. "I was standing in front of that mare over there, and I felt waves flowing through me, deep inside. The feeling was so warm and nourishing, I couldn't help but surrender to it. Then, out of the blue, a single word came at me: Baby. What do you think that means?"

The horse was pregnant, a fact which I hadn't yet admitted to participants, in part to see if someone might pick up on this little secret. Monique's jaw dropped when I told her about the mare's condition.

"Wow," she said. "I know it sounds completely weird, but now that you mention it, those waves seemed very much like amniotic fluid. Really though, don't you think it was just my imagination?"

"Imagination is never a *just*," I replied directly to Monique's inner critic. "Imagination fuels innovation. It creates great works of art and music. It designs buildings. It flies us to the moon."

"Yeah, but couldn't it just be transference?" asked a psychologist in the group. "Most of the time, I think people are just projecting their own stuff onto horses because they can't deal with it in themselves."

"That's often true," I said, "and it's something we humans constantly do with each other. But here again, the word *just* invalidates these processes also. Until we remain open to the possibility that intuition, transference, and projection all contain valuable information, we'll never learn to tell the difference. Judging or shaming ourselves for experimenting with nonrational insights, even in the subtlest way, is the surest road to shutting down a vast source of inner wisdom."

Transference occurs when a person's thoughts and feelings toward a horse are strongly influenced by attitudes originally developed in a significant past relationship. At a subsequent Tucson workshop, my self-confident Arabian gelding Max completely intimidated "Ginger," a forty-five-year-old executive secretary. Brow furrowed in disgust, she characterized the horse as "rude, presumptuous, and dangerous." This first impression, however, contrasted sharply with what I already knew about Max. Certainly no pushover, he nevertheless had a kind heart. I could always count on him to take care of beginner riders and emotionally fragile clients.

Ginger had completely misread Max, and I was curious to find out why. Rather than announce that she'd misjudged this benevolent soul, I asked her how she'd come to these conclusions.

"I don't know exactly," she said. "Something about that horse reminds me of my father. He was a real bastard, very abusive."

Through this emotionally charged statement, I glimpsed what *was* happening — and what *wanted to happen* next. The horse's true nature was obscured by Ginger's transference. If she learned to set boundaries with the strong male figure Max represented, however, she'd be able to see that the horse's typically positive response to self-assertiveness was quite different from her father's attempts to disempower and demoralize her. Sure enough, when she took Max into the round pen, her submissive body language and tendency to dissociate encouraged him to herd her around, albeit gently, in the same way that every man she had ever known felt compelled to do. Yet as she learned to stay present and hold her ground, she eventually realized that Max was affable and accommodating, not at all like her father. Ginger's transference, then, allowed her to work through behaviors and perceptions rooted in a destructive childhood relationship. Max brought to light a significant *repetition compulsion*, Freud's term for habitually acting out the same unconscious scenario with a variety of people, despite the negative results. Ginger realized that her initial impressions about men, and their subsequent reactions toward her, were heavily influenced by patterns initiated under her father's tyranny. She finally understood that to develop healthy relationships in the future, she'd need to stop dissociating, set boundaries, and see each man for who he truly was. More important, she left with the memory, *in her body*, of what it felt like to stay present and hold her ground, and she was rewarded for doing so by Max's nourishing response.

From a False Self perspective, Ginger had been wrong about Max. This mindset could easily have been reinforced by a facilitator *trying* to exercise intuition, for example, or a trainer uncomfortable with personal issues that quite naturally arise from even the most casual horse-human relationships. In both cases, Ginger would have felt considerable shame when her misconceptions were brought to light. In supporting the woman to recognize her transference as an important message, however, she found significant value in what would otherwise have been rejected as a mistake.

THE POWER OF PROJECTION

Projection is similar to transference, except that the horse's true nature is obscured by feelings the person refuses to acknowledge about herself. Projected qualities, like those related to transference, can be positive or negative. During a clinic held at Samantha McGrath King's scenic Ontario farm, KingOak, a group of horse trainers and amateur equestrians witnessed one of the most powerful, transformative examples of projection I've ever had the pleasure, and terror, of facilitating. Connecticut-based cultural anthropologist Jane Strong chose to work with a stunning, dark gray mare named Cinders because, as she put it, "Her eyes seemed so wise and alert, like she could handle anything with grace and dignity. She seemed so sure of herself, full of poise and sensuality. She possessed all those qualities I aspire to as a mature woman."

Conscious of the opportunity to change old patterns, Jane resisted the urge to work with a more troubled horse. "That's what

I'm used to in life," she says. "Adversity and challenge seem to have become my specialty." Yet when Cinders's owner, Margaret Rodman, turned the horse loose in the round pen, the mare's calm, collected demeanor evaporated. She raced around the arena, leaping and charging as if she expected a group of machine-gun-wielding terrorists infected with SARS to come barreling out of the woods. Jane's entry had no effect whatsoever — Cinders almost knocked this experienced horsewoman over *several times*. The fact that Jane didn't move out of the way until the horse was practically on top of her smacked of confusion and dissociation. I knew Jane would have to stabilize Cinders, or I would have to bring in another horse.

"Cinders seemed so wary and disconnected from me," Jane remembers. "When she wasn't fidgety and spooky, she'd graze as if to avoid me, completely disregarding my presence. 'Why wouldn't she?' I thought. 'Why would a beautiful animal like this want anything to do with me — especially when I'm not saying anything brilliant or witty?' My business is communication, and I have become so identified with reasoning people into or out of things, I'd forgotten about any other value I might have. I felt inferior to this creature and afraid — except I don't *do* fear. As Cinders spooked, my brain didn't register the fear, though my chest was pounding and my breath was all caught up there. It was so constricted that my brain was like oatmeal, and I didn't even think to put myself at a safe distance."

The woman was practically paralyzed. Attempting to bring her back to reality, I asked her what she was feeling. In a voice so serene it was eerie, she admitted her self-doubt, but not her fear. I had no time to argue with her. Though I didn't want to fix the situation, I had to intervene for safety's sake.

"Jane," I shouted. "You're in trouble, and you're not even aware of it. Move to the center of the arena. It's safer there. Stay in your body! It's the only way you'll be able to sense what Cinders might do in time to at least move out of her way."

My slim, graceful student seemed to float into position. This really worried me. In her habitual attempts to deny fear, she had jumped so far into transcendence she was oblivious to the danger. Before removing her from the round pen, I made one last ditch effort to change the dynamic. Since Jane had recently attended a Monty Roberts clinic, I decided to describe, as succinctly as possible, an extremely subtle yet powerful horse whisperer's trick used to avert a possible spook — a technique so simple in fact that most trainers do it unconsciously.

"Breathe into your belly," I said. "Keep your attention focused on Cinders, not so much through your eyes, but through your body. Feel what she's feeling and what you're feeling simultaneously. You should experience a jolt of fear shoot through your solar plexus a split second before she spooks. Rather than let that jolt tense *you* up, breathe into the fear. Let it flow through you, and you'll ground that shock like a lightening rod. But you *must* be willing to *feel the fear* to ground it."

Cinders grazed nervously. It seemed, for several minutes, like nothing was happening, yet something had shifted. Jane reported feeling a slight jolt and breathing through it. She said she couldn't tell if it worked or not.

"Well, the horse didn't spook, did she?" I asked.

Jane shook her head, still concentrating. All of a sudden, Cinders stopped grazing and looked directly at the woman, as if seeing her for the first time. The response was so startling it was as if, from the horse's perspective, Jane had suddenly materialized out of thin air. The mare sighed, walked over, and briefly rested her muzzle on Jane's shoulder.

"What happened?" I asked.

"Cinders wasn't spooking anymore," she said, "but she still had no interest in coming near or acknowledging my existence. Then, for some reason, I decided to try to feel my feet and the ground underneath them. I breathed deeply and tried to imagine the breath going down through my feet. As I felt the ground, I noticed this release in my diaphragm muscle as if someone had taken off my belt and allowed the air to fill my whole torso. I was just *barely* noticing this when Cinders raised her head, looked at me, and walked over."

"What would you like to do now?" Cinders seemed to ask as she nuzzled Jane's shoulder once more. The woman proceeded to meander around the arena with the magnificent gray mare following her every move, "joining up," as Monty Roberts would say, not through an elaborate ritual of free longeing, but through Jane's simple act of finally, completely, coming into herself.

"All of those wonderful qualities you saw in Cinders earlier today you possess, *in this moment*," I emphasized as Jane and the mare approached the gate. "Maybe it was projection, or maybe you resonated with qualities in Cinders that both of you share. Either way, you were starstruck at first. You still couldn't see her for who she truly was, in all her contradictions."

Jane gently stroked the horse's neck. The mare was alert yet relaxed, downright cheerful actually. "Thank God Cinders isn't human enough to wallow in hero worship," I continued. "She managed, instead, to embody a strong feminine figure who wasn't afraid to show fear. She did us all a favor by being who she was, nothing more, nothing less."

"Do you think she was acting out my hidden fear?" Jane asked.

"Maybe," I said. "Maybe she was spooking for her own reasons, most likely a bit of both. Either way, you gained her respect, not by denying your fear and talking a good game, but simply by *being present*. And you showed everyone outside the arena what being present really means. It looks like nothing to the untrained eye, but it means everything to a horse."

"It was like magic," Jane declared in a phone conversation two weeks later, "*practical magic!* Finally after years of repressing and disconnecting from my fear, relying on my head and my words to get through life, I found a way to ground it through my breath and my feet. Cinders recognized it before I did; she responded so directly and clearly that it shocked me and everyone who watched."

The practical side of this magic, she observed, "is that now I know the symptom of fear in me. I can breathe into it, down into my feet, and give my body the space it apparently needs to give me the correct information. I can ask, 'What's being threatened here? What does this remind me of that comes from some other association, some past situation that may cloud what's relevant now? What's *real* about this fear?' I never had access to such articulation from my own self."

Reflecting on how she projected her truest feelings, both positive and negative, onto Cinders, and other people over the years, Jane came to the conclusion that she was "counter-phobic": overly "brave, independent, and self-sufficient."

"I'm a great risk taker," she said. "I've taken on many men who were deeply troubled and angry, so many that I've turned away from relationships and shut down my sexuality. As I look at my life, I can see how my path has taken me to places over and over again that would bring up fear so that I might have a chance to integrate this emotion. I can see now that I kept fear close through the people and situations I chose so that I didn't have to own it in myself. Now I'm able to experience it fully from the inside. I can use it to serve my well-being rather than displacing my fear onto others. This very cool minister at my Unitarian Church was just saying that until we really accept where we are, we can't change. Until I accepted that fear, until I let it go all the way through to my feet, I couldn't use it or move it. And the miracle is once I did accept it, once I drew it in like the very breath that gives me life, it moved all by itself."

There was one more, completely unexpected benefit Jane experienced by embracing her body's long-neglected wisdom:

"The dynamism and aliveness I feel have awakened my libido

again. I thought that, at fifty-three, this was kind of over for me: too many disappointments, too many angry, childish men for one lifetime. Now, I feel this life coursing through my body that makes me want to enjoy my body, to express myself through dancing, sex, *real* grace, and power — exactly what I projected onto Cinders."

BUTTERFLY

In *The Drama of the Gifted Child*, psychotherapist Alice Miller discusses subtle emotional traumas that alienate people from their true selves. "The true opposite of depression," she says, "is neither gaiety nor absence of pain, but vitality — the freedom to experience spontaneous feelings."

Miller cites numerous examples of troubled people who weren't overtly abused, one of whom suffered through her parent's obsession with practicality: "Whenever she began, through her imaginative play, to have a true sense of herself, her parents would ask her to do something 'more sensible' — to achieve something — and her inner world, which was just beginning to unfold, would be closed off to her. She reacted to this interference by withdrawing her feelings and becoming depressed, because she could not take the risk of a normal reaction — rage perhaps."

So often, people who weren't literally beaten as children have trouble reclaiming their Authentic Selves precisely because they can't remember being bullied. Those growing up in "upstanding, successful families" often grapple with inexplicable surges of sadness, grief, and anger, debilitating feelings that seem completely irrational and self-indulgent. Yet a heart trained into submission cannot truly experience joy, cannot truly express love, even if parents use nonviolent methods.

"We can only try to *behave as if we were loving*," Miller emphasizes. This superficial version of love passes from parent to child, across the generations, until no one really knows what love is anymore. "No wonder, then, that even well-intended moral appeals — to be loving, caring, generous, and so forth — are fruitless," she writes. "[T]his hypocritical behavior is the opposite of love. It is confusing and deceptive, and it produces much helpless rage in the deceived person. This rage must be repressed in the presence of the pretended 'love,' especially if one is dependent, as a child is, on the person who is masquerading in this illusion of love."

As I suspected, Dinah Jeffries chose to work with Mariposa, the alpha mare of the Grizzle Gate herd, precisely because this "aloof, all business" horse "who doesn't tolerate fools" reminded her of her unemotional, exacting mother. This transference was mixed with the projection of what Dinah *thought* "every centered woman" hopes to be: "undaunted and confident." Yet some authentic part of her may also have sensed who Mariposa truly was, the horse whose name translates as "butterfly," a potent symbol of transformation. This mare, as it turned out, quietly embodied a motherly figure supportive of authenticity, one that Alice Miller describes as "empathic and open, understanding and understandable, helpful and loving, feeling, transparent, clear, without unintelligible contradictions. Such a parent was never ours, for a mother can react empathically only to the extent that she has become free of her own childhood; when she denies the vicissitudes of her early life, she wears invisible chains."

Those chains, handed down from mother to daughter, held Dinah in an emotional vice. During our brief yet powerful half-hour experience in the round pen, I learned that the woman's freeze response wasn't related to physical trauma, but to a heart frozen by conformity, practicality, and the external trappings of success. I didn't know this up front, of course; my only goal at the time was to get my paralyzed student moving. And a little voice inside told me that a reflective *ride* was in order.

Mindful that Dinah might be dealing with significant trauma and transference, I asked the rest of the group to leave so that she could explore her feelings privately. As my assistant, a Denver horsewoman and life coach named Carol Marra, held the lead rope, I invited Dinah to climb on the mare's sturdy back.

"At that point my lugubrious demeanor had consumed me," she says. "In what I can only describe as a robotic response, I mounted Mariposa. But once I was on her back, the sense of peace and presence of God was immediate."

Moving counterclockwise, I asked Dinah to tell me a bit about her childhood.

"The middle child of five siblings, I was driven by my mother's expectations for all of us," she remembered. "I was one of those kids who constantly rose the bar for herself and would only cry when the water from my shower afforded me the opportunity to wash my self-imposed hell down the drain with the rest of the day's dirt. I loved my parents, and they me, but the pressures I put on myself only set the stage for conditional love and a joyless adolescence."

As we circled the round pen, the horse's movement and her potent, accepting presence loosened the torrential emotional energies trapped in Dinah's body. "Life had been void of joy for many months since my son's trauma," she admitted to me later, "but what I didn't realize was that his trauma resurrected the sadness of my past. I felt five years old again, and the little girl on Mariposa's back began to cry and grow angry. Joy had been stolen from her at such a young age. She was riding with me as she grieved the loss of laughter, spontaneity, and lazy afternoons all surrendered to the ass that carried the burden-bag of responsibility and expectation. Joy had been stolen, and my parents, unwittingly, were the thieves. Carol later told me that Mariposa yawned incessantly whenever there was talk of my mother. I knew horses yawned to throw off stress, and there was plenty of it for Mariposa to deal with. I will be forever grateful to her for carrying me through this."

After Dinah's tears subsided, I moved to a simple clearing and releasing ceremony especially powerful on horseback. It involved, in part, walking counterclockwise while naming those limiting patterns, based on survival, that no longer support growth.

"Each step Mariposa took liberated me," she says. "Then we reversed direction and verbalized all those things I wanted to reclaim. As we walked clockwise, I was putting on hope, peace, and forgiveness, and really feeling it this time. The exercise drew to a close as we stood in the center of the round pen. I closed my eyes at what I thought was the conclusion of a very emotional journey."

I sensed, from Mariposa's concentration, that the ritual of release was not, in fact, over. I encouraged Dinah to stay with her feelings, to see what might happen if she let them unfold even further.

"At first I felt the sensation of a tornado," she remembers. "The funnel cloud enveloped my feet and climbed up my body spinning at a tremendous rate of speed only to stop mid torso. The whirling motion continued, and then stopped just as suddenly as it had begun. Next, I had a clear picture of honey dripping down from my head, slowly sliding down my body into my boots until they filled and overflowed.

"I smiled. I was home."

Later that day, when Dinah turned Mariposa out with the rest of the herd, the mare everyone described as "aloof" with humans didn't rush to rejoin the other horses, as the Schroeters were accustomed to seeing her do. She stood at the fence, looking longingly as Dinah walked away, as if the two were still connected, still holding some silent, intimate conversation about things that logic all too easily obscures.

"My father phones me now and asks, 'Are you smiling?'" Dinah told me a year later. "This is something he's never done before. He has never heard the story of my journey with Mariposa, but every time he says this, it reminds me that I must ride the butterfly."

Transformation is a natural process that flows without forcing, as simple as a pony ride, as powerful as a hurricane, as gentle and miraculous as wings unfolding in the soft shadows of a misty Kentucky pasture. Mariposa had never been trained for therapy, but she knew about healing. She knew about presence. She knew about acceptance. Most important, Mariposa convinced me that horses know something about love, something that reason can only glimpse, hovering at the edge of words.

CHAPTER SIX

RASA AND MERLIN

As I let my horses take the lead, they stretched the limits of what my human mind could fathom. Yet even when I couldn't figure out *how* or *why* they did what they did, I was able to interact on their terms, absorbing nonverbal lessons, eventually teaching people some of what I'd learned. An arrogant inner critic tried to block my way at times, but a more open, creative awareness was steadily gaining force, able to embrace mysteries and paradoxes that would have blown my circuits just a few years earlier.

I finally accepted, deep in my bones, that the universe was intelligent and meaningful, and that the earth itself was populated by conscious, imaginative beings, some of whom just happened to trot around on four legs. As if to confirm, perhaps even to celebrate, this view, several members of my herd enacted a drama blurring the lines between myth and reality, past and future, life and death. And they lured nearly a hundred people into this strange story, challenging us to realize that if we were going to talk about "authentic community" and "freedom for all sentient beings," we had to let our horses in on the conversation.

I felt the first twinge of this shift in 1999 when my Arabian mare Tabula Rasa decided it was high time she mated with the stallion I'd recently acquired. Previously obsessed with the grass outside her corral, she took to casually nibbling the green stuff when turned loose, coyly edging further from sight, finally breaking into a defiant gallop toward his stall when I wasn't looking. Midnight Merlin was fascinating and flamboyant. He was also, at that time, dangerously disturbed. I'd inherited him by default six months after his trainer skipped town, leaving no forwarding address, no money for board, and no information about the stallion's legal owner, who according to rumor, lived somewhere in New Mexico. The owners of The Ranch, where I based my practice for three years, took care of the abandoned horse for a while, but Merlin's strength and volatile temper made turnout such an ordeal that he was relegated to a roomy yet isolated corral. Good-natured souls who attempted to halter him were subjected to fits of rage; if they managed to lead him out of the gate, he'd try to wrap them around the nearest tree. Yet for some reason, I felt an affinity for this troubled horse and agreed, against all practicality, to take him on.

The account of how I formed a tenuous relationship with Midnight Merlin appeared in *The Tao of Equus*. The most profound aspect of his rehabilitation, however, came as I was finishing the book, and I didn't have the space or perspective to discuss it. Training this proud stallion to submit to a human agenda had already backfired with several experienced trainers. I knew I had to take a different approach. After experimenting with a number of innovative techniques, I finally realized that preparing Merlin to mate with my mare — a purpose he understood and valued — would prove my greatest leverage in forming a partnership with him.

It was a bit hair-raising stepping outside the breeding protocols I'd learned as an apprentice trainer seven years earlier. My
position at that time involved helping the head trainer prepare for
something that looked more like organized rape than consensual
sex. I refused to subject my own mare to the tortures I'd been
directed to impose on other horses. Yet I couldn't find anyone
with a satisfying alternative. The stallion handlers I contacted in
Tucson used variations of the same restrictive techniques. I
researched accounts of pasture breeding and wild stud behavior in
books and videos, but these stallions had been socialized by other
horses, particularly older, more experienced matriarchs. Rasa was
a "maiden mare," a virgin. Merlin had been isolated and abused; he
was as violent and domineering with other horses as he was with
human handlers. He had bred mares who were fully restrained. I
knew I couldn't just turn him loose with Rasa. If my goal was to
encourage a safe, natural breeding relationship, I had to experiment with teaching an angry stud the mating etiquette he'd normally learn from an assertive alpha mare.

Most horse professionals in town thought I was naïve, if not
crazy, for trying such a stunt. To them, in-hand breeding techniques were so scientific, so obviously safe and convenient for
"everyone" involved. No one seemed to care that the relationship
between stallion and mare had been sacrificed for efficiency's sake.
My goals, therefore, were completely alien, and the experts didn't
quite know what to do with me. I wasn't breeding Rasa and
Merlin because *I* wanted a foal, but because *they* wanted to be
together. It just so happened that they were both registered black
Arabians, which made them a respectable pair by human standards. I continued to ask for bits and pieces of help from trainers
who approved of the mating, if not my motives. But for the most
part, I communicated directly with the horses, feeling when
things were right, when they weren't, and when they might go
either way.

I'm sure my initial explorations with Merlin looked like the blind leading the blind, or more accurately, the terrified and confused leading the enraged and sexually frustrated. Yet I wasn't about to conform to standards that disregarded the mare's perspective. People thought I was sentimentalizing — and, horror of horrors, anthropomorphizing — the mating act when I discussed how disturbing it was to restrain horses who had no control whatsoever over their own breeding. I wasn't condemning the status quo completely. With some mares, a feeling of joy surrounded the mating experience; they really didn't mind, and perhaps even felt supported by human involvement. Others, however, were quite obviously traumatized. My job as an apprentice trainer had been to hold these mares through the process, and it didn't take an empathic genius to realize which of them wanted to breed and which didn't. The memory of one frightened gray continued to haunt me. We practically had to drag her into the arena. Shaking, sweating, obviously repelled by the stallion her owners had chosen, she squealed in agony as the stud threw himself on her, his front legs scraping her shoulders, his teeth sinking into her neck, his breath blasting into my face as I pushed my own weight into her chest, helping her brace against his thrusts, trying to keep her from leaping forward, despite the restraints on her legs and the chain twisted around her lip. After loosening that chain, removing the hobbles, washing her trembling body, and leading her back to her stall, I ran behind the nearest tree and threw up.

Owners of half-million-dollar studs have all kinds of reasons for taking absolute control of mating, most of them financial. A stallion who rejects a prospective mate forfeits a hefty breeding fee. He may, of course, have good reason for backing off. Hostile females can injure or even kill a stallion with a well-placed kick. These same horses, however, can be forced or deceived into fulfilling the breeding contract. Hobbles are often placed on the mare's hind legs. An especially uncooperative female might also have a front leg tied up, and most farms use a twitch, that chain twisted around the upper lip. Stallions also wear a chain and sometimes a muzzle, the latter to keep him from biting a chunk out of the mare's neck as he mounts. Yet these and other aspects of conventional breeding arise because horses in captivity are rarely allowed to decline a mate — or develop a meaningful relationship with the ones they *are* attracted to.

Documented variations in mating behavior suggest that the most "dangerous" horses are those willing to assert their own desires. Intriguing case studies can be found in *Stud: Adventures in Breeding* by Kevin Conley and *The Stallion: A Breeding Guide for Owners and Handlers* by James P. McCall, Ph.D. The latter's fifth chapter, "Unusual and Unacceptable Stallion Behavior," is a must-read for people who naïvely believe that mating is a brainless instinctual act.

"For some reason that he usually does not share with the handler, the horse will refuse to court or breed a particular mare," McCall writes — a development that's "extremely irritating to the person in charge of getting all the mares in foal." The solution rarely involves finding another mate for the mare. More often, the breeder resorts to what McCall blatantly characterizes as "tricky, manipulative, matchmaking tactics."

"Deception is a good first choice," he emphasizes. "By altering the appearance and smell of the scorned mare, it might be possible to convince the stallion that he is breeding another. This can be attempted by covering up the mare with a blanket frequently worn by a favored consort. A dab or two of menthol on his nostrils may mask the mare's odor and as a final device, the lights can be turned off by the use of a blindfold. As our deceptive plot thickens, we may let the stallion tease a mare that he finds particularly seductive and then, at the last moment, substitute the ringer. In his frenzied state, we hope our difficult stallion will not notice the switch."

Handlers who resort to such intricate tactics are often the same people who insist that horses "don't have much going on upstairs." When it comes right down to it, these people *want* their mounts to act like easily manipulated imbeciles, and in fact, the horse industry has created all kinds of techniques to make sure these animals never assert their will, never develop discerning, agile minds of their own. But for some reason, the human contingent has to add insult to injury by ceaselessly complaining that horses suffer from a hopeless case of stupidity. The seemingly more progressive among them have told me, "The horse has a little brain, but a *big heart.*"

"Horse*shit,*" I say. "You condition these animals to submit to your will without question because that's what you're paid to do. You may be dominant over your horses, but you're submissive to the system. When you talk about how your training techniques follow prey animal instincts, what you're also telling me is that you deny horses the power of innovative thought. It's so much easier to suppress someone's spirit when you see him as a child-like, mentally deficient creature whose entire life must be managed *for his own good.* But even a happy, well-cared-for slave is still a slave."

IF I ONLY HAD A BRAIN

Well, that's what I *want* to say. Usually I opt for the gentler, more cowardly approach of citing the research I've found in books like *Inside Your Horse's Mind: A Study of Equine Intelligence and Human Prejudice* by Leslie Skipper. I came across this title while desperately searching for a diagram of the horse's brain. What I found, or more accurately, didn't find, spoke volumes about our relentless efforts to suppress independent thought in horses, a habit so ingrained in the equestrian arts that it's virtually unconscious. While I found numerous texts diagramming multiple angles of the legs, muscles, and tendons, discussing every conceivable lameness problem in nauseating detail, the simplest line drawing of an equine brain took me weeks to locate. Most riders, quite obviously, just don't care about that part of the horse. If they do, it's only to figure out how to more easily bend the animal to their will. Some of the most popular nonviolent training methods literally promote "controlling your horse's body by controlling his mind." People generally see this as an innovative, even enlightened approach, completely ignoring the fact that they're advocating *mind control*. Most of these techniques work equally well on humans — as religious cults and suicide bombers have proven many times over — yet such methods aren't considered the least bit immoral or distasteful when they're used on other species.

A few innovators, most notably Linda Tellington-Jones, founder of the Tellington Touch Equine Awareness Method (TTEAM), have found ways to change behavior through non-habitual movements. Taught in a stress-free environment, these exercises prove that horses can learn quickly, without repetition. Even so, a significant number of the TTEAM practitioners I've encountered still tend to ignore, even discourage the development of personal responsibility, will, and ingenuity in horses, not to mention compassion, discernment, and emotional agility. These qualities are considered troublesome or simply unimportant to people training competitive mounts and beasts of burden, but they're immensely helpful in horses employed as co-therapists.

For this reason, I've become much more interested in *developing* a horse's mind than in *conditioning* it to respond predictably. Many of the same principles still apply: Nonviolent methods used to manage a horse's every move can be modified to empower him. Basically, the brain develops new circuitry patterns through experience. A trainer can create instructive experiences designed to produce a specific response on command. She can also devise different yet equally influential experiences to exercise a horse's confidence, sensitivity, will, or inventiveness. The problem is one of motivation. While coercing a horse to change his behavior isn't so much of an issue when mind control is the goal, it defeats the purpose when you're developing his ability to communicate opinions and make informed choices. Like humans, these animals rarely embrace new ways of behaving and perceiving for their own amusement. They do so in relation to others, usually when old patterns no longer get them what they want.

For Merlin, associating with people most often involved trotting around in meaningless circles while an egotistical, emotionally conflicted trainer shouted commands. It's no surprise that this strong-willed horse found it more entertaining to fight than submit, and he sometimes won the battle with outlandish behavior, which only served to enhance his reputation as a berserker of uncommon theatricality. It *was* impressive to watch him toy with people — as long as you weren't the object of his practical jokes. Yet even in his seemingly most frenzied state, he'd always stop just short of actually injuring anyone, which, after I got over my initial shock and terror, struck me as evidence of subtlety, grace, and, believe it or not, *self-control.*

More than once, Merlin careened across the arena and *slid* into rearing position, his front hooves flailing inches from my face. Had he been the least bit clumsy, he would have knocked me unconscious. Had he *wanted* to hurt me, I wouldn't have had a chance. After being subjected to these horrifying antics several days in a row, I noticed a pattern. He always ran toward me from the same end of the arena, reared, and then trotted away, looking over his shoulder as if to say, "Did you get it this time?" The strangest part was that he didn't seem to be communicating aggression on these occasions. It felt like he wanted me to applaud him, like he assumed this hair-raising act would win me over — to what end, I had no idea.

When The Ranch finally tracked down his original owner,

Shawnee Allen, I learned that Merlin had actually been rewarded for this behavior. When prospective breeders arrived, Shawnee stood in the center of the arena while Merlin enacted this simple yet thrilling routine to showcase his power and agility. It suddenly struck me that Merlin had been performing a ritual for me that had, in the past, motivated humans to bring him their mares. Every time Rasa ran to his stall, after all, I was the one who dragged her away. Was I the latest breeder on whom he'd been trying to work his magic?

From his perspective, I must have seemed mighty dense since it took me a good four months to get the message. Had it taken that long for a horse to learn a simple training cue, I would have assumed the poor creature must have fallen out of the womb onto his head, suffering irreparable brain damage.

MISCOMMUNICATION

This incident reminded me of a story I'd heard from a colleague. A couple of amateur horse owners, let's call them Bill and Tammy King, purchased a finely bred palomino weanling, figuring the only way they'd be able to afford a horse of this caliber was to buy him as a six-month-old and save up for the right kind of training. The colt became a family project. Every night after work, Bill and Tammy would take "Tallis" for a walk or play with him in the arena, teaching him some moves they'd learned from a trick horse instruction video. By the time he was two, the horse knew how to bow and lie down. He had no fear of humans, trails, or trailers, and seemed unusually mature for a colt his age. When it came time to start him under saddle, the Kings hired "Jan," a trainer who'd studied directly with a nationally recognized horseman. Jan at first thought Tallis was the smartest, most cooperative horse she'd ever encountered — until she worked on free-longeing in the round pen. Suddenly, for no apparent reason, Tallis raced toward her, reared up, slammed his front legs across her shoulders, and knocked her to the ground. Then, as she stared up at his belly, he calmly stepped over her and walked away.

Thinking it was a fluke, Jan brushed herself off and proceeded with the lesson. Ten minutes later Tallis tried to assault her again, though she managed to beat him off with the whip. Jan couldn't for the life of her figure out what the colt was trying to prove. Over the next week, she realized the aggression didn't stem from frustration. It escalated when Tallis successfully accomplished something new. Yet try as she might, she couldn't decipher the meaning behind this appalling behavior.

Jan finally swallowed her pride, called Bill and Tammy, and set up a meeting. Oddly enough, they weren't the least bit surprised when she told them Tallis would have to find another trainer, that he might not be trainable at all. Tammy's eyes filled with tears as her husband finally explained the origins of "The Problem." Turns out they'd invented a little trick of their own when the horse was still a weanling. Every time their sweet palomino baby did something right, Bill would hold a carrot between his teeth and encourage the colt to jump up. Resting his legs on the man's shoulders, Tallis would gently take the reward from Bill's mouth. What had initially struck them as *sooo* cute became downright lethal as Tallis approached a thousand pounds. Too embarrassed to tell the trainer what they'd done, the Kings hoped their beloved horse wouldn't attempt the behavior with a more accomplished, assertive teacher. Yet whenever Jan praised him, Tallis would come running, looking for a tasty treat in exchange for a monstrous hug.

I never did hear what became of the colt, yet I assume, from my subsequent success altering Merlin's mating ritual, that Tallis eventually learned a new way of responding to positive reinforcement. Even without knowing the outcome, however, the story has become one of my favorite teaching tools for clients. Some neophytes believe that the best way to master basic training skills is to raise their first horse from the ground up, "so we can learn together," as they always say. The problem is, most of these people refuse to solicit a trainer's help until the colt or filly becomes old enough to ride. Trying to save a few bucks during the horse's early years, they inadvertently establish bad habits that cost significant time and money for a professional to work through later.

For those who insist on taking this route, however, I offer a simple rule of thumb: Don't reward behavior in a foal that you'd find undesirable in an adult. And for God's sake, don't actively teach a hundred-pound colt a trick that you'd consider dangerous or intimidating when performed by a thousand-pound stallion.

As I worked through my own stud's misconceptions about what would win me over, I realized that experienced trainers quite often failed to follow this same guideline, especially in the breeding barn. The vast majority of stallions in this country are kept isolated from other horses, and are therefore rarely socialized by the female members of their own species. Intact males are encouraged to adopt outlandish mannerisms, not so much to excite prospective mates, but to impress other people. From halter-class judges to weekend riders toying with breeding a backyard mare, people pay more attention to, and more money for, a "spirited" stud. Yet increasingly, accounts of wild and semi-feral horse coupling illustrate that for the most part, stallions who aren't in the business of pleasing people rarely waste that much energy gearing up for the mating act. Close, constant contact with their mares has a *calming* effect.

After touring the finest barns in the country, describing the ostentatious mating antics of powerhouse studs in riveting detail, author Kevin Conley ended his book *Stud: Adventures in Breeding* on a surprisingly gentle note. Visiting the semi-feral bands of Shetland ponies based at Havemeyer Equine Behavior Lab, he learned a secret about horses who govern their own affairs: The sex act, so loud and carnal in domesticated stallions, is easy to miss when studs roam freely with their mares. Puzzled, he asked veterinary researcher Sue McDonnell for an explanation:

"The main reason I won't catch them having sex, she says, is because 'it's so quiet and unobtrusive. Because when the stallions are there all the time, there's no need for that great flamboyant entrance.'

"Quiet, frequent, amid rebuffs, and the misbehavior of children: I hadn't expected the sex life of a harem stallion to sound so much like the married version. Fine. We've seen enough by now, and I can appreciate their discretion."

The tempestuous documentary *Cloud: Wild Stallion of the Rockies* culminates in a similar realization. For five years, filmmaker Ginger Kathrens followed a striking pale white horse from childhood innocence and adolescent frustration through harrowing struggles with predators, harsh winters, and government roundups. Still, when Cloud successfully wooed his first mare, it didn't happen in "a furious clash of teeth and hooves, but in a moment of stillness. . . .

"The mare had given birth to a sickly foal," Kathrens reveals, "and when she stayed with her newborn rather than rejoining her band, Cloud found her and stood quietly by her side. When the foal died, Cloud, the mare, and [her half-grown] yearling [son by another stallion] stayed together." After seasons of rough play in bachelor bands, and serious fights with harem stallions that left him scarred and temporarily lame, it was ultimately an act of compassion that won Cloud the privilege of starting his own family.

Neither Kathrens nor Conley set out to prove that the human obsession with horsepower has, over the centuries, created a sensationalized caricature of the stallion. They barely found the words to describe these surprisingly gentle interactions, much less speculate on the institutionalized turmoil people promote in domesticated horses by disempowering the one member of equine society capable of tempering the colossal force of testosterone-infused adolescence. When the mare no longer has a choice in her own breeding, when her children are taken away from her at six months and raised by a creature with little regard for their mental and emotional development, subsequent generations suffer a loss of soul and self-control. The lack of a wise, assertive feminine presence wreaks havoc on domesticated mares *and* stallions.

I couldn't help noticing the parallels in human culture. As I struggled to help Rasa and Merlin form a relationship of equals, I felt like I was bringing to light something unconscious, yet essential, in my own species.

MATING DANCE

Teaching Merlin, who had never been properly socialized, to mate naturally (off lead, with no restraints on the mare) turned out to be an emotional ordeal for everyone involved. The first major hurdle involved my own fear — fear of failure, fear of looking foolish, fear of Merlin's incredible strength and energy. I was dealing with the most frustrating and dangerous type of high sensitive, one who, like Alexander's Bucephalus, knew he had the upper hand, er... hoof, and took pleasure in intimidating serf and warrior alike. Such horses react explosively to incongruity. As I learned on more than one occasion, Merlin's over-the-top way of mirroring the hidden emotion was much more frightening than owning up to the original feeling. The dilemma: openly acknowledging the terror Merlin inspired without letting him use it to his advantage. The solution: rewarding him for gentleness and understanding.

Of course, at that time, it took incredible courage and creativity to interact with him at all. I began by leading Rasa to Merlin's corral, modulating the intensity of their brief contact before walking the mare to another corral attached to a particularly sturdy arena. Then I haltered Merlin, which was an ordeal all its own, and escorted him to that arena, trying to keep my composure as he screamed and reared and sometimes leaped into the air. I didn't take this personally. He performed his hair-raising act with everyone, including the experienced stallion handlers I hired now and then to lend me some insight. These professionals, however, were able to take Merlin's antics in stride without the visceral fear that gripped me every time I opened his gate. To remain congruent, I had to add an extra element. I had to say, "Merlin, you're scaring me," whenever he tried to bite me or wrap me around the nearest tree. Yet running this gauntlet with him was the only way I could show him the nature of his reward: to spend an afternoon cavorting with the object of his desire over the fence — a big deal for a stallion kept completely isolated from other horses. To play with Rasa, he had to cooperate with me. It didn't take him long to realize that if he quietly accepted the halter and walked to the arena without all the time-consuming drama, he reached that sexy black mare much more efficiently.

Once he understood this, I finally had some leverage. I began to tell him, in so many words and gestures, that the more respect and self-control he showed, the more privileges he received. And I gradually raised my standards, illustrating that if he frightened me at any point during the process, he had one chance to pull himself together or he was going back to a lonely stall. After a while, the phrase "Merlin, you're scaring me" inspired an instant behavior change, just as other horses acknowledge voice commands like "walk," "trot," and "canter," or run to the gate when someone shouts, "Who wants a carrot?"

With a sturdy fence between them, Rasa and Merlin ate together, played together, and accepted a certain amount of direction from me. The only rules I enforced were those related to safety. The horses seemed to understand this and find it acceptable. I couldn't leave them alone when Rasa was in heat or the two would try to mate through the fence. Yet when faced with the choice of not spending time with Rasa the week she was in season, Merlin opted to back off on my command — and much to my surprise, masturbate by rubbing his three-foot-long penis against his abdomen.

Before I finally turned them loose together, I revisited some standard training techniques. I hoped that this time, Merlin would recognize longeing as a form of communication rather than an instrument of dominance. Initially quite happy to trot along the perimeter of the round pen on cue, the stallion suddenly stopped and tilted his head as if considering his options. Perhaps he was remembering the frustration and humiliation he'd experienced with trainers in the past. Whatever his reasons for the sudden change of heart, he ran toward me, all puffed up and ready to rumble. I managed to stop him at a respectful distance. "Merlin, you're scaring me," I said automatically, and almost as an afterthought I continued to speak out loud.

"You and I aren't meant for horse shows and trick rides," I said. The stallion sputtered and tossed his head. "Next week," I continued, "Rasa will be in heat again, and this time your dream will come true. Not because you're a flashy stud with great bloodlines, but because you've shown us that you truly can be a gentleman. But I'll only feel safe turning you loose with my mare if you show me the proper respect and self-control. One way for a human to develop that kind of trust with a horse, especially off lead, is through this silly game of running around in circles. I'm not asking you to perform these moves to stroke my ego. I have to stand in the middle because I'm much slower and weaker than you are. I have a few talents of my own, but my stubby little legs would never be able to keep up with you. When you trot *around* me, I feel your grace and strength. I feel the elation that you feel, and I'm in awe of you."

Merlin's eyes softened ever so slightly, and it seemed he understood me. Perhaps he simply sensed my humility, respect, and desire to connect riding my words. As he backed up a few steps, I felt a surge of energy in my solar plexus pulling me toward him, almost as if he was inviting me to dance. I lifted my arm like a conductor holding the potential power of an entire symphony in the palm of her hand. Merlin matched my downbeat with a flourish of artful movement, prancing, fully collected, around and around and around me. He seemed especially pleased with himself, no doubt for conceiving a new ritual, one that could finally convince a timid, two-legged creature to trust him with her favorite mare.

A NEW LIFE

Merlin and Rasa were ecstatic. After they mated successfully, I decided to let them live together in a spacious paddock for a few days. The problem was Rasa didn't quite know how to hold her own with a stallion who focused his long unrequited sexual and social needs entirely on her. In nature, a maiden mare would most likely have a few older, more experienced females to coach and protect her. In some bands, the alpha mare shields her sisters from the stallion and insists on making the proper introductions before letting him breed. I performed this function to a certain extent, but I couldn't stay with Rasa twenty-four hours a day. I saw my first marriage in a whole new light as she temporarily lost her power and vitality in the presence of a flamboyant male who wooed her respectably for a few hours, then tried to control her every move. Oddly enough, when the mare was supported in setting boundaries, Merlin lost his erection and focused on other horses. Rasa actually had to work to regain his attention, but he was a hell of a lot more sensitive to her needs and rhythms when he finally came back around.

Watching, and in some cases helping, these two horses negotiate a partnership in which each member felt respected and satisfied gave the entire Epona staff new insights into their own relationships, both romantic and platonic. It also brought to light a valuable function the harem plays for less-assertive, or simply inexperienced, mares. Female horses, it seems, need a support system to socialize the powerful "men" in their lives.

A recent UCLA study on friendship among women suggests a biological benefit as well. Five decades of research conducted mostly on men led scientists to believe that the hormones released during stress rev the body up to prepare for flight or fight. When a couple of female scientists finally thought to study the effects of stress on their own sex, they learned, much to everyone's surprise, that women sometimes have an entirely different reaction. The hormone oxytocin buffers the flight-or-fight response, encouraging females to tend children and gather with other women instead. Drs. Laura Cousins Klein and Shelley Taylor, authors of the study, call this the "tend and befriend" response, and when women engage it, more oxytocin is released, which further counteracts stress and produces a calming effect. I suspect that female animals who gather in harem-style herds have a similar biological directive, which might also contribute to the powerful cross-species relationships that women and horses develop.

It was clear in working with Rasa and Merlin, for instance, that while the stallion simply tolerated my presence when turned out with his mare, Rasa was *glad* to have me around. She appreciated time with her mate, but she had no desire to keep him to herself, which was in direct conflict with Merlin's initial impulse to possess her completely, herding her around and dictating her every move long after he was spent sexually. The experience of preparing Rasa to mate and helping her stand up to him actually strengthened our bond. After we experimented with various breeding scenarios over several heat cycles, the mare made it clear that she preferred the comfort and tranquility of a separate corral or a nice long walk with me after her conjugal visits with Merlin.

These and a number of other insights difficult to translate into words made all the time and effort I spent preparing for a more natural breeding experience well worth my while, which was good, since Rasa and Merlin had trouble conceiving. Had I been obsessed with producing a foal, I would have been mighty frustrated.

The vet performed several ultrasounds that spring, a procedure used to confirm pregnancy, but more specifically to check for the dangerous possibility of twins. Of the 18 percent of equine pregnancies that result in double conception, less than 1 percent of all births involve two foals. Left to their own devices, mares tend to lose both fetuses naturally long before they come to term. Even so, it's customary in modern veterinary medicine to abort one as early as possible to save the other. Breeding costs make it desirable to intervene. Miscarriage can mean waiting another year, hauling the mare back to the stallion's barn, boarding her for a couple weeks while she comes into heat — or, increasingly, shipping in more sperm and paying the vet to perform another artificial insemination procedure. In the few cases where twins survive the first six months, other problems arise. Most of these foals are stillborn prematurely or die soon afterward, and the mother's life is often at risk. An ultrasound forty days after mating is the only way to confirm how many fetuses are present early enough to safely remove one.

This didn't seem to be much of a concern in Rasa's case. After mating with Merlin nearly thirty times in 2000, the mare was unable to conceive. The vet came to the conclusion that one of the horses must be infertile. Since I wasn't running a breeding farm, I turned down the option of sperm counts and hormone shots, deciding the couple could cavort for fun now and then, ostensibly to hone Merlin's socialization skills. Secretly, however, I felt something akin to love growing between them, and I thought it the height of human arrogance to end their relationship just because they couldn't propagate the species. When Rasa wasn't in heat, I would turn her out in the paddock next to Merlin's. As if remembering the difficulties she faced trying to hold her own in the stallion's presence, Rasa gained confidence from the physical boundary between them. Set free to do as she wished, she would still head straight for her mate, yet she also appreciated being able to stay just out of reach. If Merlin showed signs of aggression, Rasa would squeal and strike out, then turn and walk away, confident he couldn't follow. If he was playful, the black mare would join the fun. Merlin would curl his neck, puff himself up, and dance for her just the same, yet without an erection, his movements were more jovial. The two would trot along the fence with a noticeable bounce in their steps, snorting in tandem, tails held high. Then they'd downshift into an animated walk and eventually pause next to each other, Merlin reaching casually over the top bar to lick Rasa's cheek.

The following spring, I was consumed with work on *The Tao of Equus* and had to suspend all lessons and training sessions. Consequently, I didn't feel up to facilitating any mating sessions with Rasa and Merlin. Shortly after completing the manuscript, however, one of my students, Jillian Lessner, and I did find the time to turn the pair out in the arena together. Though the temperature approached 100 degrees that late-April morning, Merlin ran toward his mare with abandon, stopping halfway to rear and leap upward from a standing position, his mane brushing the clear blue sky twenty feet in the air. Then he and Rasa efficiently reenacted the dramas of the previous year: he trying to mount her aggressively, she kicking him in the chest for his lack of respect, he losing his erection, she wooing him back from his sudden interest in playing with a couple of geldings over the fence, he finally approaching her more gently. This time, their mating ended in a kiss. As Merlin's fervent thrusting culminated in a full body sigh, Rasa turned around and licked him tenderly on the nose. I looked over at Jillian, both of us rubbing a bit of mist from our eyes. "Too bad they can't conceive," I said wistfully. "This most certainly would have been a love child."

Jillian nodded, staring back at the coal black stallion and his night-haired mare glistening in the heat of the noonday sun, the two walking side by side in perfect harmony.

I didn't order an ultrasound after that last session for several reasons. Since Rasa and Merlin had coupled numerous times the previous year without result, the idea that they might produce two foals after mating only once seemed the most incredible long shot. Rasa also showed all the signs of going into heat the following month. Still, her interest in the stallion was noticeably less intense. Twenty-one days later, she went into heat again. This time, Merlin seemed strangely low-key about the possibility of sex. Was Rasa really in heat, I wondered? Or was she like the small percentage of women who menstruate during the first months of pregnancy? With this in mind, I had Dr. Christine Staten palpate her at four months. On the outside chance the mare had conceived, I wanted to make sure she received the proper shots and nutrition. The vet didn't detect a fetus, confirming what seemed destined to be true. Once again, an ultrasound was the only way to tell for sure, she said, but knowing Rasa and Merlin's mating history, she thought it was superfluous.

The following January, however, Rasa's behavior changed suddenly. An unusually gregarious mare, she began moving to the back of her paddock when people arrived. Her eyes took on a strange, blank appearance, as if her mind was somewhere else entirely. Though she seemed comforted by my presence, she wanted little to do with anyone else, including the other horses. She actually had an air of worry about her, an emotion I had up to that point considered purely human. Yet several of my clients, unprompted, used that same word when describing her mood.

"What's up with Rasa?" asked thirteen-year-old Christie Holmes the first week in 2002. "I can't tell if she's sick or depressed, but she definitely looks worried about something."

I congratulated my student on her powers of observation, especially since she was scheduled to ride another horse that day. "Rasa *has* been acting a bit odd lately," I said. "I thought she had a case of colic a couple days ago, but when I tossed her a flake of alfalfa, she trotted right over and started munching. Actually, it looks like someone's been feeding her too much."

The next day, I discussed the situation with Epona's barn manager Xena Carpenter. The mare's ability to gain weight quickly was a constant concern. Rasa's Arabian ancestors were bred to travel vast expanses of barren land with little more than a bowl of camel's milk and a handful of dates at the end of the day. During times of plenty, these horses stored fat by developing a crest on top of the neck, an asset in preparing for drought and famine. With regular access to hay, however, this same crest became a serious precursor to *foundering*, a crippling, often deadly condition resulting from overfeeding, among other causes.

"You know," I said to Xena, assessing Rasa's appearance head on, "something's different about her weight this time. Look at her. She's actually thinner than usual everywhere except her stomach."

Xena walked over to feel Rasa's neck as I moved around to her side. "There's no crest here," she reported.

"Wow," I said, "come over here and feel her belly. It's hard . . . almost like . . . a pregnant woman's . . . belly."

Xena's eyes widened with a combination of disbelief and excitement. If Rasa was going to foal, she'd be due in early April, we calculated, thinking back on that single mating session at the end of April 2001. Horses usually give birth eleven months after conception, but it's not uncommon for them to take a year.

I ordered an ultrasound immediately, but once again Tabula Rasa managed to keep us in the dark. The morning Dr. Staten arrived, it was so windy we couldn't get the mare to stand still. We struggled for a half hour to give her a shot to calm her down for the test, to no avail. We both felt movement in her abdomen, however, and it was finally confirmed. Rasa and Merlin were going to have a baby!

EPONA'S CENTER

In the midst of all this excitement, the opportunity to rent space at a more private facility arose. The Ranch on Tucson's east side had served as a comfortable and economical place to start my fledgling practice. However, the challenges of running an EFP/EEL operation at a public boarding stable became more pronounced as Epona attracted clients from around the world. In January 2002, I realized my days at The Ranch were numbered, and I let the owner know I was looking for another facility. Yet with Rasa's foal on the way and five major workshops scheduled between January and April, I figured I wouldn't have the time to look for a place until after the birth. A few days later, I met my friend Laura Brinkerhoff for lunch. After resigning from her position as program director of a local therapeutic riding facility, she had opened her own equine experiential learning practice. We often got together to share new techniques, theories, and challenges. Laura also had an expanded view of equine intelligence and a deep appreciation for the as-yet-unexplainable aspects of the horse-human connection. The year she went away to college, for instance, she had dreamed that her pony came to say goodbye — several days *before* her father arrived to break the bad news: The pony, who had never been sick a day in his life, had died unexpectedly.

When I told Laura about my plans to move, she said she knew of the perfect setting, a rustic but scenic spot in the middle of the city. Peggy Green, a natural horsemanship practitioner, had recently bought the facility as an investment. She was looking for riding instructors, renters, and boarders to help support the operation. A few days later, The Ranch's owner visited the same property independently and told me she thought it would be ideal for my practice.

In a subsequent tour of Peggy's place, I turned down the offer to take over a twelve-stall barn in favor of renting several acres at the back. The deal included a charming yet rustic two-bedroom house that could be used as a meeting space with simple accommodations for out-of-town clients. There was enough land around the little desert cabin to set up a practice far away from the activities of other boarders and instructors. The spirit of Epona, it seemed, was looking out for her namesake operation.

The only hitch was that I had to move in a month. Looking at my calendar, I realized I would only have one brief opportunity. So, the Monday after an intensely emotional weekend workshop, I hired a couple of men to help move my entire operation to the new Epona Center. By Friday, I was seeing a couple of out-of-state clients who'd booked five days of private sessions.

Everything fell into place with remarkable ease. Transporting the horses seemed to pose the biggest challenge, but even that went smoothly. Noche, Merlin, and Amigo (a former drug-running horse acquired after he got picked up at the Mexican border) had all shown a marked aversion to trailers. I knew from experience I could eventually convince Noche to step on, if given enough time. But according to sources at The Ranch, Merlin and Amigo had vehemently refused trainers, treats, ropes, and even whips in favor of staying put. I had bought both horses at The Ranch and had never worked with them off site, so I expected some trouble. With no time for trailer lessons, I decided to tell the herd what was up and ask for cooperation.

Though I'd learned some intuitive animal communication techniques over the years, my inner critic didn't quite believe in such notions, no matter how many times I had experienced the compelling, sometimes remarkable results of connecting with the equine mind. So it was with some skepticism that I explained to the warier members of my herd that they had to take a short ride in a big moving stall if they wanted to join the three mares at their new home. I visualized the new Epona Center, emphasizing the spacious corrals and arenas. Then my dressage trainer, Shelley Rosenberg, and I loaded up Rasa, Comet, and Xena's little chestnut horse Mary. An hour later, upon returning to pick up what we assumed would be the most difficult crew, I again visualized the center, this time with the mares in place. Shelley and I were both surprised when Merlin, Noche, Max, and Amigo stepped up the ramp with little fanfare, as if they were waiting to catch the next bus to wherever the rest of the herd had gone.

Though Rasa adjusted effortlessly to her new surroundings, I continued to worry about her for some nameless reason. I stayed at the Epona Center that first week, compulsively checking on her in the wee hours of the morning. Most of the furniture had yet to be delivered and the electricity still needed to be turned on, but I was content to crash next to the blazing fireplace in the living room. Because I was staying on site, I decided to let Rasa and Merlin live in adjoining corrals until construction of her foaling stall was finished. They reveled in each other's company. Quietly protective of his expectant mate, Merlin never once showed signs of aggression — toward her anyway. The other geldings were given fair warning to stay far away. Each evening after a flake of hay and a cool drink of water, the two would stand next to each other as the sun set over the mountains, their manes blowing gently in the breeze. For the first time since I'd known him, Merlin looked content, fulfilled, and Rasa, though still worried, seemed comforted by his presence.

NIGHT VISIONS

I had just drifted off to sleep two nights after the move when I heard a rap on the floor-length windows overlooking the corrals.

It was Laura Brinkerhoff, my colleague who'd had a prescient dream about her own horse's passing.

"Something's not right," she said, pointing to Rasa's stall.

I jumped up from the couch and ran through the sliding glass door without bothering to open it, realizing then that *I* was dreaming. With an agility I don't possess in waking life, I leaped over the fence. A dozen men in crisp black suits stood around Rasa, blocking my view. "Show me the truth," I said, pushing through this crowd of grave-looking specters.

Rasa had just given birth. The group's somber mood suggested the foal was dead, but I could see movement in the thin gray membrane covering his little body. I ripped the placenta open to allow the colt to breathe and noticed he was wearing a little collar with a nametag on it. "SPRTS," it read cryptically.

"This baby is going to be fine," I said.

Then I noticed another black horse lying beside the foal, disintegrating into the earth before my eyes.

I woke up in a sweat, threw on my coat, and headed to Rasa's corral, thinking the dream meant her life was in danger. This time I made sure I actually opened the sliding glass door before braving the chilling quiet of that winter night. I sensed no fear or foreboding as I approached her stall. Rasa was grazing peacefully in the darkness, seemingly without a care in the world.

The following night, I awoke suddenly from another perplexing dream. A solid black colt stared at me through swirling clouds, the corners of his little mouth turned downward in an exaggerated, almost theatrical frown. It seemed he was trying, rather clumsily, to depict an emotion not easily expressed on the face of a horse.

"Why are you so sad?" I asked him.

He made no attempt to answer. Instead, he faded from view, seemingly satisfied with the question.

DAY VISIONS

I tried to shake off these unsettling images as I met with Pam [last name withheld] and Jana Lucaccioni the next day. The two had flown in from Chicago and San Diego respectively, eager to experience the power of equine-facilitated therapy. While attending a Ph.D. program in energy medicine, Pam and Jana found that they shared a love of horses. As part of their research, they decided to meet in Tucson and see what it would take to incorporate these animals into their own healing practices.

The Epona Center was still in relative disarray that first weekend, but the added privacy proved key in unlocking deeper intuition in horse and human alike. We quickly began exploring psychological and spiritual dimensions I wouldn't have entertained at The Ranch with a steady stream of boarders walking by.

Several years earlier, Pam had fallen from a horse. Struggling toward consciousness, she felt an angelic presence surrounding her, warning her not to move. While her daughter called the paramedics, a soothing, celestial voice told Pam that she had broken her neck, while also conveying that this life-threatening injury was a gift. The incident set the fifty-four-year-old psychotherapist on a journey that stretched far beyond the mores of her conservative Midwestern lifestyle. Yet even a Ph.D. program in alternative healing wasn't able to entertain the two most nagging questions of all. Why did Pam still yearn to work with horses, and how would she ever overcome the terror that gripped her every time she approached one?

After going over the Emotional Message Chart, I led Pam and Jana through the body scan, once again emphasizing that they shouldn't try to relax any tensions or discomforts. Rather they were to expand each sensation that arose in their interactions with the horses, and together we would decipher the meaning behind it.

Stepping into the round pen with Noche, Pam felt considerable nausea and constriction in her solar plexus. Though she practically doubled over into a fetal position, she managed to stay with the fear. So many images, feelings, and memories rushed forward that she was unable to speak coherently. Yet a potent theme began to emerge from the cacophony. Pam felt that she *deserved* to be punished by the horses, even though she swore she had never been abusive. As she voiced this perplexing thought, Noche lowered his head, stepped forward, and began licking and chewing profusely. When I told her his behavior indicated that she had hit a truth or congruency of some sort, the woman began to sob, begging for his forgiveness. Vivid descriptions of another time and place poured from her lips. Pam saw herself merge with the image of a cruel, self-possessed warrior who broke his horses' spirits in training and thoughtlessly discarded them when they fell in battle.

Standing in that dusty arena under the blinding light of the noonday sun, Pam explored a past-life memory in excruciating detail. Any skepticism I might have normally felt dissipated as I watched Noche's reaction. This horse, usually so mistrustful of strangers, moved in closer as Pam expressed the disgust, shame, and violence of the scenes unfolding before her eyes. Then, when she began to connect key elements of this ancient lifetime with the serious riding accident she had experienced in the late twentieth century, Noche took several steps backward, raising his head higher and higher, finally jerking his face from side to side, audibly *cracking his neck* as Pam saw her own life-altering neck injury from a new perspective.

Whatever beliefs about past lives I'd acquired from a conventional Christian upbringing, I couldn't deny the change in Pam's demeanor as she hugged Noche at the end of that session. The terror had subsided. In its place was a warmth, a lightness, a palpable sense of relief.

Later that afternoon, Pam announced that she was ready to get back on a horse, something she thought she might never be able to do again after the accident. She wanted to ride Noche.

"Your body will probably have some trauma memories of its own to work through," I said. "It's helpful at this stage to let someone else lead the horse. That way, you can do some mounted body scans and some gentle balancing exercises that would be difficult, if not impossible, to concentrate on if you were trying to steer."

With Jana acting as horse handler, Pam mounted the gelding bareback, and the four of us proceeded to walk slowly around the arena. After an initial feeling of elation, she began to shake uncontrollably, a response common among rape survivors, accident victims, and riders who've experienced serious falls. I knew from extensive experience that a moving horse would keep Pam from lapsing fully into freeze mode and help her body release the pent-up energy of unresolved trauma. However, I wasn't expecting the dramatic return of a past-life personality. At one point, Pam's distress escalated in such a way that I had no alternative but to stop Noche. Yet something about the horse's confidence and concentration prevented me from asking the woman to dismount. Pam was in another realm, and Noche seemed intent on carrying her between the worlds.

Speaking in a strange, undecipherable language, she raised her hands to the sky. Jana and I were poised to assist Pam if needed, but she was somehow able to keep her balance through an incredible series of physical and emotional contortions. Her rapid vocalizations increased in volume until she let out an agonizing scream. A blast of chaotic energy radiated outward in all directions. The hair on the back of my neck stood up. A split second later, Merlin jerked and surged forward in his own corral like he'd been electrocuted. Rasa shuddered and reared a split second after that, on and on until the entire herd was in an uproar, bucking and racing around the stalls as if *they* were running off the intensity of Pam's long-repressed feelings. Every horse, that is, except Noche, who stood perfectly still — as if he knew how to ground this shock wave. As if he'd been expecting it.

TRADING LEADS

The next day, Pam and Jana asked me how I had trained Noche to assist clients in this way. I told them I was probably more surprised by his behavior than they were.

"I can't imagine how you'd teach a horse to support someone moving back through time and speaking in tongues," I said. "And I have never seen a horse crack his own neck before. But I do know this: Training that's too specific or method-oriented actually prevents them from tapping wisdom we humans lost a long time ago."

"But how do you know when to move forward and when to back off?" Jana asked. "How do you keep it safe?"

"Over the years, I've learned to trust the horse's judgment," I emphasized, "and the herd hasn't let me down yet. But I have to respect their wishes. My job yesterday was to stay present and make sure that we had Noche's consent every step of the way. I was constantly checking to see if he felt threatened by what was happening. I was ready at any moment to help Pam dismount and move away from him. I never thought he'd allow things to progress as far as they did, but he actually seemed to be urging us on."

"Now that you mention it," Jana said, "I felt like Noche was in charge, and we were *his* assistants."

"I guess that's why I prefer the term equine-*facilitated* therapy, rather than equine-*assisted* therapy for my approach," I said. "More often than not I'm following the horse's lead, and because of that, we end up exploring aspects of mind, body, and spirit we couldn't possibly imagine ahead of time, much less read about in some textbook."

"It really felt like he was unlocking something in me," Pam added, "like he was drawing the memories out, but there was something about the way he did it that I've never experienced with a human being before. He was so... *non*judgmental. His spirit carried me toward a truth I couldn't have accessed on my own. He allowed me to explore something that could have been very frightening and very shameful.

"I felt *seen*," she said as her eyes filled with tears. "And he made it safe for me to *be* seen."

Pam went away from the experience convinced that her neck injury had been "a lucky break." This unexpected brush with death gave her an expanded vision of who she was, who she *could* be if she had the courage to step into the unknown. She felt connected to a higher power and sensed meaning in what had previously seemed a cold, heartless universe. "If it wasn't for that accident," she insisted, "I might still be living a complacent life. I still can't quite wrap my mind around what happened yesterday, but I feel like it was the culmination of something set into motion a long, long time ago."

"That's what I call *black horse wisdom*," I said, "wisdom shrouded in mystery, wisdom that's felt more deeply than it can ever be explained, wisdom we often ignore, unfortunately, until some inescapable tragedy opens us up to other possibilities. When Rasa went lame a decade ago, I was crushed. But that single 'accident' led me to start Epona and write my first book. I thank Rasa every day for thwarting my conventional equestrian ambitions. The arena we work in now is much bigger, and certainly more surreal, than anything I would have accessed training *her* for jumping or dressage."

Over the years, I told them, Rasa had led me into uncharted territory, literally and figuratively. In the process, I became somewhat of an expert on what the black horse represents. This universal archetype champions knowledge rejected by civilization: instinct, emotion, intuition, sensory and extrasensory awareness, and the human-nature partnership associated with tribal cultures.

"Science may never be able to dissect this wisdom, to bring it into the light of conscious understanding," I said. "But through the metaphor of the horse, and through real-life interactions with these animals, we can learn to ride these mysteries. Sometimes horses act as catalysts for dramatic shifts in consciousness that carry us to other worlds of creativity and insight, including realms associated with the collective unconscious, the spirit world, death, rebirth, and tragedy. There's a paradoxical element to this wisdom. What looks like darkness, fear, and hopelessness actually contains the seeds of transformation."

I reminded Pam and Jana how skittish Noche seemed when they first approached him. "And yet he *chose* to accompany us on an emotional journey that would have scared the wits out of most people I know," I said. "I've seen many horses volunteer to interact with clients at this level. The flight response protects these animals physically, but emotionally and spiritually, they show tremendous courage. They seem intent on helping people access the strengths that arise from what first appears as a wound, a weakness, or an injustice. They teach us to trust the universe in a way the logical mind can't fathom."

Pam and Jana talked extensively about the mystical insights various horses had inspired in them over the years. The conversation quite naturally drifted to the unsettling dreams I'd had a few nights earlier. Though we came up with multiple interpretations, it was obvious these visions foreshadowed another chapter in my own personal diary of black horse adventures.

"So what do you think about that strange nametag, SPRTS?" I asked at one point.

"You know," Jana replied as if it were obvious. "*Spirits!*"

"Yeah, but why more than one?" I asked.

That evening, I took my night-haired mare for a walk in the moonlight, mindful that my days with her might very well be numbered. These spirits who put their mark on Rasa's unexpected foal, were they supporting new life or planning to take their namesake back to the Otherworld? Would Rasa join the spirits of the

Ancestors as a result of giving birth? Either way, I realized that once again, I was following my beloved mare into unknown territory. If I'd learned anything at all from her, I knew I had to trust the outcome — no matter how painful the journey might be. The wisdom of the black horse was taking hold once more, urging me to embrace the genius that sometimes rides into town on what looks more like a dense, dark storm than a cloud with a silver lining.

HEART OF DARKNESS

Two days later, Rasa showed signs of labor. Milk began to flow from her udders, and there was a strange, reddish discharge under her tail. Dr. Staten's senior partner, Barbara Page, responded to my call.

"It looks like an infection in the placenta," she said, "which could cause the mare to abort. We'll have to do an ultrasound." Though my heart sank at the possibility of losing the foal, I was intrigued to finally catch a glimpse of Rasa's mystery baby. Yet once again, the little guy managed to elude us. As the vet scanned for signs of infection, she realized the fetus was positioned under Rasa's ribs, beyond the scope of a portable ultrasound machine.

"The good news is the placenta looks pretty clean," she said. "Whatever the problem is, we've probably caught it early enough to do something about it." Dr. Page prescribed a course of antibiotics, as well as a hormone designed to keep the mare from going into labor. "If she gives birth now, the foal won't survive," the vet cautioned. "Make sure you give her this hormone every day until it runs out."

Over the next three weeks, Rasa continued to drip milk, but there were no other signs of infection. Still, I felt the need to check on her most nights while frantically trying to finish stall construction and furnish the house before our next big event. Two dozen counselors and horse professionals from across the U.S. and Canada had signed up to study our methods for employing horses in the work of human development. They'd be arriving March 8, 2002, for a seminar called The Epona Approach.

Energy-wise, I was running on empty worrying about Rasa's condition, the new center, and the daily details of the business, while preparing for The Epona Approach, and continuing to see clients. My staff strongly encouraged me to take March 7 off.

"I gave Rasa the last of her medicine a couple days ago," I told my barn manager the night before I reluctantly headed home. "She should be fine."

Xena could see that I didn't quite believe it. "I've got lots of volunteers scheduled to help us tomorrow," she said. "I'll be in and out all day. We'll keep an eye on Rasa. Sleep in. Watch some silly, mindless videos. *Don't worry.*"

"Well, I'll keep my cell phone on just in case," I said.

At 7:30 the next morning, I awoke to an ominous ringing. It was "Sandra," a recent veterinary graduate from the East Coast. She decided to stop in Tucson on her way to the Pacific Northwest for a job interview. After school expenses, she had little money left, yet I admired her interest in exploring the emotional dimension of the horse-human connection, a subject most vets tend to ignore. Pleased to support this innovative young woman, I'd offered her the chance to stay at the center for a week and attend The Epona Approach.

I breathed a potent sigh of relief at the sound of her voice. My one chance to sleep late was blown, but at least she wasn't calling about Rasa.

"I just got into town," Sandra said. "I've been driving for days, and I'd really like to get some rest. Would it be possible to check into the Epona Center a few hours early?"

"Sure," I mumbled, rubbing my eyes, "if you don't mind that staff will be setting up until late afternoon."

"At this point I could probably sleep through a hurricane," she replied.

Exhausted yet wide awake, I dragged myself into the living room. After watching DVDs all morning, I made lunch and was just sitting down with a good book when the phone rang again. It was my colleague Kathleen Ingram.

"I think Rasa's going into labor," she said. "She's really let down her milk, and she's agitated."

I hoped it wasn't true. "Rasa's still two months early. Besides, she's had those symptoms for weeks."

"Damn it, Linda, I may not know as much about horses as you do, but I've had two kids myself. I *know* what labor looks like! Xena's not here right now. You really need to get over here."

Speeding down the road, I called Dr. Page. She also seemed skeptical when I told her that Kathleen thought the mare was about to give birth. The vet was helping a horse at the fairgrounds, a good forty-minute drive from the center. Even so, she began to coach me in some emergency measures.

"There's another call coming in," I interrupted her, racing through a yellow light. "I'll have to get back to you."

Hitting the call waiting button, I heard Kathleen's frantic voice. "Rasa's water just broke! What should I do?"

"I have no idea," I said, "and I'm still fifteen minutes away. *Wait a second.* Sandra should be there at the house. She's a *vet.*"

By the time I pulled into the driveway, the tiniest foal I had ever seen was lying in the grass. Rasa was pacing around him, her strange, high-pitched whinny barely discernable above the excited cries of the rest of the herd. Merlin, the calmest of them all, stared at his new son over the fence. Rasa's foaling stall wasn't quite finished. Her official due date was a good six weeks away, and she was still living next to her mate. Consequently, the stallion had been able to watch his mare give birth, an event few domesticated studs ever witness. Sandra waited at the edge of the corral, mindful of the need for mother and baby to bond during their first moments.

But Rasa was distracted. I felt a queasy, sinking feeling in the pit of my stomach as she approached her foal. "Something's wrong," I said after quickly introducing myself. I climbed over the fence and ran toward the mare as she started to lie down. Sandra followed, and together, we dragged the foal out of Rasa's way. A split second later and the mare would have crushed him as she rolled in agony.

Rasa stood up and trotted toward the other side of corral, twitching, straining, raising her tail to reveal a limp pair of hooves. Sandra ran over, reached into the mare's vagina, and pulled another black colt into the world, his eyes vacant and cloudy. There *had* been more than one spirit taking form in Rasa's belly, and now I knew why the little black colt in my dream had feigned a human frown. He had been dying in the cramped space of his mother's womb.

The stillborn colt was much bigger than his brother. Even so, he wouldn't have survived when Rasa showed the first signs of labor a month earlier. Some presence able to communicate through dreams foreshadowed a bittersweet ending to an impossible situation. For some as-yet-unfathomable reason, the human contingent was kept in the dark about the details of this unlikely conception, despite multiple attempts to confirm pregnancy and see into the womb. It was as if we were informed on a need-to-know basis, allowed to support the process without fully understanding what was taking place, encouraged by circumstance to employ the hormone, the one medical wonder that could delay birth for a few more precious weeks.

The larger foal was sacrificed. As his beautiful, lifeless form lay near his fragile brother, I briefly touched the face of the twin I would never get to know. "Safe journey, little one," I said.

The sadness I'd first tapped in a dream flooded my heart as I gazed into his empty, otherworldly eyes. The void came to life for one brief moment, and a piece of me went with it as the second son of two black horses receded into eternity.

RAIN IN THE DESERT

The firstborn twin seemed destined to join his brother. Try as he might, the foal was unable to stand on his own. When we propped him up to nurse, he couldn't begin to reach his mother's udders. As his spindly legs struggled to hold his weight, his knees began to bend backward. He shivered as the wind picked up and a cloud passed over the late-afternoon sun.

"That's not just a reaction to the drop in temperature," Dr. Page explained when she arrived. "His nervous system isn't fully developed, and I can see that his joints aren't either. We have to get him inside. He's going to need heat lamps and blankets. We'll have to milk the mare and bottle-feed him. But really, I must caution you, it may not be enough. He may not live through the night."

At the very least, I was thankful that we'd made the hectic move across town. The Ranch had large corrals and acres of dry pasture to run around in, but no indoor accommodations. Peggy's place, on the other hand, had exactly what we needed to save Rasa's foal: a barn. Dr. Page's assistant Leanne Garber carried the infant horse as I led his mother to a spacious stall with electricity.

A bit claustrophobic, Rasa had always resisted conventional stabling, and her companions weren't making the transition any easier for her. They bucked and squealed, encouraging her to break away and return to the herd. In response, she bolted out the door and pawed at the gate of the modest turnout attached to her new stall. Then she suddenly remembered her baby and ran back in to sniff him distractedly. With a handful of carrots and a big flake of alfalfa, we managed to distract her long enough to draw some milk. As the discomfort of her swollen udders lessened under Dr. Page's experienced hands, Rasa let out a big sigh of relief and understanding. Then she stood quietly, of her own free will, glad for the release. The question was, Would the foal be able to drink? After a moment of fumbling, he grabbed hold of the nipple and sucked the fluid down like ambrosia. Then he let out a deep, delighted whinny.

The foal's enthusiasm seemed to inflate his delicate body. Though he weighed a mere twenty pounds, a third the size of the average newborn Arabian, his presence filled the room. His rich baritone voice, the result of premature vocal chords, seemed so incongruous with his tiny frame that we couldn't help but laugh out loud when he demanded another bottle. His curious, wide-eyed gaze entranced everyone, including a vet who thought she'd seen everything. The little toy horse looked so pleased with himself, so happy to be in the world, we couldn't help but rally around him and actually revel in the challenge of keeping him alive.

"Well, one thing's for sure," I said, "he's got more spirit than body. I really feel like he wants to stay." My staff knew of the collar a newborn colt had worn in my first, most ominous dream. The foal's name, therefore, seemed obvious.

"You want some more, Spirit?" I asked as the doctor showed me how to milk Rasa. The little guy responded with an animated rumble.

As the news spread and people came to see Rasa's tenuous miracle, my husband was left with the most difficult task of all: burying Spirit's twin, who I named Sanctus, acknowledging his sacrifice and the effect his brief, sad, profound visit had on me. After everyone had left, Steve told me of carrying the little foal to his final resting place, of the power and gentleness in those silent eyes, of the insights the twins inspired in him.

"To see life and death side by side," he said, shaking his head, "to bury one colt and hear the other calling out. . . ."

Steve couldn't finish the sentence, but I knew he was, like me, swirling between the opposites: not transcending duality exactly, but feeling, really feeling, how joy spills into sadness, how beauty emerges from suffering, and how language can never touch the mystery that informs all life.

Shortly before midnight, the first storm in seven weeks raged across the desert. I crouched down in the middle of that stall for hours, hovering over Spirit, shielding him with my body as Rasa ran frantic circles around us with every blast of thunder. Torrential winds blew rain through the rafters, but I felt safe and blessed. At our previous location, we would have had no such shelter, no heat lamps, and no veterinary graduate staying on the property. Practicality suggested I should have stayed at The Ranch until after the birth, but a series of synchronicities paved the way for us to move to a new center, one that could accommodate the needs of a special foal. I still couldn't quite believe how efficiently we'd been directed to Peggy's unadvertised barn, how easily the move had taken place. I'd spent a decade collecting proof of horse intelligence, imagination, will, and compassion. Now, it seemed I had to add the ability to solicit otherworldly protection and guidance to those equine faculties usually reserved for humans.

A flash of lightning sent Rasa careening past us once more, but Spirit knew he was safe. The little black horse gazed at the drama from a cave of fragrant hay and soft blankets, content with the world, just as it was.

CHAPTER SEVEN

YEAR OF THE BLACK HORSE

W ading through the darkness beyond dreams, I sensed a distant call. A strong, feminine presence, not quite human, demanded something familiar, something I couldn't quite remember. She was kicking my shoulder, trying desperately to wake me up.

Why was I lying on the ground?

The creature jostled me again. My hands felt like ice cubes, but my belly burned hot. I was curled around something warm, something breathing. I opened my eyes and stared up at the massive black face hovering over me. Steam rose from Rasa's nostrils in the cold morning air.

A mare gently nudges her foal with the edge of her hoof when her udders are full, but Rasa's baby couldn't stand and nurse. And so she had taken to nudging me, every two hours, all night long.

I wrapped my down sleeping bag around little Spirit, who shivered ever so slightly the moment I stood up. I couldn't seem to find my left glove. I blew on my hands and rubbed them together, but Rasa still flinched when I squeezed the first stream of milk into a cold plastic cup.

Kneeling under my horse in the hazy twilight, I realized it was Tuesday morning — Spirit had successfully survived his first five days. I thought back to the night of his birth: By 2 A.M. on March 8, the clouds had begun to dissipate. Epona social worker Laurie Levon drove up in the darkness. I showed her how to milk the mare, thankful for the help and the company, especially after holding Spirit through a torrential thunderstorm for two hours while trying to calm his mother. Laurie and I talked briefly about the unsettling yet extraordinary events of the past twelve hours. (Spirit was born around 2:20 P.M. on March 7.) Then I curled up in my sleeping bag, mindful of the fact that I would be leading a workshop at 9 A.M.

None of us got much sleep. I dozed off a couple of times, hoping Rasa might feel comfortable enough to finally lie down, but she refused to close her eyes. She stood over Laurie, Spirit, and me in a strange protective trance, rarely blinking, staring down at the sleeping foal covered in blankets, his head resting on the edge of my pillow. (She wouldn't lie down for a week.) Laurie and I were drawn into an altered state of consciousness with her, as if we were vibrating sympathetically with some hormonal response new horse mothers engage to keep watch over their newborns. Tired but extremely alert, we felt intimately connected to Rasa, Spirit, and each other. We barely spoke for hours, yet it didn't seem forced or unnatural. It felt like we'd been sucked into a different reality, and our voices hadn't quite caught up with us.

A phenomenal group of counselors and horse professionals arrived the next day. Some volunteered to sit with Spirit each evening, and a few stayed on for several days after the workshop, marveling at Rasa's accommodating demeanor. Upon foaling, mares can become extremely hostile toward other horses — and people. Sometimes even a trusted owner is chased from the stall. Yet Rasa graciously welcomed total strangers, one right after the other. She endured their first clumsy attempts to milk her and stood quietly beside them as they fed her baby.

"I couldn't believe it," said Sue Ratcliffe, a talented horse-woman and EEL practitioner from Toronto. "Rasa acted like she knew exactly what was going on and was grateful for the help. She hung out with us like one of the girls, and yet there was a special feeling to the whole thing that I can't quite describe. The experience made me look at my own horses in a new way."

Charlie McGuire, founder of the American Holistic Nurses Association, attended the workshop that weekend with her partner, Robbie Nelson. The two had recently established the Buffalo William Ranch in Cortez, Colorado, and were looking for ideas on how to better incorporate horses into a multidisciplinary healing and empowerment program. The final day of our seminar, they offered to stay up all night with me before making the eleven-hour drive back home.

I was beginning to notice a pattern. People would enter the stall chattering, laughing, cooing over the little horse baby. Several hours later, they'd leave in hushed reverence.

"Spirit was extremely small and fragile," Charlie remembers. "But there was an energy about him that was strong and vital. As I walked into the stall, I felt I was entering sacred space, something akin to a manger scene."

PRESENCE

The following week, a former nun reached a deeper, purer understanding of her original faith communing with the herd and sitting with Rasa and Spirit for an hour.

Cathy [last name withheld], who had recently completed a doctoral program in alternate spirituality, stopped by the Epona Center shortly before Spirit's birth. She came on the recommendation of Pam, the psychotherapist who'd experienced those cathartic sessions with Noche. "I really wasn't sure why I felt compelled to do this," Cathy says. "I've never been around horses and have never cared to be. They were too big, and I didn't like the way they smelled. For someone who tends to live in the clouds with the angels, anything earthly did not hold a great appeal."

Cathy *was* interested in how horses help children with attention deficit disorder. Yet beyond this practical reason for checking out the program, she had to admit she felt an inexplicably "strong draw" and was surprised by her response.

"The minute I walked on the property, a feeling of sadness came over me," she says. "As we worked with this emotion in our session that day, it became clear to me that I was experiencing a sadness beyond my own. This was the sadness of generations that have forgotten . . . forgotten how to truly know and to connect. Since we've locked ourselves into the prison of our minds, we've lost connection with Mind, with the feminine way of knowing, with our connection to the earth and all life forms."

I asked Cathy to stay with that sadness and she walked among the horse corrals. She was immediately drawn to my gray (almost white) gelding Max. "I felt him speaking to me," she wrote in a letter several weeks later. "He was telling me not to be afraid of this feminine, intuitive knowing, that it wasn't just reserved for an elite few. All humans have this ability, and I did, too. I felt unconditional love sweep over me. It was as if I was being brought back to an ancient time where humans knew how to connect with horses and all of nature . . . as if, through Max, the ancient ones were calling me back.

"There were times as I walked around the horses when my [inner] judge would say: 'What are you doing? This is stupid.' Belief systems that keep us supposedly superior and separate were kicking in. But I felt the horses with me for days afterward, trying to teach me, calling me forth. I dreamed about riding a beautiful white horse. During my meditations, I felt the ancient horse energy, and I visualized myself riding the beautiful white horse. He took me through incredibly lovely areas until we reached a place of all knowing, the place of oneness. This knowing wasn't about words, it was vibrational. I felt the unconditional love of the horses dropping into my body, and I wept."

Cathy returned for another session two weeks later — on the one day I was unable to find an assistant experienced enough to be left alone with Rasa and Spirit. "I'm so sorry for the inconvenience," I said, "but when we made this appointment, I didn't expect to have a premature foal to take care of. I can't leave Spirit right now for more than ten minutes at a time. We can reschedule if you like, or you can hang out with the herd for a while and then come to Rasa's stall. We can do an informal session there."

As it turned out, Cathy was more interested in spending time with Max than she was in talking to me. Thrilled to be left alone with him for a while, she headed toward his corral. A half hour later, she told me that she'd also connected with Noche this time. "I Ic has seen and experienced much," she told me, quite accurately. "I felt his sadness and his wisdom. In a way, I felt he was mirroring me — very shy, very sensitive, and somewhat hidden."

When I invited her into Rasa's stall, Cathy acknowledged her fear of sitting with a loose horse in a confined space. The mare, however, reached out to her. "Rasa came over and began playing with my hat," she remembers, "as if to tell me not to be afraid, that she wouldn't hurt me. When I took off my hat, she put her head on mine and once again, I felt the unconditional love pass from her to me — and almost a gratefulness that I was with her baby... mother to mother, connecting."

Thick streams of tears flowed down Cathy's cheeks. She spoke about how Spirit seemed to fill the room. This tiny, fragile, helpless horse, she said, radiated pure presence. And at that moment, the former nun saw that she had been *striving* all her life for a love that was meant to be given freely.

"This love was no different than the love I feel when Mary or Jesus come into my body," she emphasized in her subsequent letter. "In a way, it was even freer because it wasn't associated with a patriarchal archetype whom I'd been trained to please. It was God expressed in the body of a horse. And this has totally blown apart all those strict Roman Catholic beliefs I'd been taught. It screams of pantheism, and yet I know that what I experienced was of God, that total unconditional energy of pure love. It has helped me to open even more to other ancient voices and to experience all of creation as magnificent expressions of God."

For Cathy, the greatest gift was that the horses transmitted a palpable feeling of this divine love without ego, without asking for anything in return — as if it were the most natural thing in the world. "Horses are just horses," she says, "not some guru or authority figure I must please, not some symbol of the patriarchal church I must worship as God. There is no competition with them, no need to win points. Heaven is right here, right now on this earth plane. It feels at times like I'm walking between the worlds."

Over the next two months, numerous people responded in similar ways. They'd stumble out of the stall with a wide-eyed look of wonder on their faces, mumbling about finally understanding the message of Christ's nativity. It was humbling to watch these two horses casually transforming people's perceptions about themselves and the universe — without a human facilitator present. One woman, who'd been unable to conceive, realized that human birth wasn't the only way to experience the miraculous nature of life. Another woman who had suffered from depression after one of her own twins was stillborn, brought her surviving son, who had been partially disabled as a result of that difficult birth. Through the experience, the family opened new lines of communication about their loss — and became more conscious of the special gifts their remaining twin, and his older sister, had brought into this world.

Clients and volunteers were inspired by the fact that Rasa and her baby were changing lives at the exact moment these two horses needed the most help. Spirit literally didn't have a leg to stand on, and yet he opened people's hearts and gave them an experience of the divinity of pure being. Psychiatrists, psychics, healers, and spiritual seekers finally understood that many of their practices were still operating from a hierarchical mentality in which people felt the need to constantly prove themselves worthy of love and respect. And yet here was a tiny horse who radiated pure, loving Presence in a state of complete openness and vulnerability.

THE POWER OF TOUCH

Spirit, as it turned out, needed twenty-four-hour care for ten weeks — during our busiest workshop season. The Epona staff was taxed to the limit. Barn manager Xena Carpenter began to comb the community for volunteers, pairing those who had never been around horses with equestrians we carefully trained.

Several experienced horse people were initially aggravated at the sight of staff members lying beside the foal, embracing him. They thought this was unnatural and indulgent. However, we had learned through experience that Spirit would shiver under mounds of blankets. They only thing that calmed him was holding him against our chests.

Stroking him like a dog was *not* helpful. Mares rub their muzzles across their foals' bodies to stimulate them, to get them to wake up and stand up. Caressing Spirit made him want to do the same thing, at a time when he wasn't allowed to stand for fear of damaging his knees.

It was really quite a scene. After resting against a series of people's bodies, the little colt spent his waking hours in a sling suspended from the barn ceiling. This allowed him to move around and put partial weight on his still-developing limbs without twisting, leaping, and running around like a normal foal. He looked like a baby in a swing — and he did enjoy the benefits of his unusual predicament. "Flying boy," we called him as he whinnied with delight, soaring back and forth through the air.

A month after his birth, one workshop participant suggested I read *Kangeroo Care: The Best You Can Do to Help Your Preterm Infant*. In this book, Susan M. Ludington-Hoe, Ph.D., and Susan K. Golant describe a program of skin-to-skin contact between parent and child that has revolutionized premature infant care. As it turns out, high-technology interventions often fail when these babies are restricted to incubators. A mother's touch is just as important to survival as the best that medical science has to offer.

Ludington-Hoe and Golant open their book with a startling anecdote. Steven was born sixteen weeks early, and the staff at Brigham and Women's Hospital in Boston, Massachusetts, had trouble keeping him alive. All their treatments were ineffective.

"Steven was slipping away," the authors wrote; "his blood values were dropping, and his immature lungs were unable to provide him with enough oxygen."

The baby was finally given to his mother, Dorothy, so that she could say goodbye, and the nurses left them alone for two hours.

"What a surprise awaited them upon their return," Ludingon-Hoe and Golant continue. "Dorothy was still holding Steven, who was still connected to all his equipment and monitors. But she had undressed him and had spontaneously placed him on her bare chest. When the nurse in charge took Steven's vital signs for what she thought was the last time, she noticed the level of oxygen in his blood had increased, the level of carbon dioxide had dropped (as one would want it to), his blood pressure was more stable, his breathing less labored."

The hospital allowed Dorothy to continue holding her baby throughout the night. "Within twenty-four hours, Steven had improved dramatically. When Dorothy grew tired, her husband Jack came in and took over holding their infant. Over the course of the next two days, Steven was continuously held in the intensive care nursery of this teaching hospital. During those three days, Steven's physiological condition reversed." He was discharged from the hospital at four months, a "miracle baby" who subsequently appeared on *Good Morning America* with his family.

Steven's story mirrors my own experiences with Spirit. The little horse thrived, not only through physical nourishment and medical attention but through the loving embraces of nearly a hundred people. Our success confirmed what many of us had always known intuitively. Horses and people may be different in many ways, but neither species can thrive without the touch of a loving presence. Children — especially those with a tenuous grip on this world — need to be cared for by someone who really *wants* them to live, someone willing to hold them through the pain and the ambiguity.

WATER HORSE

Synchronizing heartbeats and sharing breath with the little horse not only inspired him to stay, the experience transformed those who took care of him in myriad ways. Charlie McGuire returned to Tucson at the end of March to help us with another workshop. She also volunteered to sit with Spirit overnight, the hardest shift to fill. "I was a little nervous," she admits. "I had never milked a mare before, but as a nurse I thought surely I could handle the situation. When I arrived at 1 A.M., I was relieved that Spirit had just been fed. A young woman was sharing the shift with me. We shoveled some fresh hay for Rasa and talked with the other two people from the last shift. They left and a quiet enveloped the stall."

Charlie rolled into the sleeping bag next to Spirit's nest of blankets. "I placed my nose and mouth next to his and began to breathe with him," she says. "His breath was about three times to my one breath, and his lips were softly nibbling at my lips. I softly nibbled back and soon we had a very interesting connection happening. What an enchanting experience! I decided I would stay in this connection with him as long as he would allow. Something which I can only describe as 'energy' began to form between us, then enfolded us. It felt as if the two of us melted into the energy. Spirit was communing with me at a level I had never experienced with another being. Tears of absolute bliss rolled down my cheeks. We were nibbling with our lips like short, light kisses and breathing softly together. Spirit had made no attempt to move away or end this experience in any way. Nor had I.

"What's the message here? What's happening? All kinds of questions were coming up. I forced myself to let them go and totally surrender to the moment. I fell into a very deep sleep. I'm not sure for how long. All I know is that when I awakened I knew I was different. Spirit was beginning to move his legs and his head. I got the feeling that he had concluded this experience. I felt like I'd just received a powerful initiation into Horse Medicine from a master teacher, Spirit to Spirit! I also remembered that this was the Chinese Year of the Horse, and I felt that somehow Spirit's birth was heralding this event."

Sure enough, one of my clients emailed me a link to a Chinese astrology website. There I learned that 2002 was not only the year of the horse, it was the year of the black horse, black representing the water element associated with emotion, intuition, nurturing, and fluidity. Even more specifically, it was the year of the yang water horse. It seemed Spirit was in alignment with cosmic forces; he was black, he was male (yang), and the night he was born, I held him through the only rainstorm we had in the desert for more than three months. Beyond that, he was proving to be yet another carrier of what I've been calling "black horse wisdom" since *The Tao of Equus* came out. Here was a little foal who at first seemed to be surrounded by such tragedy, mystery, and vulnerability, whose brother was stillborn, who was himself not expected to live, but whose daily existence produced deep insights and little miracles in so many people's lives, including my own.

TWO REALITIES

With all these synchronicities and religious archetypes flying around the stable, I decided to investigate the symbology of twins. Some inexplicable force, after all, seemed intent on making sure Rasa gave birth to twin male foals, only one of which was destined to survive. It seemed to me that if some nonmaterial intelligence was capable of sending me two dreams about the twins before they were born, it most certainly could have warned me early enough to prevent the whole drama in the first place. Instead, circumstances prevented us from aborting one fetus at forty days — and from seeing into the womb on two other occasions.

In cultures around the world, curiously enough, male twins are often closely associated with horses. In a significant number of these myths, one brother endures the death of the other, who then connects the survivor to the otherworld. The Greek myth of Castor and Pollux is a prime example. Castor was famous for training horses, Pollux for his skill in boxing. United by the warmest affection, they accompanied Jason on his Argonautic expedition. Castor was later slain in war, and Pollux, inconsolable after the loss of his brother, begged Zeus to take his life in exchange. The Greek god instead granted Castor semi-immortality, directing him to spend half his days in the underworld, emerging every other day to visit heaven. Upon Pollux's death the two were reunited as the constellation Gemini.

In Thebes, Amphion and Zethus were, like the Roman twins Romulus and Remus, abandoned at birth, though the former were raised by a shepherd and the latter by wolves. The similarity also includes the death of Amphion, who like Remus, was the less bold of the two. While Romulus and Remus weren't hailed as great equestrians, Amphion and Zethus were called the "White Horses," "The Horsemen," or "Riders of White Horses," mirroring the equine associations of Castor and Pollux, who are collectively referred to as the Discouri, the "horseman gods."

The Irish goddess Macha gave birth to twins after winning a horse race. The twin brother of the Welsh god Lleu Llaw Gyffes jumped into the sea at birth. The Lithuanian Supreme God had twins through a union with the Great Mother Goddess Lada. These children, significantly, were born in the shape of twin horses. A number of Eastern twin myths also share the equestrian associations of their Western counterparts. Many feature a weaker brother, who perishes.

In his book *The Soul's Code*, psychologist James Hillman reflects on the mythological theme of sacrificing one of the twins to create balance between this world and the other. The Inuits speak of "another soul," he writes, "whether internal and in the same body or an external one that comes and goes, alights and leaves, inhabits things and places and animals. Anthropologists who walk with Australian aborigines call this second soul a bush-soul."

Hillman also cites fairy tales, Rumi poems, and Zen stories alluding to "this doubleness, this strange duplicity of life. There are two birds in the tree, a mortal one and an immortal one, side by side. The first chirps and nests and flies about; the other watches.

"The placenta must be carefully disposed of in many cultures, for it is born with you and must not be allowed to enter the life you live. It must remain stillborn and return to the otherworld, or else your congenital twin may form a monstrous ghost.

"Twins themselves are often considered ominous, as if a mistake has occurred; the two birds, the human and the ghost, this world and that, both present in this world. Twins literalize the doppelganger, visible and invisible both displayed. So tales tell of the murder (sacrifice) of one twin for the sake of the other. . . . The shadow, immortal, otherworldly one gives way so that the mortal one can fully enter this life."

In an Internet discussion of his paper "Twin lights of consciousness, biology, microphysics, and macropsychology," H. Teich took the symbology of twins to a much deeper level. He uses Roger Penrose's theory concerning the nature of consciousness as expressed in "three worlds": the perceptual world, the physical world, and the Platonic archetypal world of ideal forms that gives rise to creation. According to Teich the "twin nature of light as waves and particles" in quantum theory "is the common denominator of the 'three worlds.' Like the atomic world of matter, the archetypal symbolic image is based on the twin nature of light." He theorizes that the overwhelming tendency to depict mythical twins as two males, rather than as male and female, is an expression of the genetic chromosomal code. "Since females are already twinned at the chromosome level (XX), perhaps the symbolic archetypal image of twin males . . . is a mythological compensation for biology."

If your head is spinning at this point, join the club. It took me months of research and reflection to integrate these concepts, and I still have trouble verbalizing what I learned. Basically, the entire experience gave me yet another reason to believe in a vast coordinating intelligence that speaks to people through dreams, art, and visions — *and* through the physical manifestation of archetypal themes. If this is indeed the case, Spirit and his stillborn brother, Sanctus, represented yet another attempt to bring the twin nature of consciousness to our attention. We saw, for one brief moment, the two lying side by side. In naming the stillborn twin, in touching him — and in being touched emotionally by his brief, sad life

— we forged a stronger bond with the numinous, archetypal realm of origins. In quantum theory, the most basic building blocks of life have a dual nature, appearing as particles with a set location in time and space, and waves, invisible regions of influence that can flow through walls, resonate with physical matter, and yet remain unlimited by the laws that hold physical beings together.

Through this strange, unusually public horse birth, the universe was upping the ante on a cross-cultural theme. If women already contain "the twins" genetically (as XX chromosomes), it alludes to why feminine wisdom is associated with intuition — ways of knowing not limited to physical and logical laws. The two male twins were an attempt to bridge the gap between the worlds in masculine consciousness. They manifested this time, not as horsemen, but as actual horses: nonpredatory beings who, though domesticated, retain a vital connection to instinct and nature, while also being associated mythically with a strong sixth sense and the ability to carry riders between this world and the other. The fact that the stronger, larger twin was sacrificed emphasized, for me, the need for a stronger connection to the otherworld at a time when logic has become much more dominant than it was during the era of Greek myths. Spirit's ability to inspire others during his time of greatest physical weakness also underlined the paradoxical power of vulnerability — at a time when technology insulates us from the elements and allows us to destroy our enemies with remarkable ease.

Nearly a hundred volunteers, clients, and Epona staff members were drawn into horse consciousness through the act of caring for a foal as one of their own. This never would have happened if Spirit had been able to stand and nurse at birth. In this sense, Spirit also bridged the gap between horse and human, drawing nourishment and love from both species. In the wild, he never would have survived.

These synchronistic insights emerged not so much from logical consideration, but from a potent vision I had while tending Spirit late one night. I grabbed my notebook and wrote it down in a strange, archaic, mythological mindset that sometimes overtakes me, a style of writing I call the Voice of Remembering:

At the dawn of the millennium, the Horse Ancestors chose among them yet another seed spirit to bring the wisdom of the prey to a violent world.

"Who among us has the courage to be truly vulnerable?" they asked. "Who will bridge the worlds between horse and human, life and death?"

Two brothers stepped forward, their manes swirling in the wake of a distant storm.

"Yes," said the oldest, wisest mare of them all. "I see great strength in such a partnership. One will stay and one will go, but the two will be born together. We need the power of both worlds now to melt the human heart."

"But the two-legged creatures guard against the birth of twins," her regal mate argued, pawing the ground and bucking against the approaching maelstrom.

"Then let us color them black so they won't be seen in the womb of their mother," the mare replied. "And let us gather the blessings of the entire herd to keep them safe from human intervention."

Every horse who had ever lived and every horse who hadn't yet been born began to neigh in deep, long tones as the twins were engulfed by the whirlwind and carried toward a distant land.

"It will be sad at first for one to flourish and one to be buried in the ground," said the mare when the sky began to clear. "But there is power in human tears shed for horses, and great compassion will rise in those who care for a foal who cannot stand and nurse."

"Perhaps," said the stallion with a toss of his head as the herd went back to grazing. "In treating him as one of their own children, they might look at us all with softer eyes."

"And maybe," the mare surmised, "they will learn to nourish the gentle, vulnerable spirit they long ago rejected in themselves."

CHAPTER EIGHT

DISPELLING HUMAN NONSENSE

As I sat with Rasa and Spirit, attending to their simple needs, the horses drew me into a secret symphony. On windless afternoons, when birds panted in the stagnant heat and all reasonable creatures huddled under whatever shade they could find, there was a thickness to the desert silence. I could feel the rocks humming on the other side of sound, resonating with Rasa's soft, rhythmic breaths. One warm, spring night, the entire herd gave voice to this hidden music, and I realized that horses not only harmonize with something too deep to hear, they know how to sing in a miracle.

It all started innocently enough. I was waiting at the Epona house, ready to greet some clients arriving from Vancouver, when one of Epona's assistants, Dorrell-Jo MacWhinnie, knocked on the door.

"Something's wrong with Merlin," she said. "Normally he runs over and calls out when I load up the hay. But he's lying down, and he didn't even touch his dinner." I followed Dorrell-Jo out to Merlin's corral and managed to get him to stand up. It seemed like a mild case of colic, something the horse could probably handle on his own. Still, I called the vet just to be safe.

Dr. Page drove up as my guests arrived. Sending Dorrell-Jo to assist our new clients, I haltered Merlin for his examination. The horse was lethargic, but he didn't seem in significant pain. When the doctor palpated him, however, her entire face went white. "This is a surgical emergency," she told me. "He has dislocated his large intestine and his spleen."

I was in shock. Merlin was nineteen, too old to be covered under my equine insurance policy. The new Epona Center was operating at a loss during its first few months. Stall construction and Spirit's extended care had taken me over the edge financially. I always knew that when I brought older horses into the herd, I'd be hard-pressed to afford a $10,000 colic surgery. Now I faced the emotional ramifications of that reality. It seemed I had to sacrifice the father for the son.

My guests wandered out to meet me as the vet and I discussed our options. I was faced with staying up all night, giving the horse fluids and pain killers until he couldn't go on any longer, and then making the call to euthanize him, knowing full well I had to teach the next day. Why did everything seem to depend on money? My new students from Vancouver had just spent a great deal of it on plane fares, a rental car, and a trunk full of groceries. I couldn't just tell them to come back some other time. I prepared for the worst as Dr. Page called to consult with one of the most respected equine surgeons in town, Larry Shamis, the same doctor who had explored noninvasive therapies for Rasa's lameness almost a decade earlier. Knowing that surgery wasn't an option, he nonetheless agreed to drive out to the Epona Center and see what he could do.

Normally, you never let a horse lie down when he's colicking.

A natural response to abdominal pain, rolling around on the ground causes the horse to twist his intestines even more. But letting Merlin roll was exactly the advice the vet gave me. "It may be his only chance," said Dr. Shamis, pointing out that without surgery, the horse would somehow have to reposition his own internal organs, a long shot at best.

I led Merlin to the same barn where Rasa and Spirit had been living, ostensibly because of the electricity and extra shelter it offered. Deep down inside, however, I knew I couldn't bear to teach a lesson if Merlin's body was lying in the corral next to the rest of the herd. (It would take a day or two to make the proper arrangements.) Dr. Shamis set up an IV and shot the horse full of potent tranquilizers. "Give him a bag of fluids every hour," the doctor told me. "It's a very slim possibility, but this might give the bowels some motility. I have to tell you that it's very, very rare, almost unheard of, for a horse to work this out for himself." Then he loaded up his truck and drove off with a promise to return, if and when it was time to send Merlin on his final journey.

Standing in that dismal stall with my stallion, I prayed for assistance and acceptance. I called in the Horse Ancestors, that complex of equine wisdom I wrote about in my first book. I told Merlin exactly what we were dealing with, how much he meant to me, and how much I wanted him to stay. I soothed him with some Tellington-Jones T-Touches designed to help colic. I gave him fluids and painkillers. Kathleen Ingram came over to offer moral support. I asked her to bring some wine to kill *my* pain. And we waited.

The whole time, the entire Epona herd was calling out to him, not whinnying so much as wailing, almost chanting, a very odd thing for the horses to do. Merlin was antagonistic with the geldings, and the other mares had never been turned out with him. Rasa herself had been isolated from the herd for a month; she hadn't seen Merlin since Spirit was born. Yet space couldn't sever the connections these horses had made over the years. It was as if direct touch wasn't necessary to strengthen their bonds. The sound of their voices seemed to envelop Merlin, to hold and encourage him, to state plainly that he was a valued member of the herd, despite his habitually aggressive behavior.

After a solid hour of this singing, the horses ran out of steam and fell into silence. Merlin lifted his head and weakly called out to them through his drug-induced haze — and the chorus started up again. All night long, the herd continued to neigh in deep, long waves of sound as Merlin progressively grew stronger and more alert. He never did lie down and roll.

At midnight, I temporarily disconnected the IV and took him for a walk to see his mare and foal. Merlin's deflated body transformed as he exchanged breath with Rasa over the fence. The stallion in him returned full force as he reared over us both. Then he danced back to the stall in that same slow, collected, artful trot that had won him the right to breed with Rasa in the first place, and stood patiently for another round of intravenous fluids.

The next morning, much to everyone's surprise, Merlin was fine. Around 4 A.M., he had a bowel movement and began to eat, two simple bodily functions that would have been impossible with a dislocated intestine and spleen.

"Congratulations," Dr. Shamis said when I called him later that day.

"I've only ever heard of one other horse pulling through something like that without surgery," Dr. Page admitted when I told her the news.

I couldn't help wondering why Merlin had to colic that night. He had never been sick a day in his life that I knew of. My goal had been to rest up for my Vancouver clients. Debra Rafel, a life coach and yoga instructor, and Georgina Eden, an experiential counselor and animal communicator, had told me ahead of time that they were "very serious about going deeply into this work." I wanted to be operating at 100 percent capacity for them, yet there I was, so physically, mentally, and emotionally exhausted after staying up with the stallion that I couldn't fully appreciate his unexpected recovery, let alone be at my best for Debra and Georgina.

That weekend, however, my horses were at *their* best, taking these two women to places they had never been before. All I had to do was interpret. Even Merlin got into the act. The last night, I could see he was inviting Georgina into his stall. With a little prompting on how to set proper boundaries with the stallion, she connected with him and began receiving some unusually clear messages. Initially, in order to see whether she was picking up intuitive information or engaging in projection, I asked her some questions about Merlin I already knew the answers to. Satisfied with the accuracy of her insights, I decided to take advantage of Georgina's talents to get to the bottom of something that had been mystifying me all weekend. I was simply too tired and too close to the situation to trust my own intuition on the subject.

"Ask Merlin if he knows why all the other horses were calling out to him the night he almost left us," I requested.

The stallion's reply, translated instantaneously by Georgina, left both our minds reeling.

"In order to perform the miracle," he said, "I needed the vibrations of the herd to dispel the human nonsense that it was impossible."

BEYOND THE TRANCE

The idea that Merlin needed "the vibrations of the herd" to "dispel the human nonsense" about needing surgery to reposition his internal organs instantaneously changed my perspective on everything from healing, extrasensory perception, and horse-human communication to why equine-facilitated therapy is so effective. I began to see that simply being around these large, powerful, highly sensitive animals creates a vibratory field where the hypnotic effects of human conditioning are interrupted. At the Epona Center, where horses reclaim their authority as sentient beings, clients are deeply affected before they even lay eyes on the herd. New students often comment that they feel a sudden urge to cry the moment they drive onto the property. They make miraculous leaps of perception and efficiently change destructive behavior that years of office therapy had previously failed to alter. When these people return home, however, they also find the social pressure to change back almost overwhelming. The field of human nonsense is so strong, especially in big cities, that it takes colossal effort just to remember what took place among the horses, let alone believe it — yet another reason why I encourage clients to keep a journal, in their own handwriting, of what they experienced. I also recommend that workshop participants create their own support groups and seek out enlightened trainers or EFP specialists in their communities to reinforce the work they started in Tucson. Access to a herd of empowered horses, of course, provides the ultimate antidote to the trance of social conditioning. In the conscious effort to regularly step outside human influence, people begin to experience things they'd previously ignored or dismissed as impossible.

Several months before his powerful brush with death, for instance, Merlin convinced me that horses possess individual electromagnetic fields, or auras, around their bodies, something I had previously considered an unprovable New Age proposition. In a particularly relaxed state, I often saw a hazy white light surrounding other people, horses, and even trees, but my inner critic consistently sloughed this off as a worthless curiosity at best. My interactions with Merlin, however, proved to me once and for all that horses are not only conscious of their auras, they use them to set boundaries and gather information at a distance.

I came to this conclusion accidentally, after countless efforts to rehabilitate the stallion. Merlin hated to be groomed and petted. Massage, chiropractic adjustments, and even Tellington-Jones T-Touches, which had a calming effect on other herd members, drove him into fits of nervous agitation. After bringing in a half dozen experts in various bodywork disciplines, and trying just about every therapeutic technique I knew, I finally reached the point where Merlin would tolerate a single, friendly stroke across his regal neck. Rather than give up completely, I resorted to standing three feet away from him for extended periods with my hands behind my back, hoping to slowly gain his trust. Outside of breeding or leading him to the stall next to Rasa, this was the only time he seemed to actually welcome my presence. One sweltering afternoon, I felt a throbbing pulse in my solar plexus. It seemed to be coming from Merlin. I held up my hand, palm facing the horse, and felt pressure. When I pushed back every so slightly, Merlin stepped to the side — as if I had touched his body, though I was in fact several feet away. A simple yet emphatic phrase popped into my head: "I begin *here*." Over the next few days, I learned that if I treated this invisible energetic boundary as a part of the stallion's body, the horse was much calmer — and more respectful of *my* space. I also noticed that when I consciously connected to Merlin by touching his field with the edge of what I later determined to be my aura, we formed a telepathic connection in which images, intentions, and sometimes even words could be exchanged.

Once Merlin confirmed this field in front of numerous clients, I began to see that certain "problem horses" around the country consider that their bodies start anywhere from three inches to three feet away from their skin. Their misbehavior (biting, pinning their ears, kicking out, spooking) results from handlers not respecting this boundary. "Petting such a horse is like a stranger sticking his hand under your shirt," I often tell my clients. Techniques used to "desensitize" these horses, including the more enlightened techniques of T-Touch, often backfire. Stroking, even brushing the aura, however, does work. Slowly, a horse deferred to in this way invites the handler into his private space and allows her to touch him directly. The energy field retracts and expands according to the animal's mood, and could very well explain how horses can tell what emotional state a person's in long before she enters the corral.

Some people are instinctively more aware of the equine field, whether or not they "believe" in things like auras and shared emotion. Jennifer Jackson, a foster parent for troubled adolescents, was in many ways the ultimate skeptic. During a two-day workshop in Vancouver, British Columbia, she repeatedly conveyed that she wasn't particularly sensitive or intuitive. I wasn't about to bring up the subject of energy fields during our private session the day after the clinic. Yet when I asked her to gather some information about several horses over the fence, she noticed a particularly strange and unexpected sensation. "I was standing in front of this one horse named Fletch," she says. "I suddenly felt a pressure against my chest, pushing me back. And so I stepped back until it released — about ten feet. This same force seemed to reach out and pull me forward again, and then it moved me from side to side."

I asked her if she wanted to explore this sensation further, not mentioning a word about my suspicion that Fletch, like Merlin, had a particularly strong and active aura. We led the horse to the round pen and turned him loose. He came up to Jennifer and let her touch his face. I watched from the sidelines, fascinated, as the handsome bay gelding wandered over to the center and began motivating Jennifer to move around him through subtle, wholly invisible feelings of pressure and release.

"It wasn't like he was pushing me away, like to get rid of me," she remembers. "He sent me back, and then turned me this way and that. At one point, I could have sworn he said, 'Lighten up.' It was very clear that it was a game. I started grinning. It was unbelievable to me that a horse could be so conscious of what he wanted, and this skeptical voice inside began to question the whole experience."

As if to prove that he did, in fact, know what was going on, Fletch reached down, grabbed a longe whip lying at the center of the arena with his teeth and waved it at Jennifer.

"Do you think he really knows what he's doing?" she shouted at me.

"Your guess is as good as mine," I replied, whereupon Fletch picked up the whip again, brandished it Jennifer's way, dropped it, and stared right at her. The two of us burst into laughter.

"He sent me all the way around the perimeter of the round pen," she remembers. "Then the pressure stopped and he left me standing. As I questioned what he wanted me to do next, I got the message that horses often just stand. It's only humans who always have to be doing something. Only then did he agree to let me pick up the whip, and I, awkwardly at first, started moving him around me. I went over to caress his face, and he followed me as I walked around the arena. Wow! I was really grinning by then."

Throughout her interactions with Fletch, Jennifer gained confidence in trading energetic cues with the horse until it was difficult to tell who was leading whom. By the end of the session, she finally had to admit that *she* was a high sensitive — so sensitive that she'd shut down her gifts early in life and launched a never-ending search for ways to isolate and numb herself to other people's hidden emotions and chaotic energy fields. Like me, she had also been skeptical of the aura's existence, until a horse showed her, viscerally, that this invisible pressure could be intentionally extended from one being to another at a distance.

Though Fletch died several months later, his life-changing influence motivated Jennifer to join Epona's yearlong apprenticeship program. She has since refined her empathic, intuitive, and energetic abilities, coaching others to do the same through the practical magic of horses. "I always knew these animals were very aware, very sensitive," she says. "But I had no idea how intelligent and compassionate they were. They speak to me now in ways I never thought possible. I don't talk baby talk to them, and we certainly don't engage in idle conversation. Horses are profound beings, and they have as much to teach us as we can teach them."

After that pivotal session with Jennifer, I felt more confident teaching other clients how to work with the equine aura. It made no difference whatsoever that the average person couldn't see it. Highly sensitive animals visibly respond to stroking the energy field. Even skeptical cowboys have seen the difference in horses they previously thought were misbehaving. With more open-minded workshop participants, I coach them in how to extend their own auras to gently touch the field of an aloof or nervous horse. Sometimes, the entire audience can see the effects. At the moment a person, whose eyes are usually closed at first, says she feels connected, a previously distracted horse will lift his head and look directly at her as if she had touched him physically.

SPARKLING AT THE EDGE

Once I worked up the nerve to discuss this with colleagues, I learned that many of them had noticed the same phenomenon — and were, like me, sharing this information with certain clients. Barbara Rector, cofounder of EFMHA, has developed a number of techniques for connecting with the equine aura. Jill Eldredge, the psychotherapist who hosted my Platteville, Colorado, workshop, has been working extensively with horse auras at her new Spirit Horse Ranch in Westcliffe, Colorado. One of her most influential teachers, a "sage of a buckskin" named Roxanne, showed her how horses use these fields to set boundaries while remaining intimately connected to each other.

"One beautiful sunny morning," she says, "I was standing in the corral, awed as usual by the peace and tranquility I often feel in this sacred space. Roxanne came and stood before me — about five feet away, where the outer edge of both our fields could just touch. As I closed my eyes, I could feel her gently showing me how pulling in or pushing out her field had a direct impact on me. As she pulled in, I felt irresistibly drawn in. As she pushed out, I felt compelled to take several steps backward. She was underlining the fact that none of this was about disconnection or enmeshment — the two main ways humans have learned to relate. As she pushed me away, there was no sense of losing connection. If I turned my back, we were equally connected — *if* I stayed conscious of what she was offering with her energy and what I was doing with mine."

Jill's sensitivity to Roxanne's field was followed, quite predictably, by an inrush of mental pictures and the impression of engaging in telepathic conversation with the horse: "Roxanne sent me an image. All around her body was dark space full of bright particles. There were definite layers within this space, each with a different density of sparkles. At the outer edge, what we would call her boundary, was a very concentrated layer of sparkles. Roxanne said to me, 'This is where I gather information. Everything is filtered through this dense layer first, informing me of the truth of what I am experiencing. It is how I know where I am and what is happening around me.' She also made it very clear that we were the same. That she could see my aura or energy field and that it was just like hers (though I could see that it was not as distinct, and the concentration of particles at the outer edge was much thinner, whereas hers was very thick, clear, bright, and obvious) and that, in fact, it was what she paid the most attention to whenever I or anyone else came into her world. She then, in a very great booming voice (which I have heard from her on multiple occasions), told me that she wanted me to realize that we were *one.* That it was all the *same.* That there was *no division.* And yet, we were very separate, unique, sacred. That *everything* was distinct, unique vibration and yet connected. She was sharing a concept of unity that can be difficult for us humans to completely comprehend. I still don't think I've got it, but I definitely *felt* something I have caught small glimpses of before. It was a sense of wholeness, of ultimate aliveness and beauty where there was nothing and yet there was everything, and that everything was potential, that all of *us* are endless potential.

"Needless to say, this was a very powerful experience for me, as it often is with Roxanne. I came away with some validation of things I had been pondering, as well as lots of questions as to what I was to do with this information. After all, how many people can I tell that I just had a mega-conversation with my horse, and now I have all this amazing information about energy fields and the truth of endless, unrealized potential because we are all one? Not many.

"Part of what this experience did for me was to offer a possible explanation of a phenomenon many of us in EFP observe over and over again: A person steps into the corral. A horse turns and comes over and immediately puts his or her nose into, on, or next to a very particular part of that person — the exact part that is wounded — whether that wound is physical, emotional, or psychic. I have seen horses indicate in this manner that they are picking up everything from a broken heart to a scraped knee to a closed-head injury. I now believe that the horse may see a distortion in that human's energy field and then moves in to bring awareness and create an energetically compassionate, healing space into which the client can then move. I have always believed that the horse can sense and feel a distortion. I now am wondering if they also see that distortion — the block, the stagnation, the pain and inflammation, the excess or depletion."

My own mare Tabula Rasa seems to have a pronounced talent for detecting emotional blocks and areas of intensely concentrated energy. With larger groups, I sometimes ask participants to form a circle with the black horse in the center. As she walks purposefully to certain people, she gently touches her nose to body parts that invariably trigger a memory, insight, or unresolved issue. In this way, the mare has repeatedly drawn attention to women who've been secretly grappling with the pain and shame of mastectomies, sexual abuse, and, on a more positive note, the joy and anticipation of a long-awaited pregnancy. These people feel blessed and supported by the mare. They open up to other participants, who instinctively follow Rasa's example in creating that sacred space of possibility where healing occurs naturally, without the usual desperate and somewhat condescending speeches about what someone *should* do to fix the situation. The group manages to convey a feeling of authentic love and nonjudgmental support through the fewest possible words. The "wounded" person's initial tears culminate in peaceful acceptance of what is, as he or she also begins to adopt a cocreative, noncontrolling view of *what's possible.*

In short, the group falls under Rasa's field of influence, responding to intense emotional blocks in a more horse-like manner.

TUNING IN

In *The Tao of Equus,* I talked extensively about my experiences with the equine collective mind, a phenomenon I alternately referred to as the Horse Ancestors or "the wisdom that gives rise to the form of the horse." Without going into too much detail here, I discovered that horses were more consciously, more fluidly able to connect with the cumulative knowledge and memory of their own species, as well as the subconscious thoughts, memories, and intentions of people who worked with them. The same abilities tend to rub off on riders and trainers who allow the equine perspective to deeply influence them.

Two hundred years ago, a horse-inspired intuitive awakening would have been interpreted as witchcraft — brought on through the intercession of a powerful animal familiar. The stigma still exists. From the letters I received after my first book was published, I learned that many equestrians hide or actively suppress these useful yet confusing insights because they expect to be persecuted — or, at the very least, dismissed as crazy. I felt that way myself for many years. As someone with a relentlessly skeptical inner critic, I dealt with the schism between my socially conditioned beliefs and my increasingly bizarre experiences by searching for scientific theories to explain phenomena I could no longer deny. In this effort, studies by Larry Dossey, M.D., Gary R. Schwarz, Ph.D., and Rupert Sheldrake, Ph.D., were particularly helpful. Each of these scientists made a strong case for memory and consciousness existing outside the individual body. From this perspective, the mind is not fixed in space and time; it is not generated by the brain, or even the neuropeptides and neurotransmitters synthesized throughout the body. Rather, our brains act as receivers for mind, in much the same way a television translates waveforms into pictures and sound. In this sense, researchers attempting to locate consciousness in the body are operating from the same faulty perspective as someone who takes a TV apart to see how it makes old reruns of *I Love Lucy*. If you throw your new digital set out the window and watch it smash into a million pieces, your favorite programs will still be floating through the air at the usual time, even though you can't detect them with your senses. So it is with what many call "nonlocal mind," which implies that the thoughts, memories, and perspectives you hold will continue after your physical "receiver" shuts down and is buried in the ground. Some theories about nonlocal mind also assert that the consciousness flowing through you existed in some fashion before you were born.

In *The Living Energy Universe*, Schwartz makes a similar point through the metaphor of the cell phone: "Phone calls from hundreds of thousands, if not millions, of people are streaming down from satellites, going here and there and everywhere, including to my desk. But I do not hear any of them. However, my phone is tuned so that it can register a certain pattern, start ringing, and initiate communication. It serves as an antenna, tuner, and amplifier."

According to Sheldrake, living beings "tune into" information useful to their species through *morphic resonance,* or "form" resonance. His theory explains a mystery that geneticists have been grappling with for decades: namely, how DNA carries the code that somehow governs everything that happens to a developing organism. Sheldrake argues that since the bone, liver, and brain cells of an individual all contain the exact same DNA, these researchers are putting an inordinate amount of faith in genetics as they search for some all-powerful internal ordering device that supervises the different cells to develop into specialized organs and limbs. Sheldrake argues that an individual's development is shaped by a collective, nonmaterial force he calls a "morphogenetic field." The embryo in a pregnant mare becomes a horse because the fetal cells are tuned to the horse frequency and resonate with the field that carries the collective blueprint of the species, just as a string tuned to C will only resonate with another string tuned to C through invisible sound waves flowing between them. Biological entities are much more complex, of course, gaining information and altering their behavior in response to the environment in myriad ways. As a result, Sheldrake argues that ancestral thoughts and experiences not only affect existing members of the species, the thoughts and experiences of each new generation in turn add to and modify the morphogenetic field.

Sheldrake also writes that morphic fields operate less like gravitational fields and more like quantum matter fields. In quantum theory, if two particles have been part of the same system and then move apart, they retain a mysterious connection at a distance, called quantum nonlocality. He expands on this model not only to describe how members of a particular species can be affected by each other at a distance, but how interspecies associations might create their own nonmaterial fields of influence. His extensive experiments with human-animal relationships suggest that resonant fields are created when living creatures form an emotional bond. The greater the bond, the stronger the field. When members of the same social group are apart, these fields continue to connect them and act as a channel for communication, offering a theoretical framework for the concept of telepathy.

The entire apprenticeship class of 2003 observed this phenomenon during one emotionally charged event. Unbeknownst to us, an informal ring of thieves was operating near the barn where Spirit was born. The thieves would case the various neighborhoods running along a huge dry riverbed that ran through town and hide getaway bicycles behind trees, effectively eluding police cars that couldn't follow them into the wash. One particularly nervy robber managed to steal several hundred dollars of Epona funds less than twenty feet from the workshop site. Our assistant, Belle Blankley, had just gone to pick up sandwiches and cash a check. She parked adjacent to the Epona house, next to Merlin's stall, unloaded the food and began to set up the noon meal inside. Before she could return to the car and retrieve her purse, the thief managed to do it for her.

Ten minutes later, I wandered out to check on something in the tack room as the group broke for lunch. On my way back, I noticed Spirit playing with someone's wallet, scattering credit cards all over the arena. I have pretty clear picture of how that feisty horse boy ended up with half the goods. At the time, he was going through the typical yearling stud colt stage of testing his power and limits. He would sometimes rear or nip at people, *especially* if they tried to playfully run next to him. (We had actually just made it a rule that no one could enter his pen without my supervision.) The scoundrel must have raced through the arena where Rasa and Spirit were turned out for the day — it was the most direct route back to the wash. Spirit, having no fear of humans, probably chased him. The poor man no doubt grabbed the cash and threw Belle's wallet at the little pyrana horse in self-defense.

Belle and I called the police as we jumped into her car and began scanning the neighborhood. As we crossed the bridge and headed into an impossible maze of houses on the other side of the wash, my cell phone rang. It was Shawnee Allen, Merlin's former owner. I hadn't spoken to her in over a year.

"Is Merlin all right?" she asked.

"Yeah, he's fine," I replied distractedly.

"I really don't mean to bother you," she said, "but I just couldn't help myself. I got this terrible, fearful feeling in my gut about a half hour ago. Merlin kept popping into my head."

"No, no, he's been doing great lately," I assured her once more. "Sorry I can't talk right now, but I'm in the middle of something. I'll call you if anything comes up, okay?"

We never did catch our burglar. The police showed up a good fifteen minutes after Belle and I gave up and returned to Epona. That evening, when I finally had time to reflect on the days' events, I thought back on Shawnee's strange call. Then it hit me. She had felt overpowering anxiety at the exact moment we were being robbed. The car was parked two feet from Merlin's stall — the stallion had seen the whole thing. A high sensitive who tended to overreact to incongruent and disruptive emotions, he no doubt felt the man's desperation and mal-intent.

I called Shawnee back and told her what happened. She immediately experienced a marked sense of calm after worrying all day "for no apparent reason."

"I felt like such a fool calling you out of the blue like that," she said, "but I just couldn't get Merlin of my mind."

As Spirit chased our bandit and retrieved Belle's credit cards, Merlin, the master magician, had transmitted a feeling of alarm to a woman several states away. Why didn't those of us nearby hear the warning? There were several accomplished empaths and intuitives in the apprenticeship group, after all. At that moment, however, we were processing some strong emotions the horses had brought up in several people during an exercise earlier that morning; our collective, empathic anxiety was already elevated. A single bolt of lightning isn't nearly so impressive when you're already weathering a powerful thunderstorm.

Why did Shawnee hear the call? She was apparently still tuned to Merlin's frequency through the strong emotional bond they had formed years earlier. Shawnee was at home that day. She was relaxed. And she was alone. The initial fear, and the subsequent anxiety she felt, contrasted sharply with her previously quiet, uneventful morning.

This confirmation of Merlin's extended mind was, for me, well worth the "admission price" of a few hundred dollars. Though I eventually moved the Epona Center to a larger, more secluded property outside city limits, in part to guard the safety of our clients and horses, I was grateful to that wily thief for giving us yet another taste of a deeper, more exhilarating reality.

THE FIELD

As we accept that our minds and the emotional connections we make with other beings are nonlocal, space and time appear to be the practical illusions of linear thought — and feeling, not reason, becomes the gateway to a wider view.

Back when people were burning herbalists, intuitives, empaths, and animal communicators at the stake for witchcraft, the human race had no understanding of processes undetectable by the naked eye and ear. These days, the FCC licenses invisible modes of communicating at a distance. Doctors see into the body with MRIs and ultrasounds. And at the time this book was going to press, a federal judge was deciding whether to prevent the Navy from deploying far-reaching LFA sonar, based on evidence that high intensity sound waves cause hemorrhaging in whales and seizures in human divers.

Much of our modern technology works through resonance and other nonmaterial forces. In physics, electromagnetic and gravitational fields act on material entities, sometimes over incredible distances, as in the moon's gravitational pull on the earth's oceans. Yet despite the persistent technological metaphors for the human mind and body that our culture employs — such as the mind as computer and the body as machine — mainstream biologists and psychologists have been extremely resistant to theories employing nonmaterial forces to explain the mysteries of living organisms. Rupert Sheldrake's work is a classic example. Orthodox biologists have held book-burning parties in Sheldrake's honor because he has the nerve to suggest that morphic resonance can be used to describe, among other things, how a collective species memory might shape the physical structure, thoughts, behavior, and calling of an individual.

Since Sheldrake first published his ideas on morphic resonance in the 1980s, however, a number of other scientists have come up with similar explanations. In her book *The Field*, investigative journalist Lynne McTaggart draws many of these theories together into a startling new view of how the universe operates.

"We are poised on the brink of a revolution," she writes, "a revolution as daring and profound as Einstein's discovery of relativity.... At its most fundamental, this new science answers questions that have perplexed scientists for hundreds of years. At its most profound, this is a science of the miraculous.

"For a number of decades respected scientists in a variety of disciplines all over the world have been carrying out well-designed experiments whose results fly in the face of current biology and physics. . . . What they have discovered is nothing less than astonishing. At our most elemental, we are not a chemical reaction, but an energetic charge. Human beings and all living things are a coalescence of energy in a field of energy connected to every other thing in the world. This pulsating energy field is the central engine of our being and our consciousness, the alpha and the omega of our existence.

"There is no 'me' and 'not me' duality to our bodies in relation to the universe, but one underlying energy field. This field is responsible for our mind's highest functions, the information source guiding the growth of our bodies. It is our brain, our heart, our memory — indeed a blueprint of the world for all time. The field is the force, rather than germs or genes, that finally determines whether we are healthy or ill, the force which must be tapped in order to heal. We are attached and engaged, indivisible from our world, and our only fundamental truth is our relationship with it. 'The field,' as Einstein once succinctly put it, 'is the only reality.'"

When I first read these words, a barrage of sounds and images flooded my mind: the horses singing Merlin toward a miracle, the palpable yet invisible field that surrounds his body, the jolt of fear that he sent to a woman a thousand miles away, prescient dreams of Spirit's bittersweet birth, the collective mind of the Horse Ancestors, those transcendental insights Jill Eldredge received when she tapped into the energy field of her buckskin Roxanne: "She wanted me to realize that we were *one*. That there was *no division*. That *everything* was distinct, unique vibration, and yet connected."

The fact that Jill, Barbara Rector, several other EFP practitioners, and I became more conscious of the equine aura independently, in different parts of the country, in virtually the same time period also speaks to the validity of this theory. According to McTaggart, "many of humankind's greatest achievements may result from an individual suddenly gaining access to a shared accumulation of information — a collective effort in the Zero Point Field — in what we consider a moment of inspiration. What we call 'genius' may simply be a greater ability to access the Zero Point Field. In that sense, our intelligence, creativity and imagination are not locked in our brains but exist as an interaction with The Field."

McTaggart, who wrote the bestseller *What Doctors Don't Tell You* based on her successful health newsletter, cites numerous experiments that confirm these revelations, complex and fascinating studies I can't possibly go into here. Yet throughout *The Field*, I found numerous explanations that could be applied to the mysteries of horse-human connection and the musical nature of relationship in general — that constantly shifting feeling of two beings moving and feeling as one, of falling in and out and back into harmony, of dancing to the beat of the same hidden drummer.

"One of the central tenets of quantum physics," McTaggart observes, "is that subatomic entities behave as either particles (precise things with a set location in space) or waves (diffuse and unbounded regions of influence which can flow through and interfere with other waves)." Scientists Robert Jahn and Brenda Dunne of the Princeton Engineering Anomalies Research project, or PEAR, "began to chew over the idea that consciousness had a similar duality. Each individual consciousness had its own 'particulate' separateness, but was also capable of 'wave-like' behavior, in which it could flow through any barriers or distance, to exchange information and interact with the physical world. At certain times, subatomic consciousness would get in resonance with — beat at the same frequency as — certain subatomic matter."

In one experiment, Jahn and Dunne found that "bonded pairs," two people in a significant relationship, could influence a random event generator (REG) well beyond the statistics of chance, and six times more strongly than *individuals* who tried to do the same thing. "If these effects depended upon some sort of resonance between the two participating consciousnesses, it would make sense that the stronger effects would occur among those people sharing identities, such as siblings, twins, or couples in a relationship. Being close may create coherence. As two waves in phase amplified a signal, it may be that a bonded couple has an especially powerful resonance, which would enhance their joint effect on the machine."

While McTaggart, Jahn, and Dunne refuse to use the dreaded "L" word here, this experiment suggests what mystics have been saying for centuries, that love is a force to be reckoned with, that it connects us with each other and with the universal source of all being, allowing us to move mountains — or, at the very least, random event generators.

The concept of resonance figures prominently in a completely different series of studies by neurosurgeon Karl Pribram, who discovered that the brain acts as a highly discriminating frequency analyzer. In a series of experiments, he confirmed that the visual cortex of cats and monkeys responded to a limited range of frequencies, just as the individual strings on a piano respond to a limited range of frequencies. At first, Pribram wasn't sure how brain cells processed wave-interference patterns — until he thought to look at the spaces between them. There he found dendrites, "tiny filaments of nerve endings wafting back and forth, like shafts of wheat in a slow breeze," communicating with other neurons, "sending out and receiving their own electrical wave impulses."

As McTaggart so artfully described, "It is at this busy juncture, a place of a ceaseless scramble of electromagnetic communications between synapses and dendrites, where it is most likely that wave frequencies could be picked up and analyzed, and holographic images formed, since these wave patterns criss-crossing all the time are creating hundreds and thousands of wave-interference patterns. . . . When we perceive something, it's not due to the activity of the neurons themselves but to certain patches of dendrites distributed around the brain, which, like a radio station, are set to resonate only at certain frequencies. It is like having a vast number of piano strings all over your head, only some of which would vibrate when a particular note is played."

The ramifications for interspecies relations are significant. Just as humans, horses, and other animals see different frequencies of light, and hear different frequencies of sound, they can only share perception in those ranges they have in common. This concept extends to creating coherence in riding. Those trainers known as "horse whisperers" are so effective precisely because they attempt to act like the horse as much as humanly possible, harmonizing with equine behavior, gradually tuning their mounts to resonate with the rider's movements and intentions.

In this respect, the biggest mistake equestrians consistently make involves leaving emotion out of the equation. A two-legged trainer and a four-legged horse share an extremely limited range of physical attributes and behaviors. Yet the two species experience many of the same feelings. As I've so often observed in equine experiential learning, people who know nothing about training can "join up" with a horse through emotional resonance — and when they do, these same clients often receive mental pictures and words riding waves of intense feeling.

Resonance, in essence, marks that realm of horse-human interactions bordering the mystical. It describes how humans who vibrate sympathetically with horses so easily disrupt the unnatural spells of human conditioning. And it explains the almost cult-like status of whisperers who may share their methods but never reveal the true secrets of harmonizing with the equine mind and spirit, simply because they too are more conscious of technique than the nonverbal wisdom that informs it.

CHAPTER NINE

EQUUS NOETICUS

Horse voices aren't designed for idle conversation. If the herd decides to speak to you, you'll hear the rumblings of a more expansive reality. Quite often, this call comes without warning — in the seemingly most mundane situations.

Ann Alden owns a working cattle ranch, in addition to her EFP practice. One rainy Wednesday afternoon, she was dropping off some calves at a Willcox, Arizona, auction when a three-year-old mustang implored her to help.

"I saw a horse in the corral right next to my truck," she says. "I didn't pay much attention. Then I heard a voice in my head. I turned around, and it was coming from this mare. She was saying, 'I don't understand. What am I doing here? What did I do wrong?' It was *very* clear.

"She had a cut over her left eye, and she was scared. I told her I didn't need another horse and tried to reassure her that she was going to be okay. I asked the girl at the office if the eye would be treated, and she said, 'No, not tonight.' I had a problem with that. She gave me the name of the man who had brought her in, the owner, and I looked up his phone number. On the hour's drive home, I couldn't get this horse out of my mind."

That night, the mustang came to Ann in a dream: "I saw her as a vaulting horse with some kids, and then another image of her jumping. This seemed especially strange because she'd been trained as a ranch horse with Western tack. When I'd called the owner earlier, he told me that he'd adopted her as a yearling. She was really more of a pet at first. He eventually sent the horse to a trainer, who did okay with her and sent her home. Then the owner's daughter got on her — with spurs. The girl fell off and broke her ankle, and the horse stood around for three months. I think they just didn't have the experience or inclination to handle her."

The next morning, Ann awoke with a strong urge to return to the auction — with a truck and trailer.

"It was like there was some force outside of me compelling me to do this," she says. "I thought, 'I'm not going to bid unless nobody else bids. I have sixteen horses at the ranch. I need to be reasonable about this.' But I noticed that when people were checking out the horses for sale that day, nobody looked at her."

Seven horses were successfully auctioned ahead of the mustang, yet sure enough, no one bid on the sad, frightened mare.

"They even announced that she had ninety days of professional training," Ann remembers, "and still there was silence. They looked at her — she's a big stout mare — and they said, 'Let's weigh her.' This panic rose up inside of me. They were going to sell her by the pound! The meat packer, he was the only one who bid on her. The next thing I knew my hand was up in the air."

Ann saved the mustang's life. But in thinking back on the experience, she feels the horse did *her* a favor. "When I was a kid," she says, "I was able to see and hear things that other people couldn't. This was socialized out of me over the years. This horse confirmed something for me that I had been unable to believe in most of my adult life. She brought me back to a part of myself I thought had been lost."

And the horse, whom Ann named Ruby, seems intent on making Ann's dream come true. "I sent her to Beth High, an English trainer in Tucson, for some additional work under saddle," Ann says. "On a whim one day Beth pointed Ruby at some jumps, and she sailed over all of them without hesitation. I do think jumping is in her future somehow."

DREAM HORSES

When a woman has a vivid, emotionally charged dream about a horse coming into her life, psychologists generally interpret this as a reawakening of the libido or a subconscious craving for freedom and power. Sometimes, however, it means a horse really is coming into her life.

In the mid-1990s, Charlie McGuire was consumed with work for the American Holistic Nurses Association. She hadn't yet bought the Buffalo Woman Ranch, hadn't even heard of equine-facilitated therapy. Even so, she found herself repeatedly dreaming of a magical gray horse. "One morning after one of these dreams," she says, "I was having my car washed. I went into the building where there were all kinds of things to buy while you're waiting and started thumbing through a box of picture prints. I came across this very unusual print of a gray horse, just like the one in my dreams, flowing out of an ocean wave. I was so excited. I bought it and took it to be framed. It hung it over my bed for years. But I don't recall having any more dreams about this horse until I moved to Colorado and bought the Buffalo Woman Ranch."

In the summer of 1999, Charlie was working as a charge nurse at the Southwest Memorial Hospital in Cortez, Colorado. She often discussed plans for her new ranch with Betsy, a colleague who also loved horses.

"We talked several times about my desire to buy a Missouri Fox Trotter," Charlie remembers. "One day, Betsy told me she'd heard that the administrator of the geriatric center next door raised Fox Trotters. I kept meaning to meet this woman, but time passed, and I just never got around to it. Then one night, I dreamed of the gray horse again. It was clear that this horse was coming into my life very soon. When I told Betsy about it the next morning, she insisted I go and meet Joanne."

During her first break, Charlie ran over to the geriatric center and asked to see the administrator. "I followed her into her office and told her I'd heard she had some Missouri Fox Trotters," Charlie says. "She confirmed this and then looked at me questioningly. I explained that I wasn't quite sure why I had come to see her; then I blurted out that I'd had a dream the previous night about a gray horse. Her face went pale. She walked over and closed the door to her office. She told me that she had two gray Fox Trotter mares, and that she too, had had a dream that night about selling the older mare, April, who was pregnant. We just stared at each other in frozen silence."

Joanne hadn't seriously considered selling April before. "It was a difficult decision to make," Charlie says, "but she admitted that she mostly rode the other horse, Lacy, and felt April needed more attention than she'd been able to give her, especially since the foal was coming in March."

Charlie's unexpected visit and their synchronistic dreams, however, convinced Joanne that April had found the perfect home, albeit in a most unusual way. "We stood up and hugged each other with tears in our eyes," Charlie marvels. "We both knew we had just tapped into something beyond our understanding."

Eight months later, the mare gave birth, and Charlie named the colt Magic. Three years later, mother and son are working their own special brand of magic with local Native American children and people from around the country who attend holistic, equine experiential workshops at the Buffalo Woman Ranch.

Carol Roush found her horse Cindy through similarly potent dreamlike synchronicities. The former massage therapist was managing an outlet mall in Oregon when she bought a farm and rekindled a lifelong interest in horses. I first met her at Epona's 2002 Power of Authenticity workshop, an extended personal empowerment seminar designed to enhance creativity through reflective horse work and visionary musical experiences designed by my husband, composer Steve Roach. Carol proved especially receptive to this combination.

"A few weeks after the workshop, I decided to listen to one of Steve's CDs while meditating," she says, "and I ended up going on what I can only call a shamanic journey, something that never happened before. A golden horse came galloping across the desert and, without even slowing, invited me along. We galloped faster and faster. I was at once beside her and sitting on her back. She began to follow a spiral trail up a mesa, gradually slowing to a trot and then a walk. She stopped at an altar of rocks. She said that we had work to do together and that she would come to me. Then I noticed that the desert below was filled with horses as far as the eye could see. They were all facing me with rapt attention. I understood that they were from the past as well as the future, and they were eagerly anticipating some role I would play."

Two days later, the golden horse again appeared during Carol's meditation. "I climbed on her back," she remembers. "As she began to move, she invited me inside. At first I was out of sync with her movements, but then I settled comfortably into her high-stepping trot up a mountain trail."

At the top, Carol again saw horses in all directions, this time grazing peacefully. It seemed she had found her animal totem. She certainly didn't expect to encounter a real live golden horse, but three days later, when she and a friend stopped by a trail riding operation that had a horse for sale, Carol was surprised to find it was a golden palomino.

"When we walked up to the mare, the strangest thing happened," she says. "Tears began to flow from her eyes. My friend Beth asked the seller if the palomino had an eye infection. The woman said she had never seen the mare's eyes do that. I really felt like the mare recognized me, and she was shedding tears of joy."

There was one hitch. The mare was twenty-six years old. "I was looking for a horse to take riding lessons on and maybe do some barrel racing," Carol emphasizes. "Purchasing a horse her age didn't make any sense."

Carol's visions and the horse's tears, however, convinced the woman, against all logic, that the mare had something to teach her. A week later, one of the people chosen for Epona's 2003 apprenticeship class had to cancel at the last minute, and Carol stepped forward to take her place. Since then, Cindy has proven to be a consummate therapy horse, the golden matriarch of Carol's growing herd. She often visits the woman in meditation, carrying her toward other worlds of insight — surreal, imaginative landscapes that have an uncanny way of manifesting in Carol's daily life.

THE TRICKS OF COMMUNICATION

While horse-inspired visions, dreams, and direct communications always feel special — and do, in fact, have the power to change lives — these incidents are much more common than people realize. Based on letters I've received from around the world, I could put together an entire book of remarkable anecdotes. Most of these people, however, feel isolated and alone. When they try to share their stories with friends and family, they're rewarded with little more than a raised eyebrow, a doubtful sigh, or a cynical "Hmmmm," if not stern warnings that they're sliding down the slippery slope of insanity.

At the opposite end of the spectrum, we find professional animal communicators. Ten years ago, I was skeptical of these people. I still am, for different reasons. There's no doubt in my mind that many animal communicators receive valuable insights. However, how they interpret and share that information varies widely. Some are extremely aggressive in telling others what they should and shouldn't do with their horses based on potent, yet still sketchy, communications. Intuition is like briefly shining a small flashlight into a huge dark room. You may catch glimpses of some of the furnishings, but it's difficult to see how it all fits together. Some clients take an all-or-nothing approach in gauging the authenticity of what's presented. Either they think it's a bunch of hooey, or they accept it as a dictate from God's own representative. The truth lies somewhere in between.

An intuitive once told my friend Julia Coleman that she'd soon be practicing *hypnotherapy* with horses. A year later, Julia developed a significant clientele teaching riding lessons for persons with physical disabilities, a field officially known as *hippotherapy* when a licensed therapist facilitates. In the late 1990s, the two of us launched a multidisciplinary riding school emphasizing the therapeutic value of horse-human relationships. Julia often employed my horse Noche in teaching students with cerebral palsy, autism, and other developmental disabilities. The old sage mustang showed a patience with these people that he didn't extend to able-bodied riders. I, on the other hand, felt drawn toward clients with emotional difficulties. When "Janice," a talented, West Coast animal communicator, came to The Ranch, she told me that Noche didn't want to help with this side of the business; he was too deeply affected by chaotic human feelings.

That was true — *at the time*. As it turned out, Noche felt unsafe around incongruent emotions. Once he understood that we were helping people become more congruent and responsive, he preferred the emotional work. He suddenly and quite emphatically objected to teaching riding lessons for persons with disabilities. Compared to the varied activities I used in my practice, and the instantaneous release we all felt when clients deciphered the message behind a troublesome emotion (rather than projecting it onto the horse), Noche found it boring to carry students around in endless circles, day after day, week after week. (Hippotherapy horses work hard to balance people with physical issues. While the results are fulfilling, the process can be tedious, requiring incredible self-control and concentration from both the instructor and her equine colleague.)

The animal communicators who advised us during that period provided some accurate insights, but their interpretations suffered from their limited experience. The first woman had no idea there *was* such a thing as hippotherapy. Her mind automatically grabbed onto something recognizable: namely, hypnotherapy. The second woman was very much like the spiritual teachers Karla McLaren encountered in her search: Janice saw negative feelings as evidence of psychological imbalance in horses and humans alike. She didn't understand the true nature of my practice, and I didn't have time to explain the nuances. Consequently, when she asked Noche if he'd be interested in facilitating clients with unresolved emotions, she transferred her own vision of what that might look like. And I'm sure it wasn't pretty.

An element of projection was involved. As I later discovered, Janice's ability to handle her personal emotional challenges didn't match up with her intuitive gifts. She engaged in spiritual bypassing, continually searching for peace and tranquility through complex meditative practices. The idea of exposing a horse to anything having to do with negative feelings was confusing and distasteful to her.

MOTHER EARTH AND FATHER SKY

Even the best communicators occasionally lapse into transference. Feelings and images coming from the horse or the human client can trigger subconscious memories of past relationships or personal traumas in the communicator. This is not a sign of ineptitude. It happens to psychotherapists so often that they have a special term for it: *countertransference.*

As Jungian analysts often say, "The brighter the light, the darker the shadow." An intuitive with an inflated ego may actually become hostile when clients question her insights. Figuratively speaking, she's afraid of her own shadow. She sees negative emotions, transference, and projection as weakness, but ultimately, they are simply information. Horses, after all, experience transference, and they're not ashamed of it. Noche, a former ranch horse, spooked wildly the first time he saw me in a cowboy hat. I wasn't the cowboy who abused him, but he raced around his corral like I'd suddenly transformed into the devil himself — until I thought to remove the objectionable article from my head. Sometimes the cure is as simple as recognizing the trigger — but you'll never get there if you erroneously assume you're too evolved for such nonsense.

Professional psychics and animal communicators must be willing to do their own personal work, and they can't bypass the pain through perpetual transcendence. Transcendence is a form of creative dissociation, useful   sometimes miraculously so   yet easily abused by those who don't want to deal with life's realities. As I've learned over the years, horses can be extremely antagonistic toward what I call "habitual transcendentals," intuitives and artists who reject the inconveniences of earthly existence. Some of these people can give you startlingly accurate information about your horse over the phone, through nonlocal mind-to-mind exchanges, but they make ineffective trainers because they're perpetually out of their bodies. (Grounded, emotionally balanced animal communicators, on the other hand, make excellent trainers.) If their egos become inflated by success, these people become incredibly dangerous. As long as you're willing to worship their talents, they'll

shower love on you like the benevolent guru they believe themselves to be. The moment you question their authority — and
heaven forbid you should bring up projection and transference —
they'll attack you with the repressed rage they long ago rejected
in themselves. I've received dozens of desperate letters and phone
calls from people who've been treated this way by highly talented
animal communicators, and the results are devastating. These
intuitives are *not* evil or insane. They've merely succumbed to one
of the pitfalls of the field. People put them on pedestals and treat
them like saints. It takes an emotionally agile, *fully grounded* person
to handle the adulation, to see it for what it really is — positive
projection coming from clients who can't yet own these qualities
in themselves.

In this respect, as in many others, horses can be insightful
guides, modeling an embodied spirituality that treats emotion as
information. They can help a high-powered intuitive adopt the
equine "wide view," a physical and psychological way of seeing
the world that integrates the nonlocal, wave-like nature of consciousness with its earthier, seemingly separate, particle-like nature.
Horses quite naturally embrace this paradox, what Jill Eldredge's
horse Roxanne referred to when she declared that everything is
"distinct, unique vibration, and yet connected."

In the past, habitual transcendentals were *cultivated* to maintain
an otherworldly perspective. The Greek Oracle of Delphi is one
such example. This person was segregated from mainstream culture and waited on hand and foot, so that she could strengthen a
nonlocal wave-like form of consciousness capable of communing
with The Field. Modern visionaries, on the other hand, must integrate more fully into society — unless they lock themselves away
in a monastery or find a group of followers to serve them without
question. The challenges are significant. Many empaths and intuitives developed their gifts as victims of childhood sexual abuse —
they learned to assess people's unspoken emotions and intentions

at a distance as a *survival mechanism*. They used out-of-body experiences to escape impossible situations. Their sometimes fanatical desire to save abused animals, while admirable, is mixed with considerable projection, transference, and constant, overpowering episodes of emotional resonance. The good news is that once these people get the help they need to resolve a horrifying past, their shamanic abilities blossom.

In tribal cultures, the shaman is known as "the wounded healer." Most are called to this position through a trauma that distinguishes them from people leading a calmer, more idyllic existence. An apprentice shaman spends years studying with an experienced medicine man, in part to integrate the intuitive gifts and the personal difficulties that arise from whatever brutal initiation "the gods" originally put him through. *This apprenticeship is necessary in part so that he doesn't project his unresolved trauma onto the people who come to him for help.* In addition to herbal remedies, psychedelic enhancements, and ritual, many shamans work with Father Sky *and* Mother Earth — in other words, they learn to both transcend and ground the powerful emotions, energies, and insights flowing through them. Successful shamans become more horse-like over time: intimately connected with nature *and* conscious of The Field that informs it. For this reason, equine-facilitated activities are remarkably effective in helping the wounded healers of our own society to hone their hard-won gifts.

ARTFUL INTEGRATION

After a decade of boarding my growing herd at various stables around Tucson, I finally live with my horses. The window above my computer overlooks the corrals. I've written half this book watching Rasa, Merlin, and Spirit perfect the lost art of doing nothing. Chinese Taoists call it *wu wei*, "not doing," and horses are particularly good at it. Just as Fletch made sure that Jennifer

Jackson understood the power of standing still, I've watched my own equine family perform strangely synchronous movements I would never have witnessed if I hadn't been staring languidly out the window, daydreaming when I "should" have been concentrating on the task at hand.

Spirit lives in the corral between those of Rasa and Merlin, and sometimes he's still turned out with his mother, though he was weaned several months ago. It's 107 degrees out there, serious wu wei weather. The horses stand quietly under three separate trees with dreamy, half-closed eyes. A subtle wave moves between father and son. Spirit pulls his right back leg forward, stretches it out far behind him, and finally cocks it next to his left leg in a more relaxed position. Two seconds later, Merlin does the exact same thing with the exact same leg, though he's a good fifteen feet from his son — looking the other way. A week ago, I saw the stallion shake his head at the colt from the same distance, and Spirit bowed down slightly, smacking his lips like a suckling foal, a signal all young horses use to placate their elders.

I think about the magic of touch, how humans so often overuse it, abuse it, and then refuse it when it's really needed. Spirit might not be here if it weren't for the loving embraces of those who took care of him. Holding his fragile, shaking body against my own stabilized his nervous system and kept him warm when he should have been floating around in the womb, synchronizing with his mother's heartbeat.

And now that he's a stud colt, I must teach him to stand away from me. I do this without sadness or nostalgia for the days when I could pick him up and carry him around. We're learning a new form of magic: how to use the fields around our bodies. Because I, too, want to feel those waves of connection with him when I'm twenty feet away, daydreaming under a big mesquite, perfecting my own brand of wu wei.

In *The Field*, Lynne McTaggart talks about a researcher named

William Braud, a behavioral psychologist with a penchant for "white crows," William James's term for scientific anomalies — those things that don't quite fit, "assumptions that could be turned askew." What Braud found, among other things, was that people could influence the laws of nature as readily as they could influence a random event generator. But it only seemed to work "when he used gentle wishing, rather than intense willing or striving. It was like trying to will yourself to sleep; the harder you try, the more you interfere with the process. It seemed to Braud that humans operated on two levels — the hard, motivated striving of the world and the relaxed, passive, receptive world of The Field — and the two seemed incompatible."

Horses are experts at straddling these twin realities. The more time I spend with them, the more I feel the music of total integration rumbling from the depths. They're tuning me to sing a new song, gently wishing me toward an expanded view of what's possible.

We're all riding between the worlds right now, shifting, clumsily at times, between freedom and captivity, spirit and nature, mind and heart. Yet I believe that someday, if more people are willing to take counsel from their four-legged friends, human consciousness will embrace these paradoxes and expand beyond them

Then, there will be no separation.

APPENDIX

EMOTIONAL MESSAGE CHART

(INSPIRED, IN PART, BY THE WORK OF KARLA MCLAREN*)

EMOTION	MESSAGE	QUESTIONS TO ASK OF THE EMOTION	INTENSIFICATION
FEAR	INTUITIVE, FOCUSED AWARENESS OF SOMETHING THAT IS A THREAT TO OUR PHYSICAL, MENTAL, EMOTIONAL, OR SPIRITUAL WELL-BEING	WHAT IS THE THREAT? WHAT ACTION MUST I TAKE TO MOVE TO A POSITION OF SAFETY?	WORRY, ANXIETY CONFUSION DULLING OF SENSES PANIC, TERROR DISSOCIATION

COMMENTARY: Panic and terror result from a true and urgent endangerment that is being ignored, often pointing back to and accentuated by an injury or trauma the person wasn't allowed to work through. The work of Peter Levine, author of *Waking the Tiger*, and writings in the field of somatic psychotherapy have important insights to offer therapists who work with trauma survivors. Dissociation — a state that results from not being able to flee a seemingly deadly situation — can be seen in many horses who have been "broken" through dominance techniques. Survivors of sexual assault often relate profoundly to horses that have been trained in this aggressive manner.

Sometimes fear intensifies when we begin to dissociate or intellectualize in a situation where full-bodied awareness is essential. In this case, the fear will often dissipate simply by breathing into the constricted solar plexus. In this case, the emotion was merely saying, "Stay in your body!"

---

* Quotes from Karla McLaren were taken from her audiobook *Becoming an Empath*. The form of this chart, most notably the "Message," "Questions to Ask of the Emotion," and "Intensification" categories were inspired by the vocabulary McLaren uses to speak about emotion, though I have added additional emotions, messages, and questions I've found useful in work with horses.

EMOTION	MESSAGE	QUESTIONS TO ASK OF THE EMOTION	INTENSIFICATION
VULNERABILITY	SOMETHING SIGNIFICANT IS ABOUT TO CHANGE OR BE REVEALED	WHAT WANTS TO HAPPEN AND HOW DOES THIS SEEM TO THREATEN THE STATUS QUO? WHAT BELIEF, BEHAVIOR, OR PERCEPTION IS BEING CHALLENGED?	PANIC ANGER

COMMENTARY: Vulnerability commonly arises in equine-facilitated psychotherapy and experiential learning. The key to understanding its meaning lies in separating it from fear, our natural warning system. If, upon checking in with your body, no discernable threat appears in the immediate environment, determine if the threat instead arises from a conflict within the self. Vulnerability marks the point at which an old coping strategy, behavior pattern, or perception of the world is being challenged — or a previously repressed part of the self is being revealed. This threatens the conditioned personality because the "False Self," as we call it, is merely a collection of habits and has no creative power to imagine a new way of acting in response to this insight. The feeling intensifies into panic or anger as the conditioned personality goes into flight-or-fight mode. The False Self can literally feel like its life is threatened — indeed the way of life in which the False Self thrives may be altered significantly, precipitating drastic changes in one's job and relationships. Panic results when the conditioned mind feels a need to "run away" from the insight. Anger arises when the False Self tries to fight or violently suppress the insight.

EMOTION	MESSAGE	QUESTIONS TO ASK OF THE EMOTION	INTENSIFICATION
ANGER	PROPER BOUNDARIES SHOULD BE MAINTAINED OR REBUILT INCONGRUENCE	WHAT MUST BE PROTECTED? WHAT MUST BE RESTORED? WHAT IS THE EMOTION BEHIND THE MASK, AND IS IT DIRECTED TOWARD ME?	RAGE, FURY (EXPLODING AT THOSE WHO'VE VIOLATED OUR BOUNDARIES) SHAME, GUILT (ANGER TOWARD SELF WHEN WE'VE VIOLATED OTHERS' BOUNDARIES) BOREDOM, APATHY (MASKS ANGER THAT CAN'T BE DEALT WITH — A NONVIOLENT COPING STRATEGY)

COMMENTARY: Shame can be dumped on us by parents, spouses, and authority figures. By asking the questions above, however, we can tell if our shame originated in our behavior, which we can do something about, or if it really belongs to someone else projecting it onto us to make him/herself feel better without changing his/her own behavior. Projected shame is common in abusive relationships where an emotionally sensitive scapegoat in the family carries and expresses the shame that actually belongs to the abuser(s).

McLaren's insights into boredom and apathy as repressed anger are intriguing. Someone who uses boredom or apathy as a coping strategy for dealing with anger can be resentful and sarcastic without causing anyone serious physical damage, but the emotional toll on significant others, especially children, can be equally damaging. And there are never any visible bruises that might alert teachers, doctors, and extended family members that the child is suffering from the covert expression of this anger.

I have also noticed over the years that highly sensitive people will experience anger in the presence of someone who is incongruent. In this case, the anger is an alarm that lets us know we're interacting with a person who is not what he or she appears to be, who is in fact wearing a mask of happiness, friendliness, courage, or control when he or she is actually feeling aggressive, fearful, sad.

(continued on next page)

The most efficient way to read the message behind anger is to first check if someone has stepped over a boundary. If not, then the person may simply be incongruent. By asking the question, "What is the emotion behind the mask, and is it directed toward me?" we may determine whether the person is hiding something in order to take unfair advantage of us, or if he or she is simply sad (angry, fearful) for personal reasons and doesn't want to bring it up. In the case of the latter, the anger often dissipates when we notice the incongruity and realize the person has the potential to act unpredictably because of his or her conflicted emotional state. In the case of the former, the anger will not lift until we take more specific action to protect ourselves.

It is important to note that sadness and anger are sometimes used to mask each other. Women will sometimes cry and assume they're sad when they're actually feeling anger because they're afraid of standing up for themselves. Men are more likely to express anger when they actually feel sad because they're afraid to show vulnerability. This is not a hard-and-fast rule, however. Sometimes men are afraid of the explosive forces of their own repressed anger and will opt to show sadness instead. Some women would rather get angry than feel sad because they're afraid they'll never stop crying if they allow the tears to flow.

EMOTION	MESSAGE	QUESTIONS TO ASK OF THE EMOTION	INTENSIFICATION
FRUSTRATION	THE ACTION YOU'RE TAKING IS NOT EFFECTIVE	WHAT IS THE BLOCK? WHAT CAN I DO DIFFERENTLY? WHO CAN I ASK FOR IDEAS AND ASSISTANCE?	RAGE POWERLESSNESS

COMMENTARY: I recently added frustration to the chart because it's so common in horse-human interactions. Commonly mistaken for anger, the two emotions do in fact feel similar and can both intensify into rage. The difference, however, lies in the message. Frustration arises when we employ a technique in work or life, or an influence in relationship with another being, that simply isn't effective. Rather than look for alternatives, or ask for help, we continue to force a breakthrough using familiar coping strategies that, while they may have worked in the past, produce little or no result in the current situation. Frustration continues to build to the point of rage if we refuse to adapt or explore other alternatives. Powerlessness arises when we give up without asking for help.

EMOTION	MESSAGE	QUESTIONS TO ASK OF THE EMOTION	INTENSIFICATION
SADNESS	RESTORES FLOW TO THE PSYCHE WHEN LOSS IS IMMANENT AND IN OUR BEST INTEREST	WHAT MUST BE RELEASED? WHAT MUST BE REJUVENATED?	DESPAIR DESPONDENCE

COMMENTARY: McLaren emphasizes that we must ask both questions to complete the cycle. Sadness "brings the healing waters of tears and physical release to us" and "removes logjams in our psyches" so that we can live authentically again. If we can't let go of old patterns and destructive relationships, we can't be rejuvenated, and the sadness persists. Sadness is often a part of grief or depression, but in its purest form, it is a healing agent that motivates us to let go of what no longer serves us so that we can be rejuvenated for a new stage of growth, development, and creativity "If we wallow in sadness and self-pity and refuse to let go, our sadness will have to intensify into despair and despondence."

EMOTION	MESSAGE	QUESTIONS TO ASK OF THE EMOTION	INTENSIFICATION
GRIEF	NO CHOICE ABOUT RELEASING SOMETHING, THE LOSS OR DEATH HAS ALREADY OCCURRED	WHAT MUST BE MOURNED?	DEPRESSION

COMMENTARY: According to McLaren, grief doesn't just bring waters of release to our psyches as sadness does, it drops us directly into the deepest rivers of the soul. In my experience, grief is so painful because any form that comes into existence, any form used with some success, solidifies and then tries to endure beyond its capacity for further innovation. This includes coping strategies, relationship patterns, and of course, our attachment to the physical bodies we are given.

EMOTION	MESSAGE	QUESTIONS TO ASK OF THE EMOTION	INTENSIFICATION
DEPRESSION	INGENIOUS STAGNATION STOP SIGN OF THE SOUL	WHERE HAS MY ENERGY GONE? WHERE IS IT NOW? WHAT NEW DIRECTION GIVES ME ENERGY?	LOSS OF SELF LOSS OF LIFE'S PURPOSE SUICIDAL URGES PHYSICAL ILLNESS

COMMENTARY: Depression often follows a period when we didn't listen to sadness, fear, anger, or grief. McLaren emphasizes that depression is not a sign of stupidity; it is, in fact, a most ingenious survival mechanism where the psyche is given no choice but to hinder our ability to move forward. People who don't feel depression and doubt often blindly stumble into situations that endanger their souls, their health, their purpose in life. "In a world where we're taught to ignore our emotions, dreams and true passions," McLaren says, "where we enter blindly into the wrong relationships and the wrong jobs, depression is our emergency break." Depression takes over when "what we were doing and where we were going didn't match up with our inner desires."

EMOTION	MESSAGE	QUESTIONS TO ASK OF THE EMOTION	INTENSIFICATION
SUICIDAL URGE	THE LIFE BEING LIVED IS ENDANGERING BODY AND SOUL AT SUCH AN EXTREME LEVEL THAT IT WILL CAUSE PERMANENT DAMAGE	WHAT MUST END NOW? WHAT MUST BE KILLED?	SOUL DEATH PHYSICAL DEATH

COMMENTARY: Sometimes the suicidal urge results from depression related to chemical imbalance and/or chronic pain. In these cases, medical, psychological, and spiritual support are needed, or the person may successfully commit suicide in a moment of extreme fatigue to simply end the pain.

Yet McLaren emphasizes that the suicidal urge absolutely does not want an end to physical existence; rather it emerges when the difference between who we are in our deepest, most authentic selves and who we've become to fit into a materialistic social system are completely out of alignment. The suicidal urge, she says, often "emerges when our lives are already endangering our souls.... What needs to die is our attachment to falseness, lovelessness, lies, and spiritual emptiness" — basically whatever stops us from living authentically. The dark night of the soul experienced in this state "exists in direct proportion to the dawn that awaits" us.

While McLaren's comments emphasize the imminent death of the soul — the person is about to become an automaton if she doesn't take action — I would also like to suggest research that implies the development of serious physical disease over time. The levels of stress, abuse, or emotional repression leading to this extreme state have been shown to suppress the immune system beyond its capacity to fight off disease. If a person experiencing the suicidal urge does not get the help she needs to change her life, she may indeed die a slow, agonizing death from a physical affliction. The refusal to take care of ourselves when every fiber of our being is calling out for help is arguably a passive form of suicide.

People experiencing a suicidal urge must be taken seriously, but the Epona staff has seen these times to be most empowering and transformational if the impulse is listened to as an urgent emotional message capable of rallying untapped resources. The questions, then, are the most extreme for this reason. As McLaren so eloquently conveys, "If you ask these questions prayerfully and ceremonially, your suicidal urge will tell you this draining behavior, this soul-killing relationship, this painful addiction, this weakness and self pity, this pathetic story about why you can't do your art [shows that] you've forgotten who you are, but I remember. If you let it speak, your suicidal urge will stand up for your lost dreams, and it will help you clear away everything that threatens to kill them. It will remind you of your forgotten goals, and it will help you move toward them again.... You'll be given your own life back."

ACKNOWLEDGMENTS

Writing *Riding between the Worlds* was a labor of love involving significant periods of reclusive incubation and painful birthing. I can't thank my husband, Steve Roach, enough for his support. He is the best literary Lamaze coach I could ever imagine. And as a composer who lives in the "soundcurrent," he understands very well the music of connection and the power of resonance. Among the two-legged creatures who have touched my life so deeply, he continues to be my main inspiration.

I completed this book in nine months, a feat that would not have been possible without the exceptional dedication and motivation of the Epona staff. These professionals not only kept things going during my long, fitful hours at the computer, they took the entire organization to a new level of innovation. Senior counselor Kathleen Barry Ingram far exceeded her responsibilities as Epona's clinical coordinator, acting as business partner, confidant, friend, and sounding board for my most adventurous insights.

Barn manager and volunteer coordinator Xena Carpenter oversees care of the horses, not just physically, but emotionally and spiritually as well. Her organizational skills and ingenuity really came to light in the weeks following Spirit's birth. In addition to finding and training nearly a hundred volunteers and staff during that crucial time, she designed, along with trainer Cathie Hook, the sling that kept our little horse baby safe and healthy.

Program coordinator Nicole Christine has been a real blessing. An accomplished writer and clinician in her own right, she handles the details of running Epona with uncommon grace and sensitivity. Social worker and shamanic practitioner Laurie Levon brings so many talents to the organization, supporting horse and human alike through her innate ability to ride between this world and the other. Special projects coordinator Melissa Shandley has that all-too-rare combination of artistic inclination, computer savvy, and organizational abilities crucial to establishing the Epona Apprenticeship Program. Assistant workshop coordinator Belle Blankley has also been essential to the development of the Epona Center and its myriad offerings.

The unexpectedly rapid expansion of Epona has made it necessary to train facilitators capable of establishing their own practices to serve people and horses who can't travel to Tucson. I've been inspired by the creativity, adaptability, and sensitivity the Apprenticeship Class of 2003 has shown throughout their year-long initiation into the Way of the Horse. These professionals continually find news ways of combining Epona theories and techniques with their own unique talents and perspectives. My blessings for carrying on this work go to Paula Bixby, Joe Esparza, Mary-Louise Gould, Jennifer Jackson, Laurie Levon, Charlie McGuire, Fran Nachtigall, Sue Ratcliffe, Carol Roush, Leigh Shambo, Bonnie Treece, Sandra Wallin, and Sara Willerson.

Photographer Tony Stromberg, whose work graces the cover of this book, is a talented horseman and clinician in his own right. His unique ability to capture the spirit of the horse on film has provided much inspiration during the writing of *Riding between the Worlds*.

Special thanks to equine artist J. C. Delano for her rendering of the False Self dilemma on page 124. Amazingly, she added significant emotion, and even a bit of class, to my primitive stick figure metaphor.

I would also like to thank the following people for their continued faith, help, and moral support: Shelley Rosenberg, Renee Waldman, Ris Higgins, Peggy Green, Betty Franklin, Janet Holmes, Robbie Nelson, Elizabeth Lasater, Jerry Petersen, Jillian Lessner, Dianna McPhail, Jill and Dave Eldredge, Carol Dickman, Maureen Luikart, Betsy Lundell, Laurie and Terry Christiansen, Laura Brinkerhoff, Barbara Rector, Sue Roach, Kathy and Myron Vrabel, Ann Alden, Cathy Schreiber, Sue Newman, Gina Morrissey, Michelle Ross, Autum Busarow, Cheryl McChesney, the Allen family, Jenna Andersen, Dennis and Margaret Hadley, Melanie Sauer, Suzanna Thomas, Isaiah Heun, and Mariah Heun.

Immense appreciation goes to the people who shared their powerful stories in this book. It takes great courage to reveal these intimate details, even under a pseudonym.

I don't have nearly enough space to name all the volunteers who supported Spirit during his rough ride into this world. Please know that your dedication and generosity are appreciated every time I see "our boy" run like the wind on four solid legs. This book is dedicated to you.

I would also like to thank veterinarians Barbara Page, Christine Staten, and Larry Shamis for their life-saving, innovative treatments.

I give special thanks once again to my agent, Felicia Eth, and my editor, Jason Gardner, whose initial faith in the way of the horse cannot be underestimated. I appreciate more than ever Jason's unique ability to guide the writing process by creating that "sacred space of possibility" the horses themselves hold so dear.

Ultimately, I could not have ridden between the worlds without a herd capable of inspiring so much black horse wisdom. The strange and miraculous course my life has taken is due to their quiet yet powerful guidance. Eternal gratefulness to Tabula Rasa, Midnight Merlin, Spirit of Epona, Noche the Incredible Desert Horse, Comet's Promise, Firehorse Mary, Tigger, Max, Amigo, and Julie for living the stories that begged to be written.

SOURCES

Aron, Elaine N. *The Highly Sensitive Person: How to Thrive When the World Overwhelms You.* New York: Broadway, 1996.

Buchanan, Lyn. *The Seventh Sense.* New York: Paraview/Pocket Books, 2003.

Conley, Kevin. *Stud: Adventures in Breeding.* New York: Bloomsbury, 2002.

Frattaroli, Elio. *Healing the Soul in the Age of the Brain: Becoming Conscious in an Unconscious World.* New York: Viking, 2001.

Grigg, Ray. *The Tao of Zen.* Edison, NJ: Alva Press, 1994.

Hillman, James. *The Soul's Code: In Search of Character and Calling.* New York: Random House, 1996.

Irwin, Chris. "E.A.P.-ed Off!" www.chrisirwin.com/articles_eapedoff.htm.

Kathryns, Ginger. *Cloud: Wild Stallion of the Rockies.* New York: Nature Video Library, produced by Thirteen/WNET, 2001.

Kidd, Sue Monk. *When the Heart Waits: Spiritual Direction for Life's Sacred Questions.* San Francisco: HarperSanFrancisco, 1992.

Lerner, Harriet. *The Dance of Anger.* New York: HarperCollins, 1988.

Luddington-Hoe, Susan M., with Susan K. Golant. *Kangaroo Care: The Best You Can Do to Help Your Preterm Infant.* New York: Bantam, 1993.

McCall, James P. *The Stallion: A Breeding Guide for Owners and Handlers.* New York: Howell Books, 1995.

McLaren, Karla. *Emotional Genius: Discovering the Deepest Language of the Soul.* Columbia, CA: Laughing Tree Press, 2001.

————. *Becoming an Empath.* Boulder, CO: Sounds True Audio, 2000.

McTaggart, Lynne. *The Field: The Quest for the Secret Force of the Universe.* New York: HarperCollins, 2002.

Miller, Alice. *The Drama of the Gifted Child: The Search for Self.* New York: Perennial, 1997.

Myss, Caroline. *Advanced Energy Anatomy.* Boulder, CO: Sounds True Audio, 2001.

Nelson, Todd R. "Dacher Keltner: Compassion Is Good for You." *Hope,* January/February 2003.

Scanlan, Lawrence. *Wild About Horses: Our Timeless Passion for the Horse.* New York: HarperCollins/Perennial Press, 2001.

Schnurnberger, Lynn. "Bag-Lady Syndrome: Are You Suddenly Afraid of Losing it All?" *More,* December 2002.

Schwartz, Gary E. R., and Linda G. S. Russek. *The Living Energy Universe.* Charlottesville, VA: Hampton Roads Publishing Company, 1999.

Soren, Ingrid. *Zen and Horses.* Emmaus, PA: Rodale Press, 2002.

Teich, H. "Twin Lights of Consciousness, Biology, Microphysics and Macropsychology." Abstract. www.imprint-academic.demon.co.uk/SPECIAL/08_07.html

Watts, Alan. 1957. *The Way of Zen.* New York: Vintage, 1989.

Welwood, John. *Toward a Psychology of Awakening.* Boston: Shambhala, 2000.

Williamson, Marianne. *A Return to Love.* New York: HarperPerennial, 1992.

INDEX

F

G

H

ABOUT THE AUTHOR

Linda Kohanov is an author, speaker, riding instructor, and horse trainer who specializes in Equine Experiential Learning and Equine Facilitated Psychotherapy. In 1997, she founded Epona Equestrian Services, a Tucson-based collective of riding instructors and counselors exploring the healing potential of working with horses. In addition to formal equine-facilitated psychotherapy sessions, Epona offers equine experiential learning programs in stress reduction, parenting skills, leadership techniques, consensus-building, mindfulness, intuition, creativity, sensory aware-ness, and women's empowerment. The author of the groundbreaking book *The Tao of Equus*, Linda speaks and gives workshops around the world. She lives with her husband, composer and musician Steve Roach, and their horses outside Tucson, Arizona. Her website is http://www.taoofequus.com.

If you enjoyed *Riding between the Worlds*, read Linda Kohanov's first book, *The Tao of Equus: A Woman's Journey of Healing and Transformation Through the Way of the Horse.*

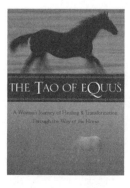

"*The Tao of Equus* reveals the transformative, healing power that is implicit in the human-animal bond. . . . a startling challenge to anyone wishing to limit consciousness to humans."

— Larry Dossey, M.D., author of *Healing Beyond the Body* and *Reinventing Medicine*

New World Library is dedicated to
publishing books and audio projects that inspire
and challenge us to improve the quality
of our lives and our world.

Our books and audios are available
at bookstores everywhere.
For a complete catalog, contact:

New World Library
14 Pamaron Way
Novato, California 94949

Phone: (415) 884-2100
Fax: (415) 884-2199
Or call toll-free: (800) 972-6657
Catalog requests: Ext. 50
Orders: Ext. 52

E-mail: escort@newworldlibrary.com
Website: www.newworldlibrary.com